We'Moon 201

Gaia Rhythms for Womyn

Born to Drum
© Annie Ocean 2008

Reinvent the Wheel

29th Edition of We'Moon

published by
Mother Tongue Ink

We'Moon 2010: Gaia Rhythms for Womyn
Spiral, Layflat and Unbound Editions

We'Moon Founder/Crone Editor: Musawa
We'Moonagers: Sue Burns, Barb Dickinson
Special Editor: Bethroot Gwynn
Graphic Design: Sequoia Watterson
We'Moon Creatrix/Editorial Team: Bethroot Gwynn, Musawa, Barb Dickinson, Sequoia Watterson, Sue Burns, EagleHawk
Promotion: Lous Chain, Sue Burns
Customer Relations/Retail Sales: Myshkin
Order Fullfillment: Lous Chain
Production Assistants: Myshkin, Renée Côté
Proofing: Sandra Pastorius, EagleHawk, Beth Freewomon

Astrological data provided by Astro Communications Services (copyright 2007), PO Box 1646, El Cajon, CA 92022-1646. www.astrocom.com

This eco-audit applies to all We'Moon 2010 datebooks:

NEW LEAF PAPER®
ENVIRONMENTAL BENEFITS STATEMENT
of using post-consumer waste fiber vs. virgin fiber

Mother Tongue Ink saved the following resources by using New Leaf Reincarnation Matte, made with a minimum of 50% recycled fiber and a minimum of 30% post consumer waste, processed chlorine free and elemental chlorine free, and manufactured with electricity that is offset with Green-e® certified renewable energy certificates.

trees	water	energy	solid waste	greenhouse gases
259 fully grown	50,122 gallons	122 million Btu	12,712 pounds	19,253 pounds

Calculations based on research by Environmental Defense and other members of the Paper Task Force.

©2008 New Leaf Paper www.newleafpaper.com

ANCIENT FOREST FRIENDLY™ Green-e NEW LEAF PAPER manufactured with wind power

Mother Tongue Ink
P.O. Box 1586, Estacada, Oregon 97023

To Order:
US toll Free: 877-693-6666
Local/International: 541-956-6052
email: weorder@wemoon.ws
www.wemoon.ws

© Hrana Janto 1991

Changing Woman

As a moon calendar, this book is recyclable: every 19 years the moon completes a metatonic cycle, returning to the same phase, sign and degree of the zodiac.

We'Moon 2010 is printed in South Korea by Sung In Printing America on recycled paper using soy based inks.

We'Moon is proud to be a signatory to TREEty, a partnership between New Leaf Paper and The Breast Cancer Fund.

Order directly from Mother Tongue Ink (see p. 229)

NEW!
The Last Wild Witch
by Starhawk, illustrated by Lindy Kehoe
An Eco-Fable for Kids and Other Free Spirits
ISBN: 978-1-890931-59-4 • $18.95

We'Moon 2010 Datebooks: $17.95
We'Moon 2010 Spiral
ISBN: 978-1-890931-60-5
We'Moon 2010 Layflat
ISBN: 978-1-890931-61-2
We'Moon 2010 Unbound
ISBN: 978-1-890931-62-9

Other We'Moon 2010 Products:
Art and writing from We'Moon 2010 also appear in the wall calendar and note cards available from MT Ink:
We'Moon on the Wall • $13.95
ISBN: 978-1-890931-63-6
We'Moon Cover Poster • $10
ISBN: 978-1-890931-66-7
We'Moon Cards • $10:
Greeting • ISBN: 978-1-890931-64-3
Solstice • ISBN: 978-1-890931-65-0

2010

JANUARY

S	M	T	W	T	F	S
					1	2
3	4	5	6	7	8	9
10	11	12	13	14	15	16
17	18	19	20	21	22	23
24	25	26	27	28	29	30
31						

FEBRUARY

S	M	T	W	T	F	S
	1	2	3	4	5	6
7	8	9	10	11	12	13
14	15	16	17	18	19	20
21	22	23	24	25	26	27
28						

MARCH

S	M	T	W	T	F	S
	1	2	3	4	5	6
7	8	9	10	11	12	13
14	15	16	17	18	19	20
21	22	23	24	25	26	27
28	29	30	31			

APRIL

S	M	T	W	T	F	S
				1	2	3
4	5	6	7	8	9	10
11	12	13	14	15	16	17
18	19	20	21	22	23	24
25	26	27	28	29	30	

MAY

S	M	T	W	T	F	S
						1
2	3	4	5	6	7	8
9	10	11	12	13	14	15
16	17	18	19	20	21	22
23	24	25	26	27	28	29
30	31					

JUNE

S	M	T	W	T	F	S
		1	2	3	4	5
6	7	8	9	10	11	12
13	14	15	16	17	18	19
20	21	22	23	24	25	26
27	28	29	30			

JULY

S	M	T	W	T	F	S
				1	2	3
4	5	6	7	8	9	10
11	12	13	14	15	16	17
18	19	20	21	22	23	24
25	26	27	28	29	30	31

AUGUST

S	M	T	W	T	F	S
1	2	3	4	5	6	7
8	9	10	11	12	13	14
15	16	17	18	19	20	21
22	23	24	25	26	27	28
29	30	31				

SEPTEMBER

S	M	T	W	T	F	S
			1	2	3	4
5	6	7	8	9	10	11
12	13	14	15	16	17	18
19	20	21	22	23	24	25
26	27	28	29	30		

OCTOBER

S	M	T	W	T	F	S
					1	2
3	4	5	6	7	8	9
10	11	12	13	14	15	16
17	18	19	20	21	22	23
24	25	26	27	28	29	30
31						

NOVEMBER

S	M	T	W	T	F	S
	1	2	3	4	5	6
7	8	9	10	11	12	13
14	15	16	17	18	19	20
21	22	23	24	25	26	27
28	29	30				

DECEMBER

S	M	T	W	T	F	S
			1	2	3	4
5	6	7	8	9	10	11
12	13	14	15	16	17	18
19	20	21	22	23	24	25
26	27	28	29	30	31	

● = NEW MOON, PST/PDT

Climbing

○ = FULL MOON, PST/PDT

Cover Notes

Front Cover Art: Firedancer ¤ ***Teresa Wild 2007***

Elemental magic-maker—Paper sky lanterns are big, and can't fly wet. It was pouring the night the villagers gathered to release them. Drums began, hoops were lit, the dancers twirled—suddenly the clouds parted! The lanterns were quickly ignited and sent up to the ancestors. As the last disappeared into the darkness, the rain blew back in and drove everyone home!

Back Cover Art: Mothering the Fire Egg © ***Lisa Noble 2005***

Dragons are our contact with the spirit world. Here by mandala magick they bring forth the Fire Egg spiraling in the rhythm of the dragon circle. The Egg, a gift from the Goddess of Fire, is a promise of transformation and potential. Empowered, we journey past our daily boundaries, for beyond here there be dragons!

Dedication

Kali Cobwoman

© Becky Bee 1998

We'Moon 2010 is dedicated to women who are reinventing the wheel by re-imagining our dwellings. As building trades are industrialized around the world, people lose touch with the basic empowerment of creating our own shelter, a job traditionally done by women in many cultures. Our modern buildings are expensive, often toxic, and giant wasters of energy. The natural building movement, pioneered in large part by women such as Becky Bee, Linda Smiley and Athena Swentzell Steen, addresses these issues by combining ancient techniques with new innovations.

Working with unprocessed, local materials like earth, stone and straw, and using salvaged resources, permaculture design principles, and a small-is-beautiful aesthetic, MudGirls is one organization putting these ideas into motion. The women of this consensus-based, non-hierarchical collective based in BC, Canada, seek to empower themselves and others by sharing natural building knowledge and skills. MudGirls works mostly with cob: a durable, sculptural mixture of sand, clay, straw and water. They barter their work, offer affordable owner-builder assistance, organize low-cost workshops, and work to facilitate the creation of not only beautiful, healing homes, but a joyful, connecting process of building. We dedicate a portion of the proceeds from this year's We'Moon to MudGirls for furthering their mission. See www.Mudgirls.ca to donate directly, and for more inspiration to get muddy!

Myshkin © Mother Tongue Ink 2009

Table of Contents

Introduction

Moon Calendar: Reinvent the Wheel

Calendar Page Features

Holydays: Ffiona Morgan; Astrological Predictions: Gretchen Lawlor

Appendix

Introduction and Appendix Features

We'Moon Cycles: Musawa; Astrologers: Gretchen Lawlor, Heather Roan Robbins, Sandra Pastorius, Susan Levitt, Beate Metz; Introduction to the Theme: Musawa; Introduction to the Holy Days: Ffiona Morgan; 2010 Lunar Phase Card: Susan Baylies.

What Is *We'Moon*? A Handbook in Natural Cycles

We'Moon: Gaia Rhythms for Womyn is more than an appointment book, it's a way of life! **We'Moon** is a lunar calendar, a handbook in natural rhythm, and comes out of international womyn's culture. Art and writing by we'moon from many lands give a glimpse of the great diversity and uniqueness of a world we create in our own image. **We'Moon** is about *womyn's spirituality* (spirit'reality). We share how we live our truth, what inspires us, how we envision our reality in connection with the whole earth and all our relations.

***We'moon* means "women."** Instead of defining ourselves in relation to men (as in *wo*man or *fe*male), we use the word *we'moon* to define ourselves by our primary relation to the natural sources of cosmic flow. Other terms we'moon use are *womyn, wimmin, womon, womb-one.* **We'Moon** is a moon calendar for we'moon. As we'moon, we seek to be whole in ourselves, rather than dividing ourselves in half and hoping that some "other half" will complete the picture. We see the whole range of life's potential embodied and expressed by we'moon and do not divide the universe into sex-role stereotypes. **We'Moon** is sacred space in which to explore and celebrate the diversity of she-ness on Earth. **We'Moon** is created by, for and about womyn: in Her image.

***We'moon* means "we of the moon."** The Moon, whose cycles run in our blood, is the original womyn's calendar. Like the Moon, we'moon circle the Earth. We are drawn to one another. We come in different shapes, colors and sizes. We are continually transforming. With all our different hues and points of view, we are one.

We'moon culture exists in the diversity and the oneness of our experience as we'moon. *We honor both.* We come from many different ways of life. At the same time, as we'moon, we share a common mother root. We are glad when we'moon from varied backgrounds contribute art and writing. When material is borrowed from cultures other than your own, we ask that it be acknowledged and something given in return. Being conscious of our sources keeps us from engaging in the divisiveness of either *cultural appropriation* (taking what belongs to others) or *cultural fascism* (controlling creative expression). We invite you to share how the "Mother Tongue" speaks to you, with respect for both cultural integrity and individual freedom.

Lunar Rhythms: Everything that flows moves in rhythm with the Moon. She rules the water element on Earth. She pulls on the ocean's tides, the weather, female reproductive cycles and the life fluids in plants, animals and people. She influences the underground currents in earth energy, the mood swings of mind, body, behavior and emotion. The Moon's phases reflect her dance with Sun and Earth, her closest relatives in the sky. Together, these three heavenly bodies weave the web of light and dark into our lives.

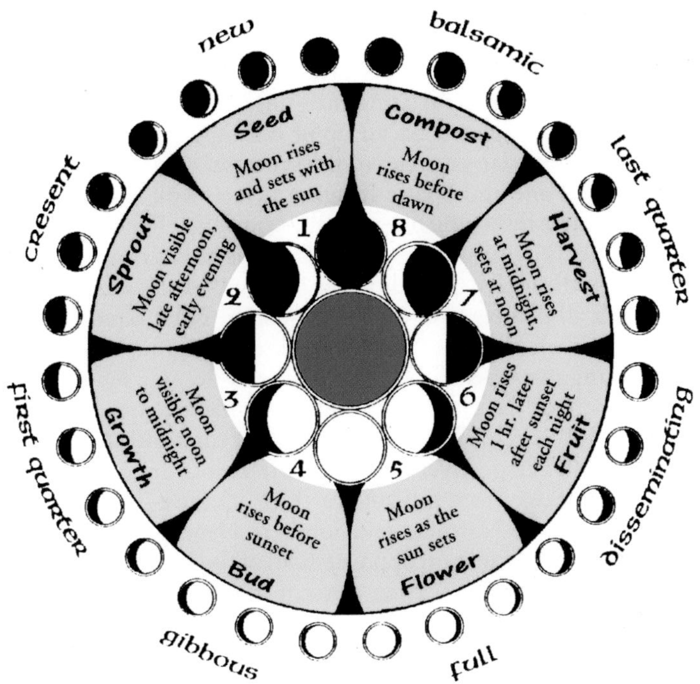

Susan Levitt © Mother Tongue Ink 2004

Gaia Rhythms: We show the natural cycles of the Moon, Sun, planets and stars as they relate to Earth. By recording our own activities side by side with those of other heavenly bodies, we may notice what connection, if any, there is for us. The Earth revolves around her axis in one day; the Moon orbits around the Earth in one month ($29^1/_2$ days); the Earth orbits around the Sun in one year. We experience each of these cycles in the alternating rhythms of day and night, waxing and waning, summer and winter. The Earth/Moon/Sun are our inner circle of kin in the universe. We know where we are in relation to them at all times by the dance of light and shadow as they circle around one another.

The Eyes of Heaven: As seen from Earth, the Moon and the Sun are equal in size: "the left and right eye of heaven," according to Hindu (Eastern) astrology. Unlike the solar-dominated calendars of Christian (Western) patriarchy, the **We'Moon** looks at our experience through both eyes at once. The **lunar eye** of heaven is seen each day in the phases of the Moon as she is both reflector and shadow, traveling her $29^1/_2$-day path through the zodiac. The **solar eye** of heaven is apparent at the turning points in the Sun's cycle. The year begins with Winter Solstice (in the Northern Hemisphere), the dark renewal time, and journeys through the full cycle of seasons and balance points (solstices, equinoxes and the cross-quarter days in between). The **third eye** of heaven may be seen in the stars. Astrology measures the cycles by relating the Sun, Moon and all other planets in our universe through the backdrop of star signs (the zodiac), helping us to tell time in the larger cycles of the universe.

Measuring Time and Space: Imagine a clock with many hands. The Earth is the center from which we view our universe. The Sun, Moon and planets are like the hands of the clock. Each one has its own rate of movement through the cycle. The ecliptic, a 17° band of sky around the earth within which all planets have their orbits, is the outer band of the clock where the numbers are. Stars along the ecliptic are grouped into constellations forming the signs of the zodiac—the twelve star signs are like the twelve numbers of the clock. They mark the movements of the planets through the 360° circle of the sky, the clock of time and space.

Whole Earth Perspective: It is important to note that all natural cycles have a mirror image from a whole earth perspective—seasons occur at opposite times in the Northern and Southern Hemispheres, and day and night are at opposite times on opposite sides of the Earth as well. Even the Moon plays this game—a waxing crescent moon in Australia faces right (e.g. ☾), while in North America it faces left (e.g.☽). **We'Moon** uses a Northern Hemisphere perspective regarding times, holy days, seasons and lunar phases. We'moon who live in the Southern hemisphere may want to transpose descriptions of the holy days to match seasons in their area. We honor a whole earth cultural perspective by including, among the four rotating languarges for the days of the week, two from the Southern Hemisphere: Swahili (a pan-African language spoken primarily in East Africa) and Quechua (the most common Amerindian language, spoken primarily in the Andes).

Whole Sky Perspective:

It is also important to note that all over the Earth, in varied cultures and times, the dome of the sky has been interacted with in countless ways. The zodiac we speak of is just one of many ways that hu-moons have pictured and related to the stars. In this calendar, we use the tropical zodiac.

Musawa
© Mother Tongue Ink 2008

Eternal Moon *© Nevas 2007*

How to Use This Book
Useful Information about *We'Moon*

Time Zones: All aspects are in Pacific Standard/Daylight Time, with the adjustment for GMT and EDT given at the bottom of each page. To calculate for other areas, see "World Time Zones" (p. 226).

Signs and Symbols at a Glance is an easily accessible handy guide that gives brief definitions of commonly used astrological symbols (p. 227).

Pages are numbered throughout the calendar to facilitate cross referencing. See Table of Contents (p. 5) and Contributor Bylines and Index (pp. 191–201). The names of the days of the week and months are in English with additional foreign language translations included (Spanish, Swahili, Quechua and Hawaiian).

Lunar Calendar Moon Theme Pages mark the beginning of each moon cycle with a two-page spread near the new moon. Each *Moon Page* is numbered with Roman numerals followed by the theme for that month (e.g. **II: Turn It Around!**) and contains the dates of that *Moon's* new and full moon and solar ingress.

Year at a Glance Calendar is on p. 3 (2010) and p. 228 (2011). **Month at a Glance Calendar** can be found on pp. 212–223 and includes daily lunar phases. At-a-glance lunar phases for 2010 can be found on pp. 224–225.

Annual Predictions: For your astrological portrait for 2010, turn to Gretchen Lawlor's Year at a Glance for your sun sign. See "Astrological Year at a Glance" (p. 21) for the page number of your portrait.

Holy Days: There is a two-page holy day spread for all 2010 equinoxes, solstices and cross-quarter days. These include feature writings by Ffiona Morgan, and are accompanied by art and writing.

Planetary Ephemeris: Exact planetary positions for every day are given on pp. 206–211. These ephemerides show where each planet is in a zodiac sign at noon GMT, measured by degree in longitude in Universal Time.

Asteroid Ephemeris: Exact positions of asteroids for every ten days are given for sixteen asteroids in the zodiac at midnight GMT on p. 205. See "Goddess Planets" (pp. 203–204) for more information.

Astrology Basics (Refer to sample on page 10)

Planets: Planets are like chakras in our solar system, allowing for different frequencies or types of energies to be expressed.

Signs: The twelve signs of the zodiac are a mandala in the sky, marking off 30° segments in the 360° circle around the earth. Signs show major shifts in planetary energy through the cycles.

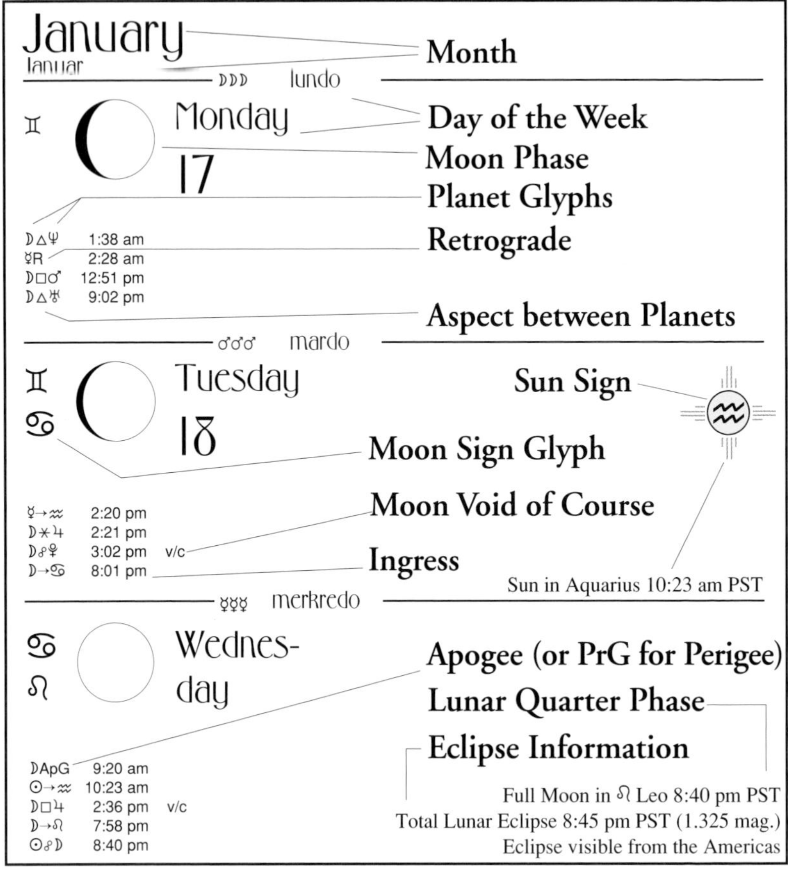

Sample calendar page for reference only

Glyphs: Glyphs are the symbols used to represent planets and signs.

Sun Sign: The Sun enters a new sign once a month (around the 20th or so), completing the whole cycle of the zodiac in one year. The sun sign reflects qualities of your outward shining self. For a description of sign qualities, see "Sun Signs" (pp. 12–14).

Moon Sign: The Moon changes signs approximately every 2 1/2 days, going through all twelve signs of the zodiac every 29 1/2 days (the sidereal month). The moon sign reflects qualities of your core inner self. For descriptions see "Moon Signs and Transits" (pp. 15–17).

Moon Phase: Each calendar day is marked with a graphic representing the phase of the Moon. Although the Moon is not usually visible in the sky during the new or dark moon, we represent her using miniscule crescent moon graphics for the days immediately before and after the actual new moon or conjunction.

Lunar Quarter Phase: At the four quarter-points of the lunar cycle waxing half, full and waning halfmoons) we indicate the phase, sign a. exact time for each. These points mark off the "lunar week."

Day of the Week: Each day is associated with a planet whose symbol appears in the line above it (e.g., ☽☽☽ is for Moon: Moonday, Monday, Luna Day, lundi, lunes). The names of the days of the week are displayed prominently in English with translations appearing in the line above them. Four languages—Spanish, Swahili, Quechua and Hawaiian—rotate weekly in this order throughout the calendar.

Eclipse: The time of greatest eclipse is given, which is near to, but not at the exact time of the conjunction (☉☌☽) or opposition (☉☍☽). Locations from where eclipses are visible are also given. For lunar and partial solar eclipses, magnitude is given in decimal form (e.g., 1.325 mag.), denoting the fraction of the Moon's diameter obscured by the shadow of Earth. For total and annular solar eclipses, the duration of the eclipse in minutes and seconds is given. For more information, see "Eclipses" (p. 18).

Aspects (□△☍☌⚹⚻): These show the angle of relation between different planets. Daily aspects provide something like an astrological weather forecast for the day, indicating which energies are working together easily and which combinations are more challenging. See "Signs and Symbols at a Glance" (p. 227) for a brief explanation of each kind.

Ingresses (→): Indicates when the Sun, Moon and other planets move into new signs.

Moon Void of Course (☽ v/c): The Moon is said to be void of course from the last significant lunar aspect in each sign until the Moon enters a new sign. This is a good time to ground and center yourself.

Apogee (ApG): This is the point in the orbit of a planet or the Moon that is farthest from Earth. At this time, the effects of transits (when planets pass across the path of another planet) may be less noticeable immediately, but may appear later on.

Perigee (PrG): This is the point in the orbit of a planet or the Moon that is nearest to Earth. Transits with the Moon or other planets when they are at perigee will be more intense.

Direct or Retrograde (D or R): These are times when a planet moves forward (D) or backward (R) through the signs of the zodiac (an optical illusion, as when a moving train passes a slower train that appears to be going backward). When a planet is in direct motion, planetary energies are more straightforward; in retrograde, planetary energies turn back in on themselves and are more involuted.

Musawa © Mother Tongue Ink 2000

Sun Signs and Sun Transits: 2010

Each month the Sun walks us through a unique gift and a lesson on our spiraling path; we choose how we respond at each crossroads. Our Birth Sun Sign describes the skeleton of personality underlying our unique being. (For discussion of elements and qualities, see page 20.)

♒ **Aquarius** (January 19–Febrary 18) The Sun in Fixed Air Aquarius immerses us in our responsibility to the collective community. It's time to gather in circles, converse with opponents and cultivate allies. Spin theory, then turn it into action.

If you're born under the Aquarius Sun, you see the big picture and understand the group gestalt. You find the theory to encompass the facts. You can choose to get stuck in this airy realm of mind and distance, or choose intimacy as well as collectivity—if you're honest with what you feel and see the beauty right here, right now.

Transformation Mandala #1
© S. Grace Mantle 2002

♓ **Pisces** (February18–March 20) The Sun in Mutable Water Pisces reminds us of how subtle and complicated the truth really is. Our antennae and nerves vibrate; if we don't overload, this translates into compassion and creativity. It's time to pray deep, honor ritual, dream new dreams.

If you're born under the Pisces Sun, you have the intuition and flexibility to add harmony to the song, your music vibrating to life's motion. You can choose to be overwhelmed in the collective's song, or choose instead to stay flexible, remembering your own heart's song, adding to the world's orchestra.

♈ **Aries** (March 20–April 19) The Sun in Cardinal Fire Aries offers us a yearly rebirth, asking us to remember why we're alive and what motivates us. Our raw life force reaches past last year's compost and seeks new answers. A clear, healthy goal can focus this fresh, rude, self-focused passion wisely.

If you're born under Sun in Aries, you reek of life-force, simple and direct, strong and willful, ready to speak your mind. Your choice, at the crossroads: will you choose your own path rather than rebel from the ones given you by others?

♉ **Taurus** (April 19–May 20) Fixed Earth Taurus Sun is a rich loam that feeds the flowers and fertilizes our plans. It teaches us to work in a sacred way with the material world as we celebrate the burgeoning green magic. It asks us to choose embodied life.

If you're born under the Taurus Sun, you embody the sacred in the material world, see beauty in the earth and all her bounty, and tend to move like a rooting tree: slow, deep and strong. Will you choose to see the sacredness of matter, rather than attach to the matter itself?

♊ **Gemini** (May 20–June 21) The Sun in Mutable Air Gemini trains us in the language of the birds; it's time to talk, network, buzz, cross-pollinate. We explore possibilities, choose which way to go and whom to talk to along the way.

If you're born under the Gemini Sun, you're a born web-weaver and can be a hub of communications that networks your community together. You can choose not to get lost in the web, and instead remember your focus: who you are, where you're going, and what is the deeper meaning.

♋ **Cancer** (June 21–July 22) When the Sun enters Cardinal Water Cancer, we're called back to home and tribe to nourish our hearts and gardens, water them with emotional honesty and domestic care. What is home? First we connect with our nest, then we can expand home into community, country, planet and solar system.

If you're born under the Cancer Sun, your feelings dive deep to the oceanic wells that nurture us all. With such tender depth, it's a daily choice to care for self and other, and, instead of brittle protection, create dynamic safety to grow in peace.

♌ **Leo** (July 22–August 22) When the Sun enters Fixed Fiery Leo we're called to shine, to ripen our talents and our love as the fruit reddens around us, and to renew our souls with sunshine and our culture's bounty. We're challenged to remember that when we care for ourselves, we have more to offer others.

If you're born under the Leo Sun, you're here to shine without reservation and warm the world with your charismatic abundance. Will you follow the path of self centeredness, or will you see and honor the light in all others, as well?

♍ **Virgo** (August 22–September 22) The Sun's run though Mutable Earthy Virgo asks us to wake up our minds, harvest our summer's bounty, and reinvest in our life's work. We turn inwards and investigate the health of our bodies, minds and systems, decide what seeds to harvest, what to compost.

If you're born under the Virgo Sun, you naturally introspect, analyze and empathize. You harvest great ideas and turn them into useful and nourishing bread; you teach others not to skim the surface. Can you let go of the problem and seek creative solutions instead?

♎ **Libra** (September 22–October 23) The Sun in Cardinal Air Libra asks us to balance our life and bring ourselves into right relations with lover and work, with ecosystem and economy. It's karma time; we harvest what we've sown. Let's soften our extremes and walk the beauty way.

If you're born under the Libra Sun, you have a gift for relationships of all types; you can see all sides, understand many perspectives and mediate between. The crossroad can be a hard place as you see the benefit and cost of all paths; all paths have worth, so listen for which one speaks to you.

♏ **Scorpio** (October 23–November 22) The Sun in Fixed Water Scorpio sends us spelunking; we look under rocks, investigate dark corners of our culture, heart, and soul, and wake up our musky curiosity. We can choose to get stuck in the dark or seek mystery and transformation instead.

If you're born under a Scorpio Sun, you take pride in embodying mystery. You get real, and handle the tough stuff where your interests lie; you're intense and focused where they shine, distant where they don't. Can you choose breadth as well as depth, and keep your interests in context and in compassion?

♐ **Sagittarius** (November 22–December 21) The Sun in Mutable Fire Sagittarius opens our hearts and puts on our traveling shoes; explore the bigger picture, socialize, philosophize, politicize, and speak with unusual honesty, if not tact. The natural world and its many species can soothe our restless souls.

If you're born under the Sagittarius Sun, you can shoot from the hip without rancor, and so get away with speaking truths that just start fights for others. You're a global citizen, and can often see the far horizon better than those close-by. Instead of disconnecting, you can choose depth with freedom.

♑ **Capricorn** (December 21–January 19) The Sun in Cardinal Earth Capricorn calls us to the roots of our traditions, calls forth layers of family karma and asks us to walk forward with integrity. We are asked to reconsider our purpose, sort what to take into the new year and what to leave behind. If you're born under the Capricorn Sun, you can embody the strength and flintiness of the mountain crags, and potentially its visionary leadership—we all look to the mountains. It's your choice to choose the heights, a clear goal achieved with integrity, control over self and not others.

Heather Roan Robbins © Mother Tongue Ink 2008

MOON SIGNS AND MOON TRANSITS

Time Dancer
© Jakki Moore 2008

The Moon changes signs every 2 ½ days and sets the mood and tone of the time. The Moon's placement at our birth describes our relation to our home, soul, family and emotional lineage; it symbolizes our inner spiritual river and our lifetime mode of operations.

♒ **Aquarius**: The Moon in Aquarius connects us to our community, reminds us that we are in this together. It asks us to make sure we walk our talk and integrate our philosophy with our politics. We abstract, communicate and work the crowd, but may be less intimate. One born under Aquarius Moon is far sighted with a gentle stubbornness; she understands group dynamics and may be more aware in family, tribe, community than she is in her most intimate relations.

♓ **Pisces**: The Moon in Pisces reveals our permeability. We dream, and need to ground our dreams. We care, but can become overwhelmed by our awareness unless we feel spirit working though us. Time to: imagine, share, sense, meditate, nurture, soak, and find constructive ways to be sensitive. One born under the Moon in Pisces has extra perceptions and needs to build the strength (not defense) to match. She is sensitive, intuitive, responsive and compassionate; her dreams are a gift.

♈ **Aries**: The Moon in Aries lights a fire under our tail, it wakes us up, strips away our complications and our patience. We can make a fresh start but tend to shoot from the hip, move fast, argue quickly. Time to: initiate, speak up, weed, honor independence.

One born under Aries Moon is passionate, honest and fierce; big-hearted but intensely self-directed. She is happy to loan her fire to inspire others, just don't tell her what to do.

♉ **Taurus**: The Moon in Taurus grounds us, it slows us down and wakes our sensual nature and stubbornness, helps us dig deeper roots. Time to: garden, plant, cultivate seeds, relationships and ideas, make love, nurture, take a stand, embody. One born under a Taurus Moon roots deeply and changes slowly; she collects, touches, supports, sees the sacred in the world of matter. Steady, she can loan her strength to others, but may need to learn the beauty in change.

♊ **Gemini**: The Moon in Gemini wakes us up; we lose our concentration but quicken our communication. The conversation sparkles, our thinking broadens but doesn't deepen. Time to: network, investigate, translate, brainstorm, mediate, prune, edit, explain, broadcast. One born under a Gemini Moon can talk to anyone, think fast, multi-task, shift moods with grace, but needs to choose depth and focus.

♋ **Cancer**: The Moon in Cancer deepens our feelings; our moods are stormy and vast, our hunger and desire to feed others sharpen. We protect our own, nest in our cave, need to know we're safe. Hunger grows, but for more than food. Time to: water, plant, feed, nest, comfort, secure, dive deep into feelings. One born under Cancer Moon can be wonderfully nurturing to our culture, body, and soul when she feels safe. Early mother/home issues can be composted into empathic understanding.

♌ **Leo**: The Moon in Leo illuminates our extroverted sides; we brim with generosity but can get stuck in our own perspective. Time to: shine, express, dramatize, celebrate, create, appreciate, stage, reach out and be generous with our attention; watch assumptions and do not push the stubborn. One born under Leo Moon can fill a room with personality and make the most of any situation, but may need to learn to honor the quiet, mundane or another's reality.

♍ **Virgo**: The Moon in Virgo sends us back to work and gives us a to-do list. We become impatiently aware of what needs to be improved, fixed, or healed. Our compassion is strong, but we can get irritated at less industrious folk. Time to: weed, edit, critique, care, exercise, investigate, study, heal, but be gentle with others.

One born under a Virgo Moon is curious, responsible, caring, but needs to cultivate gentle acceptance of self and others.

♎ **Libra**: The Moon in Libra opens our sociability, brings a friendly, egalitarian vibe and encourages us to connect. Bread and roses: we need beauty like we need air. Time to: seek justice, romance, meet, approach, create, beautify, find our core balance, and balance our needs with others. One born under a Libra Moon is a peacemaker, but she needs to remember to keep herself in the equation. She sees the beauty and seeks fairness, helps us understand one another.

♏ **Scorpio**: The Moon in Scorpio gives us attitude, and brings out our primal side; it sharpens our curiosity and our edges, our focus to the point of obsession. Fluff doesn't cut it; get real or let it go; honor privacy, don't crowd. Time to: dig deep, weed, investigate, do surgery, keep secrets and love each other up. One born under Scorpio Moon is intense, fiercely curious, and needs to create solitude with healthy boundaries rather than isolation.

♐ **Sagittarius**: The Moon in Sagittarius gets us moving; it brings cheerful impatience and refreshing honesty. We need wide open minds, souls, attitudes but can't sit still. Time to: get honest, forgive, dance, hike, explore, and connect to the natural world. One born under a Sagittarius Moon is funny, restless, freedom-loving, and direct; she is a natural global citizen but needs also to look for answers at home. She accepts the wild in all sentient beings.

♑ **Capricorn**: The Moon in Capricorn inspires our ambitions for good or ill, we just have to be gentle on our souls if we're not there yet. Lead and manage, but do not manipulate or control. Time to: build, dig, organize, exercise discipline, work on foundations and make practical progress on a dream. One born under Capricorn Moon has a strong work ethic, competence, and leadership capacity, but may need to learn to love herself holding still.

Heather Roan Robbins © Mother Tongue Ink 2009

Moon *© Dorrie Joy 2007*

Eclipses: 2010

Solar and lunar eclipses occur only when the Earth, Sun and Moon align at the Moon's nodal axis, usually four times a year, during new moon and full moon, respectively. The South (past) and North (future) Nodes symbolize our greater evolutionary path. Eclipses catalyze our destiny's deeper calling. Use eclipse degrees in your birth chart to identify potential release points.

Two solar and two lunar eclipses take place in 2010. On January 14th a very long annular solar eclipse occurs at 25° Capricorn. Entrenched investments that no longer serve us can get released, clearing the path ahead. Pilgrims unite. On July 11th a total solar eclipse occurs at 19° Cancer. Clarify values around home and family security issues. Refresh your kinship circle.

On June 26th a partial lunar eclipse occurs at 4° Capricorn and conjuncts Pluto, activating a planetary grand cross. A shake down of our ruling power base reveals what communal commitments we actually honor. Get involved to evolve. On December 21st a total lunar eclipse occurs at 29° Gemini, highlighting our friendships and peers. Cultivate qualities within yourself to become a better friend, and find your reflection everywhere. Practice compassion.

Sandra Pastorius © Mother Tongue Ink 2009

Mercury Retrograde: 2010

Mercury, planetary muse and mentor of our mental and communicative lives, appears to reverse its course three or four times a year. We may benefit from less stress when it retrogrades by making allowances for a symbolic "sleep cycle." These periods give us permission to pause and go back over familiar territory, reflecting and giving second thoughts to dropped projects or miscommunications. Breakdowns can help us attend to the safety of mechanical and mobility modes. It's time to "recall the now" of the past and pay attention to underlying issues. Leave matters that lock in future commitments until Mercury goes direct.

This year begins with Mercury retrograde in Capricorn on December 26th, 2009. Tease out serious concerns in finances, and be thorough with checks and balances. Move forward after the 15th with confidence. From April 17th to May 11th with Mercury in Taurus, security is served through taking a grounded and deliberate approach to all practical affairs.

From August 20th to September 12th use Mercury in Virgo to repair and restore your credibility. Mercury retrogrades in Capricorn again from December 10th through 29th; revisit your goals for the year to cull any excuses or excesses, and then reinvent your promise for the year ahead.

Sandra Pastorius © Mother Tongue Ink 2009

Vibrational Medicines for 2010

Flower essences align us with the potent healing gifts of nature, supporting us in our awakening to a new way of being. California Wild Rose, a universal remedy for 2010, stimulates gratitude in the heart for being alive here on the Earth. By strengthening our loving appreciation for all of life, we shift from apathy, resignation and isolation to compassionate participation. California Wild Rose lifts the numbing fog, and rouses passion for caring, giving and serving.

Combine California Wild Rose with the remedy for the soul intention of your Sun or rising sign in 2010, and take it as needed orally or topically. Gentle enough to be used by children and animals as well as anyone in distress, they are available in many health stores or visit www.FlowerEssenceMagazine.com for sources.

Aries: Tiger Lily to shift from competitive instincts to cooperative/inclusive efforts for common good.

Taurus: Tansy lifts one from entrenched habits into new, more vital, purposeful action.

Gemini: Yellow Star Tulip for empathy to hear the meaning behind words/actions of others.

Cancer: Chicory helps loosen self-protectiveness to give and receive tender care.

Leo: Canyon Dudleya to experience deep joy and contentment in making art of daily routines.

Virgo: Dandelion to listen more closely to messages from a body desiring more ease.

Libra: Bleeding Heart to support more freedom and objectivity in relationships.

Sorpio: Sage provides wise review and appreciation when completing a chapter of life.

Sagittarius: Blackberry to contribute your optimism and perspective to group projects.

Capricorn: Black-eyed Susan supports recovery and transformation of unclaimed selves.

Aquarius: Mullein strengthens realignment of work with principles.

Pisces: Mountain Pennyroyal and Self-heal assist in clearing your psychic filters of collective toxins.

Gretchen Lawlor

Pema's Garden *© Beth Lenco 2005*

Astrology's Elemental Weave

Nature's webs weave our reality on every level, from inner to outer space. Astrology attempts to interpret the whole span. The **four elements** and the **three qualities** are the warp and woof of the astrological web, weaving unique combinations, as they alternate in sequence around the cycle of the year. If you know nothing else about astrology, you can navigate your birth chart simply by having a sense of the elements and qualities of the signs your planets are in.

Keys for the 4 Elements: Fire=spirit/transforming energy; **Earth**=physical form/matter-realizing energy; **Air**=consciousness/creative energy; **Water**=emotion/psyche, flowing energy.

Keys for the 3 Qualities: Cardinal signs initiate; **Fixed** signs maintain; **Mutable** signs dissolve and transform.

You can imagine what the qualities of each element might be like, by building on these key strands. Take the fire signs, for example: Aries (a cardinal fire sign) is like kindling wood: a temperment that burns hot and quick; Leo (a fixed fire sign) warms with a steady big fire of the heart/hearth; Sagittarius (a mutable fire sign) is like the embers that burn long after the flames have gone out, cool like contemplation and long-lasting. Each quality has both positive and negative manifestations: fixed earth can be loyal and stubborn; fixed water can be deep and stagnant; fixed air can be idealistic and rigid; fixed fire can be radiant and self-centered.

Such is life!

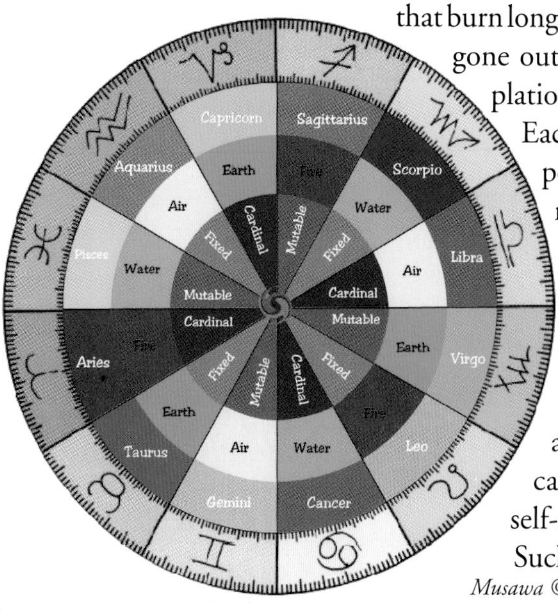

Astrological Year at a Glance

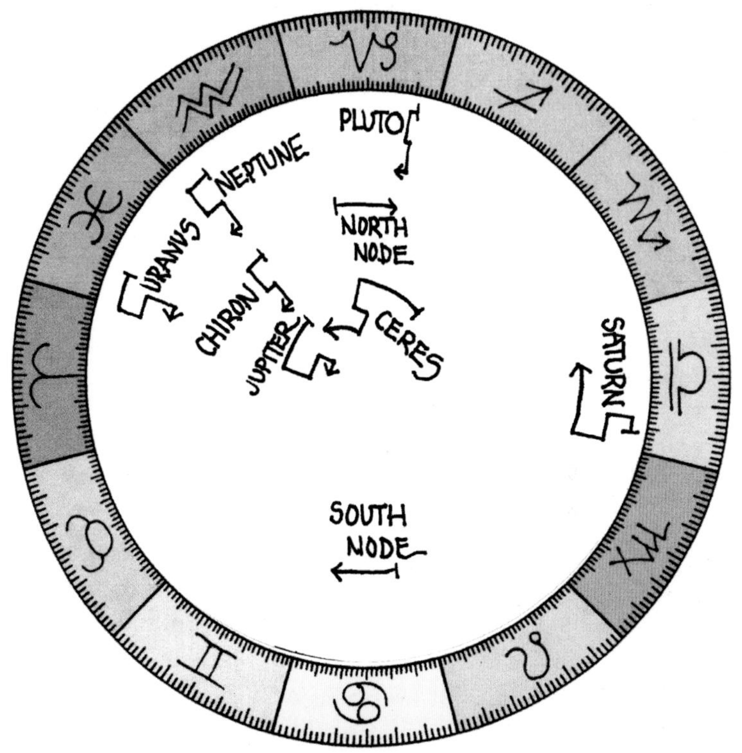

"As above, so below"—an ancient reminder of the parallel between planetary movements and life here on Earth. Uranus awakens and unsettles—and in 2010 Pisces and Aries-born will feel it most. Neptune inspires especially the Aquarians; Pluto transforms the Capricorns and all who hold positions of authority, while reactivating ancient wisdom in each of us. Chiron encourages us to share our healing stories; Jupiter rewards us when we release what no longer serves, while Saturn builds powerful alliances, encourages social activism, not only in Libran-born. The Moon's Nodes are not planets but signposts. When in doubt in 2010, take the path of self-mastery rather than reactive entrenchment in old ways.

The sky maps ways to optimize the best of the year and mitigate the challenges. For your own specific Year at a Glance for 2010 turn to the pages of your birth month.

Astro Overview: 2010

We need to find our core, our center of gravity, first and foremost this year, and operate from there. We have the opportunity to reinvent our wheel of life, but our axis needs to be well-centered for us to stay on track over rocky terrain as Saturn and change-making Uranus shift signs from adaptable Virgo and Pisces into proactive, dynamic Libra and Aries, and both form an unsettling, innovative T-square with Pluto in Capricorn.

This line-up describes the peak of a four-year pivot point in history. We left one era as structural, disciplinarian Saturn perfected an opposition to electrical, chaotic Uranus exactly on Election Day 2008. We learned to adjust as this aspect peaked twice in 2009, and can feel the foundations of our world shift as this opposition peaks on 4/26 and 7/26. It's time to reinvent, not retread; transform into something completely new without throwing away the wisdom we've worked so hard to acquire.

While this wild astrological earthquake can break open the potential of the future, it also puts stress on the cracks in the culture. War zones will feel this hot breath, as will any clash that tempts us to demonize the opposition. Stress along the fault lines can shake the ground; the elements will remind us of their primordial power. It's a freedom-loving rollercoaster ride, though sometimes freedom is having nothing left to lose.

Saturn in Libra can help us find partnership through our work. Our vital and loving relationships will strengthen if we give them room to breathe and encourage each one to their largest self as Uranus in Aries calls us to be our most authentic, uncompromising self. But relationships that are just kept together out of habit will feel the pressure. Both sides could feel held back by the other, but most likely it's how we relate that's the problem, not the needs of the other person involved.

We need to listen to our dreams and brainstorm our vision as Jupiter conjuncts intuitive Neptune on New Year's, then enters Pisces 1/17. As Neptune conjuncts healing Chiron 2/10, it offers us a chance to compost our pain and fertilize our spiritual or creative growth. All this soggy Neptune energy can leave us feeling flooded or awash early in the year; watch for water damage and consider making a spiritual journey or retreat. Jupiter in Pisces asks us to seek our freedom in Piscean imagination and sensitivity to the spiritual pulse.

Spinning Your Dreams
© Melissa Harris 1999

As Saturn squares Pluto exactly (1/31 and 8/21, though we feel it all year) we may be tempted to misuse our power as another misuses theirs; this can test the power dynamics of romances and international relations alike. We're pressured to birth new forms of power in all its dimensions; renewable utilities, healthy political power and empowered individual souls. We just need to stop arguing and get to work.

As Saturn dances between Libra and Virgo it reminds us that it takes hard work to create beautiful dreams and healthy egalitarian partnerships. We get the vision, go back to do the homework, and then sort the results as Saturn retrogrades in Libra 1/13, reenters Virgo 4/7, turns direct 5/30 and reenters Libra 7/21. By the fall we'll assess which new creative projects and love interests are bearing fruit, and which aren't.

Jupiter pumps up the volume on whatever it touches; as it dances with Uranus from April onwards, it will intensify our potential for change. Together they speed up technological breakthroughs and empower the youth, but can leave us feeling unanchored. Uranus enters Aries 5/27, Jupiter enters 6/5, and they conjunct 6/8 to offer a taste of the future. They both retrograde back into Pisces (Uranus on 8/10, Jupiter 9/8), conjunct again 9/18, and then do this dance in reverse in 2011.

As Uranus enters Aries it feeds the revolutionary spirit and births innovation. We want to do things our way, avoid the rule book and push horizons for the next 8 years. Old traditions may be temporarily ignored unless they're stated afresh. The whole cultural center of gravity shifts to a younger focus, but we still need to learn from the past to avoid repeating it. If we feel a new generational gap growing, let's bridge it but not fight it; empower the next generation while honoring the unique wisdom of the last.

A lunar eclipse 6/26 and solar eclipse 7/11 help us break into the next level of our work or personal evolution if we take personal responsibility for the change. Let's work towards a potential breakthrough around 7/30 as Jupiter, Moon and Uranus conjunct in Aries, all oppose Saturn conjunct Mars in Libra, and all 5 planets square Pluto in Capricorn. This could be a make or break time; it turns up the heat on our search for self-realization and independence, both on the international front and in our bedroom.

If we ask anyone to choose between Aries' self-realization and Libran connection, they'll choose realization or explode. But this dichotomy is illusory; we need both. To get there we need leadership without oppression, leadership towards fresh goals and not just in rebellion. We need to be true to ourselves and also be spacious and real with one another; drop the delusion that anyone but ourselves can hold us back and appreciate the glorious contribution each one makes.

In the fall, we'd better make sure we're headed in a good direction. Mars forms a series of dynamic aspects which spark our life and energize our journey, finishing the year with a powerful Mars-Pluto conjunction on 12/13. 2010 is potential-packed; if we can work dynamically within our constraints we'll break barriers and enlighten our darkest corner. But we need to move forward with integrity and spiritual connection; what happens to the least of us happens to us all.

Heather Roan Robbins

www.roanrobbins.com

Moon Glow
© Maria Silmon 2007

Flight of Spring © *Jacqueline Young 2008*

The Year of the Tiger: 2010

The year of the Tiger begins on the New Moon of February 13th. (Chinese New Year begins on the second New Moon after Winter Solstice.) Anticipate a dynamic year of sudden opportunities, bold actions, and life experiences on a grand scale. Mighty Tiger brings a year of extremes when drama and excitement reign, tempers flare, and the wildest dreams can become reality. There is little restraint as brave Tiger pounces on new endeavors. Expect massive social change, political rebellion, and military coups all over the world.

We'Moon born in Tiger years (1902, 1914, 1926, 1938, 1950, 1962, 1974, 1986, 1998, 2010) have a regal quality and assume the leadership role whenever possible. Tiger gals naturally possess strength, determination, and charisma. No matter how many obstacles are in their path, they will courageously pursue their goals. Tigers are free thinkers and non-conformists like their Western counterpart Aquarius. But despite the independent and dynamic mask they wear to the world, underneath their fur the Tiger is sensitive and emotional. A Tiger gal demands much attention from her partner, but when given enough love and support she turns into a gentle pussy cat.

Thank Goddess for the Women's Movement because Tiger daughters were not valued in sexist patriarchal cultures. The Confucian "Three Virtues for Women" state that a daughter obey her father, a wife obey her husband, and a crone obey her eldest son. But we'moon Tigers are warrioresses who will not willingly submit to rules; they bow down to no one. Tiger is a formidable animal totem to contact in the shamanic realm to assist in banishments and purifications because Tigers scare off thieves, ghosts, and fires.

Susan Levitt © Mother Tongue Ink 2009

The Wheel of the Year: Holy Days

The seasonal cycle of the year is created by the tilt of the Earth's axis, leaning toward or away from the Sun, north to south, as the Earth orbits the Sun. Solstices are the extreme points all over the world when days and nights are longest or shortest. On equinoxes, days and nights are equal in all parts of the world. The four cross-quarter days roughly mark the mid-points in between solstices and equinoxes. These natural turning points in the Earth's annual cycle are the holidays we commemorate in **We'Moon**. We use the dates in the ancient Celtic calendar, which closely approximate the eight spokes of the wheel of the year.* Seasonal celebrations of most cultures cluster around these same natural turning points; we list here a very few of the world's many holy days/holidays.

Dec. 21 Solstice/Winter: returning of the light—Kwanzaa (African-American), Soyal (Hopi), Jul (Scandanavian), Cassave/Dreaming (Taino), Chanukah (Jewish), Christmas (Christian), Festival of Hummingbirds (Quecha). Goddess Festivals: Freya (Norse), Lucia (Italy), Sarasvati (India).

Feb. 2 Imbolc/Mid-Winter: celebration, prophecy, purification, initiation—Candlemas (Christian), New Year (Tibetan, Chinese, Iroquois), Tu Bi-Shevat (Jewish). Goddess Festivals: Brigit, Brighid, Brigid (Celtic).

Mar. 20 Equinox/Spring: rebirth, fertility, eggs—Passover (Jewish), Easter (Christian). Goddess Festivals: Eostare, Ostara, Oestre (German), Astarte (Semite), Persephone (Greek), Flora (Roman).

May 1 Beltane/Mid-Spring: planting, fertility, sexuality—May Day (Euro-American), Walpurgisnacht/Valborg (German and Scandanavian), Root Festival (Yakima), Ching Ming (Chinese), Whitsuntide (Dutch). Goddess Festivals: Aphrodite (Greek), Venus (Roman), Lada (Slavic).

June 21 Solstice/Summer: sun, fire festivals—Niman Kachina (Hopi). Goddess Festivals: Isis (Egyptian), Litha (N. African), Yellow Corn Mother (Taino), Ishtar (Babylonian), Hestia (Greek), Sunna (Norse).

Aug. 2 Lammas/Mid-Summer: first harvest, breaking bread, abundance—Green Corn Ceremony (Creek), Sundance (Lakota). Goddess Festivals: Corn Mother (Hopi), Amaterasu (Japanese), Hatshepsut's Day (Egyptian), Ziva (Ukraine), Habondia (Celtic).

Sept. 22 Equinox/Fall: gather and store, ripeness—Goddess Festivals: Tari Pennu (Bengali), Old Woman Who Never Dies (Mandan), Chicomecoatl (Aztec), Black Bean Mother (Taino), Epona (Roman), Demeter (Greek)

Oct. 31 Samhain/Mid-Fall: underworld journey, ancestor spirits—Hallowmas/Halloween, All Souls Day (Christian), Sukkoth (Jewish harvest). Goddess Festivals: Baba Yaga (Russia), Inanna (Sumer), Hecate (Greek).

*** Note: Traditional pagan Celtic/N. European holy days start earlier than the customary Native/North American ones—they are seen to begin in the embryonic dark phase: e.g., at sunset, the night before the holy day.**

 Sources: The Grandmother of Time *by Z. Budapest, 1989;* Celestially Auspicious Occasions *by Donna Henes, 1996 and* Songs of Bleeding *by Spider, 1992*

SUN CYCLE
Lammas
LUGHNASADH
FEAST OF LOAVES
summer solstice
Midsummers Eve
fall equinox
Harvest Moon
WALPURGISNACHT
BELTANE
MAY DAY
ALL HALLOWS EVE
SAMHAIN
ALL SOULS DAY
spring equinox
Ostara
winter solstice
Yuletide
CANDLEMAS
IMBOLC
FEAST OF LIGHTS
PAGAN
HOLY DAYS
OF THE YEAR
Max Dashu

Introduction to the Holy Days

The Wheel of Life is a constantly moving, changing circle of life. In European traditions, the Wheel contains eight spokes, or Holydays, which are celebrated to honor the rhythmic change of the seasons. Just as there are special holy places on our planet which hold great magic, there are also intense holy times when a door of power swings open, and we can experience that same mystery.

These ancient festivals celebrate and revere the cycles of growing things and of all life: birth, maturity and death. They are also a personal celebration of our womanly cycles, a natural rhythm that ebbs and flows, like the ocean tides. Rituals are a medium for transcending everyday reality and experiencing a place "out of time." They link our inner and outer worlds by honoring our changes, connecting us to each other and to the universe. On each Holyday we remember the one we celebrated last year, and the year before; our present experience and knowledge are deepened by those memories.

The solstices and equinoxes are celebrated as each astrological quarter begins with its initiating Cardinal sign (see page 20: "Astrologies Elemental Weave"). Then, at the potent Cross-quarter festivals of Brigit/Imbolc, Beltane, Lammas and Samhain, an energy surge releases the intense force of the Fixed signs—Power Gates, through which profound, sacred energy flows, recharging our spiritual batteries. The Mutable signs end each quarter, to culminate, dissolve and change.

Transformative energy is available for healing and strength on Holydays. It is especially important to utilize it now, when mending the heart of the planet is such a formidable task. We live in a fast-moving world gone out of control. We must continually repair ourselves, as well as the pulsing threads that comprise the living web in which we exist. It took eons to create the world and its life forms, yet how quickly it all could be destroyed!

We call on the timeless Goddesses of destiny and karma to restore wholeness to the cycle, and we implore all earthlings, as guardians of the mundane world, to work tirelessly for healing the Web.

With your magic broom, sweep the earth's floor to clear your path, then move forward, in faith that you are participating in the Great Healing.

Introduction to the Theme: We'Moon 2010: Reinvent the Wheel

We'Moon 2010 is a wake up call. In recent years, our themes have honed in on womyn's creative response to the planetary urgency of these times: *On Purpose* (**We'Moon '07**), *Mending the Web* (**We'Moon '08**), *At the Crossroads* (**We'Moon '09**). Now as life-support systems continue to break down and reel out of control on a global scale, we are called to *Reinvent the Wheel* to restore balance for survival of life on earth.

The Wheel is an ancient metaphor for the great cycles of Karma/Destiny/Fate, of Life and Death. From the nucleus of an atom to the hub of the universe, through the Wheel of the Year and the flux of life cycles, we are caught up in the mysterious turns of personal, planetary and galactic rhythms. The art and writing in **We'Moon 2010** celebrate Gaia Rhythms for Womyn in the manifold cycles of change, the spinning of the Wheel. The Great Round of the seasons is the secure ground for the 13 Moons of this year, as the Earth spins us through the cycles of solar, lunar, astrological revolutions. Riding on the thin rim between alarm at what humankind has wrought and trust in Spirit at the center, we are moved to *Reinvent the Wheel* to transform and repair Her sacred order.

At this cusp of the second decade of the 21st century, we include all four digits of the year in our title, **We'Moon 2010**, and expand our numerological perspective in considering the theme. Drawing from the Major Arcana of Tarot to read the winds of cosmic currents, this year's theme is a spin-off from Tarot card #10 (X), The Wheel of Fortune. 20/10 could be seen as different octaves on the same scale,

Spider Woman: Life Weaver D.O.M. *Tarot* © *Ffiona Morgan* 1986

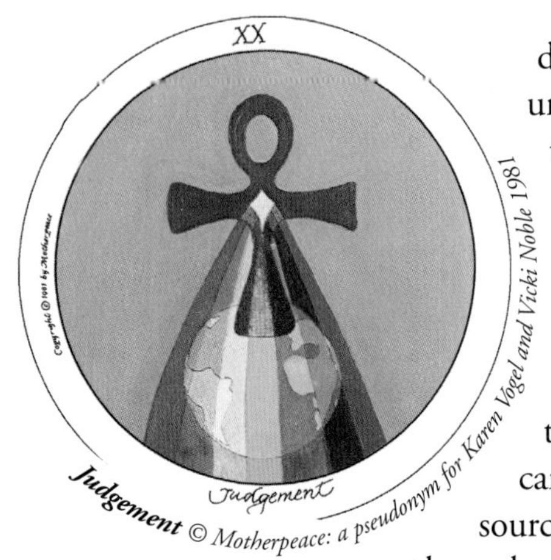

Judgement © *Motherpeace: a pseudonym for Karen Vogel and Vicki Noble 1981*

doubling the overtones of urgency, and calling in XX, the Judgment card. The numerology of the year 2010 distills down further to 3 (III, the Empress or Earth Mother), unleashing the power of womyn to change the World (21 or XXI). We can align ourselves with the true source of our power and let it shine through our hearts, as reflected in this Judgment card image. If we miss our chance to *Reinvent the Wheel*, the Wheel of Fortune will continue spinning out of control. The choices we make now may well determine our fate for millennia to come. *Where will this spin of the Wheel stop?*

As of this writing, the international economy is in collapse; global war, terror, poverty, hunger, disease, the threat of nuclear and natural disasters are on the rise; and the ability of the planet to support life is breaking down all over. The most basic natural rhythms have been thrown off balance. We are shaken by extremes of climate change—severe local weather, melting polar ice caps, extinction of species and eco-systems. With steady and sudden demise of "the birds and the bees," disrupted patterns of migration and reproduction of plants, animals, humans—our life force is diminishing. From genetically modified organisms (GMO's) to rampant mutations in nature to cosmic shifts: all forms of life are systemically thrown off balance as even the Earth, our vehicle through space, wobbles ever more erratically on Her axis. What we have counted on to sustain our lives can no longer be taken for granted, personally or planetarily. When intensifying man-made forces of destruction, dissention and dissolution interact with increasingly unpredictable natural forces and the vagaries of choice and chance—*What role is left for us to play in shaping our destiny?*

As ancient prophecies foresaw, we are going through a period of great suffering and destruction. Caught in the crosscurrents of the "Old Order" collapsing and the labor pains of a "New Order" emerging, we are thrown into a cauldron of total transformation. In native traditions, prophecies are not predictions set in stone about a pre-destined future; they are ongoing messages from Spirit unfolding in the hearts of people who are open to receive them. Nature is the primary source of prophecy: natural wisdom in action. Traditional ceremonies and practices help keep alive connection with Spirit whose guidance people depend on for survival. As long as the Earth was revered as the Mother of all creation—a living organism, the embodiment of Spirit in all forms—the Wheel of Life was held in balance naturally and life on Earth was sustainable. *If it ain't broke, don't fix it*—and if it is broken, fix the cause: Man's relation to the Wheel . . . and the solutions will come naturally. Every point in a circle is equidistant from the center: the spokes of the wheel balanced perfectly in Nature's blueprint. Radiating out in all directions, different spokes for different folks, equally valued, all one circle: may the circle be unbroken! In designing solutions to today's problems, the innovative science of Biomimicry asks what indigenous earth-keepers have always understood: *How would Nature do it?*

The rise in ecological awareness, green technologies, environmental justice, holistic healing, natural foods and medicines, earth-based spirituality, indigenous and women's wisdom traditions, leadership by and for the people—all these energies are seismic shifts in consciousness. The polarity is beginning to shift back toward a more life-affirming stance with a growing commitment to clean up our act on a global scale. As the ground shifts beneath us, we are being called to create a new way of being that supports a whole and healthy planet. As of this writing, news of the first African-American family moving into the White House is being celebrated the world over with high hopes for people joining in a new paradigm to turn the tide. By the time you read this, that will be old news, but time will tell which way the tide is turning. *Can we hold the balance?*

We'Moon artists and writers offer hopeful images of next steps for 2010. They invite us deep into the wisdoms of past generations and indigenous earth-loving peoples. **We'Moon** voices call us to the land, where women have renewed passion for growing organic food, saving seed, preserving harvests, where indigenous movements struggle against corporate control of vital life processes like water, traditional medicines and foods. Urgency about war and climate change is framed with visual beauty and graceful word, conjuring reinventions of self, celebrating diversities of ethnic origins and traditions, embracing the cycles of life and death wholeheartedly. Changing Woman is in charge here, as women work on personal healing and on restoring planetary balance. "*...the womyn who goes back to change the future*" (Patti Sinclair, p. 134) has her hands on the karmic Wheel, turning and being turned in the great revolutions that cycle through this moment in herstory. **We'Moon 2010** serves as chronicle and oracle of these changes.

The line along the bottom of the pages of this *Introduction to the Theme* represents how long Earth Mother's natural wisdom has held sway—in contrast to the dot at the end, the drop in the bucket that is the current time of imbalance. Does it mark "the end," period? The ancient Mayan calendar stops abruptly in 2012. Or could it be a synapse, a period of re-organization for a quantum leap to a new orbit of possibility? The International Council of Thirteen Indigenous Grandmothers* speaks of hope for balance returning: balance among all our relations, balance in harmony with Mother Earth. The open space that follows is the synapse between now and what is to come. What will you fill it with this year? We offer the creative expression of we'moon in the following pages as inspiration to connect with your center and the ground you stand on, to bring balance in your life and sustain the vehicle that carries us all, this Great Mother Earth.

Musawa © Mother Tongue Ink 2009

**www.GrandmothersCouncil.com*

O Goddesses of The Great Round!
Gaia, Mother Nature, Changing Woman
We are in awe of your mighty spinning
Your Great Cycles of Life/Death/Re-birth
Up and Down and Around
Fortuna and Tyche—Mothers of Destiny
Norns and Moerae—The Three Fates
Arianrhod—Keeper of the Silver Star-Wheel
Kali—Time Dancer, Goddess of the Karmic Wheel
Help us repair the world
Reinvent the human spin
Even as we swing round toward the unthinkable
Help us to trust in your Wholeness.

Nehiyaw Medicine *© Leah Marie Dorion 2005*

GAIA'S MESSAGE

I am here
in the scent of a flower
in the living rainbow of light
on a dew drop
on a blade of grass

I am in every ray of the sun's light
in every grain of sand and drop of rain
in the rising mist
in the heat of the morning sun

and I am living through you

I whisper my secrets to you
when you are waking
and sing to you my song
while you sleep

I teach you of love
and its unfolding
and hold you when you weep

I am a reflection of life's unfolding
and I too,
as you,
am evolving

I am growing and changing
just as you do

I am vast
and, like you
I am part of the great cosmic dance
of awakening and becoming

I dance with the planets and the stars
and sparkle
as a radiant emerald jewel
in the bed of the universe

I. THE GREAT ROUND

Moon 1: December 16–January 14

New Moon in ♐ Sagittarius Dec. 16; Sun in ♑ Capricorn Dec. 21; Full Moon in ♋ Cancer Dec. 31

Gaia Mandala

Be the Goddess

In this time of the Great Shift,
Let us make love without regret
No love is wasted.
Let us sing the old songs again.
Let us remember how to be
Magical creatures,
Animals of light,
Creating new life
In the spirit of our ancestors who loved us.

excerpt ¤ Silvie Jensen 2007

December 2009

Ayamarq'ay killa

☿☿☿ Quyllurchaw

♐ ♑

Wednesday 16

☽□♅ 12:22 am
☽✶♃ 1:32 am
☽✶♆ 3:05 am
☉☌☽ 4:02 am v/c
☽→♑ 2:32 pm
☽☌♇ 8:00 pm
☽□♄ 10:24 pm

New Moon in ♐ Sagittarius 4:02 am PST

♃♃♃ Illapachaw

♑

Thursday 17

♀△♂ 4:39 am
☽☌☿ 11:52 pm

♀♀♀ Ch'askachaw

♑

Friday 18

☽✶♅ 12:08 pm v/c

The Goddess Re-Turns ¤ *Selina Maria Di Girolamo 2008*

♄♄♄ K'uychichaw

♑
♒

Saturday

19

☽→♒ 2:39 am
♀⚹⚷ 10:45 am
☽△♄ 10:58 am
♀□♅ 5:52 pm

☉☉☉ Intichaw

♒

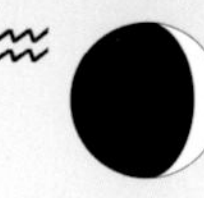

Sunday

20

♂R 5:26 am
☽ApG 6:55 am
☽☍♂ 6:44 pm
♀⚹♃ 8:53 pm
♀⚹♆ 9:24 pm

December 2009
Kēkēmapa

☽☽☽ pō 'akahi

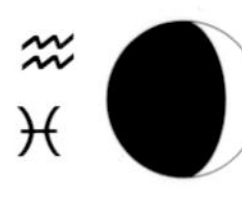

Monday 21

Winter Solstice

♃☌♆ 12:51 am
☽☌♆ 4:06 am
☽☌♃ 4:09 am
☿⊼♂ 4:33 am
☽✶♀ 4:54 am v/c
☉→♑ 9:47 am
21 ☽→♓ 3:42 pm
21 ☉✶☽ 4:15 pm
21 ☽✶♇ 9:42 pm

Sun in ♑ Capricorn 9:47 am PST

♂♂♂ pō 'alua

Tuesday 22

No Exact Aspects

☿☿☿ pō 'akolu

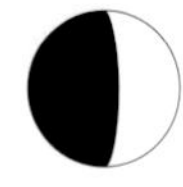

Wednesday 23

☽✶☿ 10:06 am
☽☌♅ 1:43 pm

♃♃♃ pō 'aha

Thursday 24

☽□♀ 12:09 am v/c
☽→♈ 3:39 am
☉☌♇ 9:32 am
☽□♇ 9:36 am
☉□☽ 9:36 am
☽☍♄ 12:01 pm

Waxing Half Moon in ♈ Aries 9:36 am PST

♀♀♀ pō 'alima

♈

Friday 25

♀→♑ 10:17 am
☉□♄ 3:58 pm
☽△♂ 5:00 pm
☽□☿ 9:16 pm
♇ApG 11:55 pm

All aspects in Pacific Standard Time; add 3 hours for EST; add 8 hours for GMT

Ring Around the Rosy International *© Joan Watterson 1996*

It has taken scientists until the twentieth century
to prove what we've known since time out of mind:
that we are all connected.

Agnes Baker Pilgrim, Takilma Grandmother
From Grandmothers Councel the World, *by Carol Schaefer © 2006 Reprinted by arrangement with Shambhala Publications Inc., Boston MA. www.shambhala.com*

♄♄♄ pō 'aono

♈ ♉

Saturday

26

☽⚹♆ 2:11 am
☽⚹♃ 3:44 am v/c
☿R 6:38 am
☽→♉ 12:26 pm
☽△♀ 3:12 pm
☽△♇ 6:08 pm
☉△☽ 10:39 pm

☉☉☉ lā pule

♉

Sunday

27

♀☌♇ 10:49 pm
☽□♂ 10:49 pm

December/January

diciembre / enero ☽☽☽ lunes

♉
♊

Monday
28

☽△☿ 2:36 am
☽⚹♅ 5:15 am
☽□♆ 7:48 am
☽□♃ 9:54 am v/c
☽→♊ 5:13 pm
♀□♄ 10:55 pm

♂♂♂ martes

♊

Tuesday
29

☽△♄ 12:43 am

☿☿☿ miércoles

♊
♋

Wednesday
30

☽⚹♂ 12:57 am
☽□♅ 7:30 am
☽△♆ 9:55 am
☽△♃ 12:29 pm v/c
☽→♋ 6:45 pm

♃♃♃ jueves

♋

Thursday
31

☽☍♇ 12:03 am
☽□♄ 1:59 am
☽☍♀ 6:35 am
☉☍☽ 11:13 am
☿⚻♂ 8:52 pm

Full Moon in ♋ Cancer 11:13 am PST
Partial lunar Eclipse 11:23 am PST *

♀♀♀ viernes

♋
♌

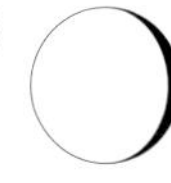

Friday
1

January 2010

☽☍☿ 12:34 am
☽△♅ 7:43 am v/c
☽PrG 12:44 pm
☽→♌ 6:41 pm

*Eclipse visible over most of Asia, Australia, Europe and Africa

The Dance of Changing Woman

Changing Woman was born on a sacred mountain, a rainbow arched over her as a quilt. Goddess of the seasons, of the constellations turning above, of sunrise and sunset, of moon's waning and waxing—she governs all of the mysteries of death and rebirth. She is the spring becoming summer turning towards fall and dying into winter's cold, the continual dance of birth, growth, death and the restoration to rebirth again.

Goddess of Laussel
© Lisa Aerianna Tayerle 2000

In the beginning, she gathered together her precious stones—jet, abalone, white shell, red-white stone—and mixed these with her skin, with clay, pollen, sand and water. She sang ritual songs over them and with great ceremony of covering and uncovering, she made the first beings.

She gave us her gifts of rites and ceremonies, her teachings of youth and age, time and eternity, her forever moving, forever evolving cycles. She gave women her House of Change which we enter at birth, and then again at first blood, at pregnancy, at midlife and on until the end of our life spirals.

She is the eternal rhythm and cycle of the moon, the hanging of the seasons, the ebb and flow of the tide. New moon, full and waning moon, then new again. We live in a universe where *everything* changes. Nothing remains static, rigid or fixed. We are Changing Woman.

excerpt © Beth Beurkens 2008

♄♄♄ sábado

♌

Saturday

2

☽✶♄ 1:55 am

☉☉☉ domingo

♌ ♍

Sunday

3

☽☌♂ 12:08 am
☽☍♆ 10:12 am
☽☍♃ 1:55 pm v/c
☽→♍ 6:52 pm

January

Januari

☽☽☽ Jumatatu

© Compago Creative 1999

♍

Monday

4

☽△♇ 12:29 am
☉☌☿ 11:06 am
☽△♀ 4:05 pm
☽△☿ 5:50 pm
☉△☽ 7:01 pm

♂♂♂ Jumanne

♍ ♎

Tuesday

5

☿☌♀ 2:39 am
☿PrG 4:46 am
☽☍♅ 9:25 am v/c
☽→♎ 8:58 pm

☿☿☿ Jumatano

♎

Wednesday

6

☽□♇ 3:00 am
☽☌♄ 4:54 am
☽□☿ 4:40 pm

♃♃♃ Alhamisi

♎

Thursday

7

☽□♀ 12:35 am
☉□☽ 2:39 am
☽✶♂ 3:34 am
☉⚻♂ 12:39 pm
☽△♆ 4:34 pm
☽△♃ 10:07 pm v/c

Waning Half Moon in ♎ Libra 2:39 am PST

♀♀♀ Ijumaa

♎ ♏

Friday

8

☽→♏ 2:00 am
♀⚻♂ 3:56 am
☽✶♇ 8:33 am
☽✶☿ 6:26 pm

The Garden of Divinity

We have the power
to keep the cycle turning,
But the seeds of change
must be planted now.
As we encourage admiration
for everyone and everything,
The flowers we plant
will bloom and burst with life—
A garden to yield
a harvest of true revival.

© Melanie Livengood
2008

The Great Wheel
¤ Colleen 1996

♄♄♄ Jumamosi

♏

Saturday
9

☽□♂ 9:24 am
☽⚹♀ 1:18 pm
☉⚹☽ 2:16 pm
☽△♅ 9:29 pm

☉☉☉ Jumapili

♏ ♐

Sunday
10

☽□♆ 12:22 am
☽□♃ 7:02 am v/c
☽→♐ 10:10 am
☽⚹♄ 7:07 pm

January

Qhapaqintiraymi killa

☽☽☽ Killachaw

She Who Spins the World Into Being
© Laura Amazzone 2006

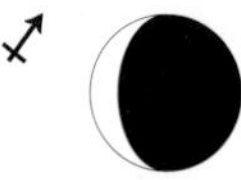

♐

Monday
11

☉☌♀ 1:06 pm
☽△♂ 5:48 pm

♂♂♂ Atichaw

♐
♑

Tuesday
12

☽□♅ 7:52 am
☽✶♆ 10:52 am
☽✶♃ 6:43 pm v/c
☽→♑ 8:54 pm

☿☿☿ Quyllurchaw

♑

Wednesday
13

♀✶♅ 1:48 am
☽☌♇ 4:23 am
☽□♄ 6:11 am
♄R 7:56 am
♀ApG 8:12 am
☽☌☿ 8:35 am
☉✶♅ 10:42 am

♃♃♃ Illapachaw

♑

Thursday
14

☽✶♅ 8:09 pm
☉☌☽ 11:11 pm

*Annular Solar Eclipse 11:06 pm PST
New Moon in ♑ Capricorn 11:11 pm PST

♀♀♀ Ch'askachaw

♑
♒

Friday
15

☽☌♀ 1:02 am v/c
☿D 8:52 am
☽→♒ 9:17 am
☽△♄ 6:43 pm

*Eclipse visible Central Africa, Indian Ocean into the South tip of India, and China.

The Three Fates

The Three Norns
© Sandra Stanton 2001

One to spin the thread of life,
One to measure its length,
One to snip
when our time is up.

When the veil
between worlds thins,
when Owl shines on you
with both her eyes,
you shiver my blood.
You who yanked me

by my umbilicus,
you who measure
and count my days
with finger songs, you
who sharpen your blade on a whirring wheel,

waiting, to you I bow. I dream you show me
the dark side of the spinning moon.
I go to my loom, like Spider, and weave

silk with your whispering words. To my
three sisters, this offering, tensile, light-filled.
The earth is a skein of silver thread.

© Joanne Rocky Delaplaine 2008

♄♄♄ K'uychichaw

Saturday
16

☽☍♂ 3:13 pm
☽ApG 5:42 pm

☉☉☉ Intichaw

Sunday
17

☽☌♆ 12:22 pm v/c
♃→♓ 6:10 pm
☽→♓ 10:17 pm
☽☌♃ 10:22 pm

Seison

When I was a little girl, just fifty years ago,
Wild geese filled the autumn skies with
harsh cacophonous song: thousands shouting south!
They were calling me out to feel the wild of their ways.
Hundreds of shifting and reshaping V's quivering,
as the compass needle inside them spoke south, south.
Gathering and going as just they ought, they turned
the earth with their near-winter work, with the tuck
and the stretch and the beat of their wings.

My people used to move with the seasons, too,
And my people turned the wheel of the stars
by their chanting and their dancing, by their
telling of what was told to them—that the seasons
are grace and goodness—that once upon a time
there were no seasons, only ice and cold and the
dark and the light, and the great beasts grew thick hair
and my people moved into the caves for eons.

But the ice finally melted and the rivers ran
and the fish jumped in the lakes, and the
trees blossomed and brought out warm fruit
when the days were long. And then leaves fell
and the fruits dried, along with the hunted meat.
And my people made thick dwellings and deep beds
for the time of rest that was just long enough
before the time for sowing, and the time
for tending, and the time for gathering in.

My people's hearts grew happy inside them,
Because they knew what to do when, and they
made great clocks of stone to celebrate the seasons.
They worshipped the clocks with songs and chants
and long processional dances down aisles of trees.
It was not really the stone they worshipped but the stars
and not the stars so much as what ordered the stars
and measured the days and glowed from the stones.

Sometime, at some point, someone forgot to tell
the story; and someone forgot to sing the songs;
and someone forgot the processional steps; and
others forgot to hear, and to worship, and to
turn the stars on the rhythm of their knowing feet.

II. TURN IT AROUND!

Moon II: January 14–February 13

New Moon in ♑ Capricorn Jan. 14; Sun in ♒ Aquarius Jan. 19; Full Moon in ♌ Leo Jan. 29

Global Cooling Incantation

My people no longer know when to do what;
Twenty-four and seven, they cry more, more, more.
But a cold panic rises within them, as the seasons,
left so long untended, begin to misbehave.

This morning I saw two wobbly V's as the snow geese
formed and gathered on the ancient route. Twenty-one
there were, and seventeen. Where are the thousand wild voices?
and the quivering shadow of all those wings?
Perhaps they have found a new south or a new way south.
But it was this morning I saw them forming and flying.
Now the night draws down, and from the heavens
fall the fair bright stars.

January
Ianuali

ᴅᴅᴅ pō 'akahi

© Jeannine Chappell 2008

Turning

♓ 

Monday
18

☽⚹♇ 6:15 am
♀→♒ 6:35 am
☽⚹☿ 10:48 am

♂♂♂ pō 'alua

♓ 

Tuesday
19

☉→♒ 8:28 pm
☽☌♅ 10:06 pm v/c

Sun in ♒ Aquarius 8:28 pm PST

☿☿☿ pō 'akolu

♓
♈

Wednesday
20

☽→♈ 10:36 am
☉⚹☽ 11:54 am
☽⚹♀ 4:37 pm
☽□♇ 6:32 pm
☽☍♄ 7:42 pm

♃♃♃ pō 'aha

♈ 

Thursday
21

☽□☿ 1:26 am
☽△♂ 12:02 pm
♀△♄ 10:07 pm

♀♀♀ pō 'alima

♈
♉

Friday
22

☽⚹♆ 11:46 am v/c
☽→♉ 8:39 pm
☽⚹♃ 10:51 pm

All aspects in Pacific Standard Time; add 3 hours for EST; add 8 hours for GMT

Year at a Glance for ♒ Aquarius (Jan. 19–Feb. 18)

This year you may think you're reaching a peak, but be willing to review and fine-tune your course to amplify your effectiveness in the next few years. Your big picture may be too small, your team may be moving in a direction that no longer suits you, or you may be too isolated. Your attitude is limiting your potential.

What different visions for the future do you have to offer to these changing times? What humanitarian causes and communities make you feel most happy and accepted? Aquarius is a natural inventor, instinctively attuned to future trends and needs. Developing talents in new technologies or progressive fields ignites your wildest genius and boosts your earning power.

From the end of May through the beginning of August you'll feel the excitement of new possibilities, new opportunities. The latter part of the year, however, may find you pulled back into what seems like "old stuff." Revise, prepare, replot your route. There'll be plenty of time for decisive action soon ahead.

If you are in school, you may consider changing majors or institutions in the next year. A profound mentor may appear, or you may find yourself in the role of guide/inspiration to younger souls.

In love, be a little more emotionally available. April–July months give you a chance to break out of an old uncomfortable shell. Changing the way you look helps you interact differently. As always, companions who share your ideals are the most likely to win your heart.

Gretchen Lawlor © Mother Tongue Ink 2009

Aphrodite Pouring Libation of Chocolate *© Kat Beyer 2007*

♄♄♄ pō 'aono

♉ 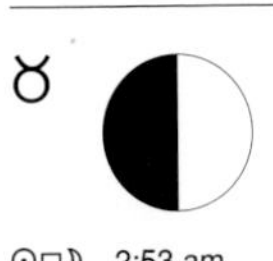

Saturday

23

☉□☽ 2:53 am
☽△♇ 4:19 am
☽□♀ 8:36 am
☽△☿ 2:07 pm
☽□♂ 7:03 pm

Waxing Half Moon in ♉ Taurus 2:53 am PST

☉☉☉ lā pule

♉ 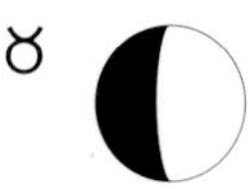

Sunday

24

☉△♄ 7:37 am
☽⚹♅ 4:25 pm
☽□♆ 7:02 pm v/c

January
enero

I speak of total revolution
and must therefore
turn around.
excerpt ¤ Elizabeth Page Roberts 2008

☽☽☽ lunes

♉ ♊

Monday 25

☽→♊ 3:11 am
☽□♃ 6:09 am
☽△♄ 11:04 am
☉△☽ 1:17 pm
☿⊼♂ 5:40 pm
☽△♀ 7:37 pm
☽✶♂ 10:35 pm

♂♂♂ martes

♊

Tuesday 26

☽□♅ 8:07 pm
♀☍♂ 9:29 pm
☽△♆ 10:32 pm v/c

☿☿☿ miércoles

♊ ♋

Wednesday 27

☽→♋ 6:01 am
☽△♃ 9:36 am
♂PrG 11:14 am
☽☍♇ 12:56 pm
☽□♄ 1:20 pm

♃♃♃ jueves

♋

Thursday 28

☽☍☿ 4:21 am
☽△♅ 8:48 pm v/c

♀♀♀ viernes

♋ ♌

Friday 29

☽→♌ 6:10 am
☉☍♂ 11:43 am
☽✶♄ 1:08 pm
☽☌♂ 9:20 pm
☉☍☽ 10:18 pm

Full Moon in ♌ Leo 10:18 pm PST

ALL ASPECTS IN PACIFIC STANDARD TIME; ADD 3 HOURS FOR EST; ADD 8 HOURS FOR GMT

Turning Swords into Plowshares

Walking down 8th Street
in the Village
this evening,
I passed
the Army/Navy Store,
displaying in its windows
army camouflage helmets
filled with earth,
in which were planted
white flowers.
Let us hope
this is what
we have come to,
or soon will,
soon will.

¤ *Karen Ethelsdattar 2008*

Finding Peace
© Cathy McClelland 2008

♄♄♄ sábado

♌ Saturday 30

☽PrG 1:01 am
☽☍♀ 5:49 am
☽☍♆ 10:27 pm v/c

☉☉☉ domingo

♌ ♍ Sunday 31

☽→♍ 5:23 am
☽☍♃ 10:19 am
☽△♇ 12:17 pm
♄□♇ 1:27 pm

February
Februari

☽☽☽ Jumatatu

Path of Tears © *Toni Truesdale 2006*

♍

Monday
1

☽△☿ 11:12 am
☽☍♅ 8:17 pm v/c

♂♂♂ Jumanne

♍ ♎

Tuesday
2

Imbolc/Candlemas

☽→♎ 5:42 am
☽☌♄ 12:48 pm
☽□♇ 1:01 pm
☽✶♂ 7:09 pm

☿☿☿ Jumatano

♎
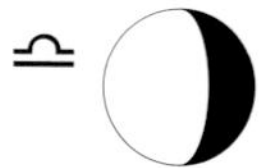

Wednesday
3

☉△☽ 6:14 am
☽△♀ 4:30 pm
☽□☿ 6:05 pm

♃♃♃ Alhamisi

♎ ♏
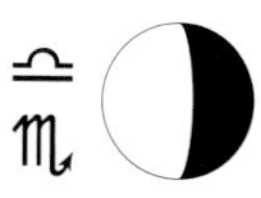

Thursday
4

☽△♆ 1:27 am v/c
☽→♏ 8:55 am
☽△♃ 4:15 pm
☽✶♇ 4:54 pm
☽□♂ 9:55 pm

♀♀♀ Ijumaa

♏

Friday
5

♃⚻♄ 12:14 am
☉□☽ 3:48 pm

Waning Half Moon in ♏ Scorpio 3:48 pm PST

All aspects in Pacific Standard Time; add 3 hours for EST; add 8 hours for GMT

Imbolc

A pure, new light sparks as we emerge from winter's dark sleep. The Power Gate of Aquarius opens, releasing the Air element and heralding returning light. We recharge our psychic batteries as the entire universe begins to quiver and pulse its cosmic rhythm. Earthlings feel Her intensity acutely as the Wheel shifts in these troubled times.

We meet in the temple's outer chamber. Since childhood we have trained as Priestesses of Brigit and keepers of Her eternal flame. Our lifework is committed to social justice and feeding the poor, sick and hungry; inspired by Brigit, we ask nothing in return.

Wemoon construct moonpoles with slender birch trees, parchment frames and votive candles. Dressed in white, we proceed into the dimmed temple, where our community waits. We can hear their soft humming. Our moonpoles are lit, held high they cast a beautiful glow of hope. We slowly circle the room, ending in a spiral. Everyone chants encouragement to the returning Sun; then we pledge our yearly commitments to Goddess—within and without. We devote ourselves to peace, caring for our precious earth and ending hatred among Her people. Our community is blessed!

Ffiona Morgan © Mother Tongue Ink 2009

Nature Diva ¤ *Diane Melanie 2002*

Silver Wheel

lightning
cracking open darks,
concealments, secret deals
Arianrhod is fierce
in her knowledge of Balance
and Beauty, she has Wisdom
flared in her hands, her mind
clear logic: She will countenance
no more from masters of illusion
who shuffle the laws of the Universe
to their gain. Her lightning-stars
are cracking the old order open
her power straking the land
back to life

Seeds of Change

Scattered throughout our Salmon Nation,
and across our planet, are the seeds of change.

Buried underground,
awaiting Spring's quickening,
curled up seedlings of change,
ready to pop their seed coats, unfurl,
push above ground, reach for the sun,
harness the wind, generate energy
to homes and businesses, everywhere.

Time is wasting.
We must move quickly
before the polar ice caps disappear forever,
drinking water is no longer available,
and the weather is perpetually altered.
"We are the change we wish to see in the world."
We are it. If not us, who?

Crack your seedpod.
Scatter your promise.
Nurture your soil.
Protect your waters.
Stretch your branches far and wide.
Grow! Grow!! Grow!!!

¤ *Stacy Anne Murphy 2008*

♄♄♄ Jumamosi

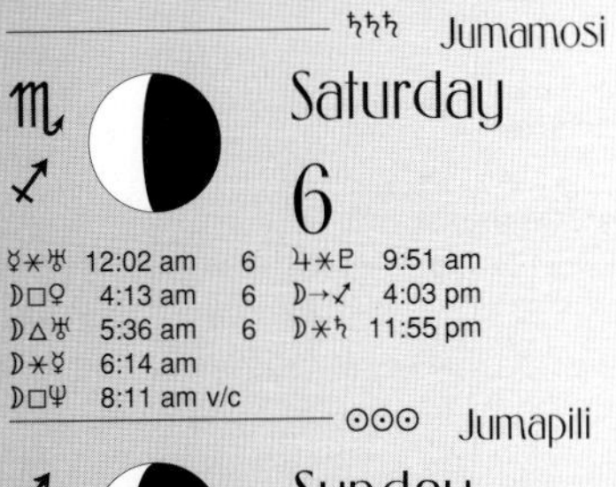

♏ ♐

Saturday
6

☿✶♅ 12:02 am
☽□♀ 4:13 am
☽△♅ 5:36 am
☽✶☿ 6:14 am
☽□♆ 8:11 am v/c
6 ♃✶♇ 9:51 am
6 ☽→♐ 4:03 pm
6 ☽✶♄ 11:55 pm

☉☉☉ Jumapili

♐

Sunday
7

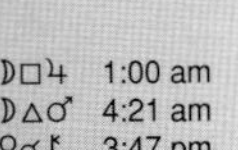

☽□♃ 1:00 am
☽△♂ 4:21 am
♀☌⚷ 3:47 pm
♀☌♆ 9:44 pm

February
Qhaqmiy Killa

☽☽☽ Killachaw

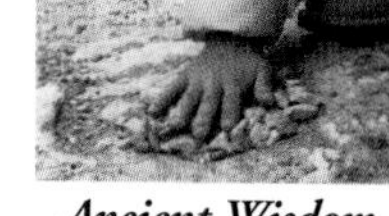

Ancient Wisdom
¤ *J. Stauber 2007*

 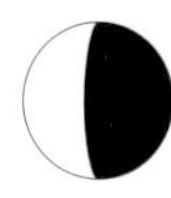

Monday
8

☉✶☽ 6:17 am
☽□♅ 3:57 pm
☽✶♆ 6:37 pm
☽✶♀ 8:58 pm v/c

♂♂♂ Atichaw

♐ ♑ 

Tuesday
9

☽→♑ 2:43 am
☽□♄ 10:45 am
☽☌♇ 11:58 am
☽✶♃ 1:18 pm

☿☿☿ Quyllurchaw

♑ 

Wednesday
10

☿→♒ 1:06 am
♂⚻♃ 1:24 am

♃♃♃ Illapachaw

♑ ♒ 

Thursday
11

♀→♓ 4:10 am
☽✶♅ 4:39 am v/c
☽→♒ 3:24 pm
☽☌☿ 8:39 pm
☽△♄ 11:18 pm

♀♀♀ Ch'askachaw

♒ 

Friday
12

☽☍♂ 1:01 am
♂⚻♇ 4:00 am
☿△♄ 5:34 pm
☽ApG 6:11 pm

I grew up in a remote part of the Okanagan on the Penticton Indian reservation in B.C., Canada. I was born on the reservation, at home, and was fortunate to be born into what was considered by many people in our area to be a traditional Okanagan family. Our first language was Okanagan and we practiced hunting/gathering traditions on the land. I'm still immersed in that family today....

And while I've lived that life and I continue to practice with my family, my community was one that had been fractionalized by colonization...Thus I have these two perspectives in terms of looking at society: the perspective of the small extended, traditional family support system that I grew up in, and that of the larger community fractionalized by colonization.

The relationships we have with each other impact what we do to the land. We grew up loving the land. We grew up loving each other on the land and loving each plant and each species the way we love our brothers and sisters.

In our language, the word for our bodies contains the word for land. Everytime I say that word...I'm saying that I'm from the land and my body is the land.

What our grandparents have said is that the land feeds us but we feed the land as well. We live on the land and we use the land and, in so doing, we impact the land: we can destroy it, or we can love the land and it can love us back.

Excerpts adapted from An Okanagan Worldview of Society *by Jeannette Armstrong*
from Original Instructions: Indigenous Teachings for a Sustainable Future
ed. by Melissa K Nelson © 2008 Bear & Company in collaboration with Bioneers

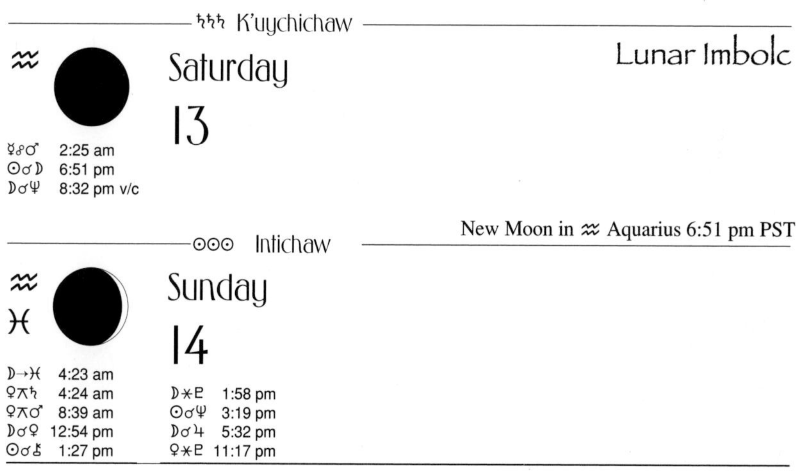

We Are All in This Together

We all come from the earth and return to her belly. We are all made of the same substance, same as the sea, the soil, the stars. Birth, growth, death, development, change, adaptation, transformation, evolution, it is all really just about recycling.

We breathe the same air as our cave-dwelling ancestors—inhaling and exhaling, exchanging carbon dioxide and oxygen with our plant relatives untold billions of times over the millennia. And the same holds true for water. We drink the tears of crocodiles and elephants. It rains, it pools, it evaporates, it rains. We drink, we pee. Again and again and again, in a grand scale cosmic round robin.

All borders and boundaries and separations are pure illusion. Each time we touch someone, we leave some particles of our skin atoms behind and pick up a parcel of new ones. Thus we merge, literally becoming part of each other. I am you and you are me and we are we.

We are all in this together, inextricably bound on our beautiful blue planet spinning through space. Remember that extraordinary photograph of Earth taken from the moon? We are one family, one community, one world, one living, breathing entity. And the sooner we realize it, the happier, safer and saner we will be.

excerpt ¤ *Mama Donna Henes 2006*

Cosmic Turtle
© Christina Smith 1999

III. CIRCLE OF LIFE

Moon III: February 13–March 15

New Moon in ♒ Aquarius Feb. 13; Sun in ♓ Pisces Feb. 18; Full Moon in ♍ Virgo Feb. 28

Deja View

© Robyn Waters 1998

February
Pepeluali

Whale Song
© S. Grace Mantle 2004

☽☽☽ pō 'akahi

Monday
15

♆ApG 5:10 am
♂✶♄ 7:20 am

♂♂♂ pō 'alua

♓
♈

Tuesday
16

☽☌♅ 6:32 am v/c
☽→♈ 4:30 pm
♀☌♃ 6:14 pm
♆☌⚷ 9:07 pm
☽△♂ 10:55 pm
☽☍♄ 11:39 pm

☿☿☿ pō 'akolu

♈

Wednesday
17

☽□♇ 2:00 am
☽✶☿ 2:23 pm

♃♃♃ pō 'aha

♈

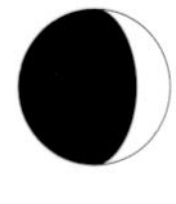

Thursday
18

☉→♓ 10:36 am
☽✶♆ 7:52 pm v/c

Sun in ♓ Pisces 10:36 am PST

♀♀♀ pō 'alima

♈
♉

Friday
19

☽→♉ 2:55 am
☉✶☽ 4:20 am
☽□♂ 7:55 am
☽△♇ 12:10 pm
☽✶♃ 5:33 pm
⚷ApG 11:23 pm
☽✶♀ 11:49 pm

ALL ASPECTS IN PACIFIC STANDARD TIME; ADD 3 HOURS FOR EST; ADD 8 HOURS FOR GMT

Year at a Glance for ♓ Pisces (Feb. 18–Mar. 20)

Pisceans are natural filters of the zodiac, able to absorb and transmute distress in an environment just by being present. You heal your system and restore your equilibrium through a devotion to art, music, dance—and tend to be unusually gifted in these areas.

In 2010, champion a dream; it may have been long in the coming, or is the latest in a series of urges that have electrified you in recent years. Your enthusiasm and devotion inspires others to join in with this one. You will be drawing people and resources like a magnet.

Many Pisces-born will be traveling or relocating this year. Especially during 6/6–8/8, watch for glimpses of where this all could go. You are just at the beginning of a new cycle of growth. To steady your course, join forces with an accomplished companion, perhaps older.

You're getting to know yourself more deeply through your relationships, in particular by learning to respect the differences between you. You may have to face some hard truths about yourself. If you have been single, issues that have been confining or mysterious are cleared away, making you more available for an alliance. It's a case of "the truth will set you free" in 2010, and launch you on a fresh path.

Be generous and have faith in yourself; your willingness to take risks will startle some people. You will prefer the company of those with whom you can share your experiences at the most profound levels.

Gretchen Lawlor © Mother Tongue Ink 2009

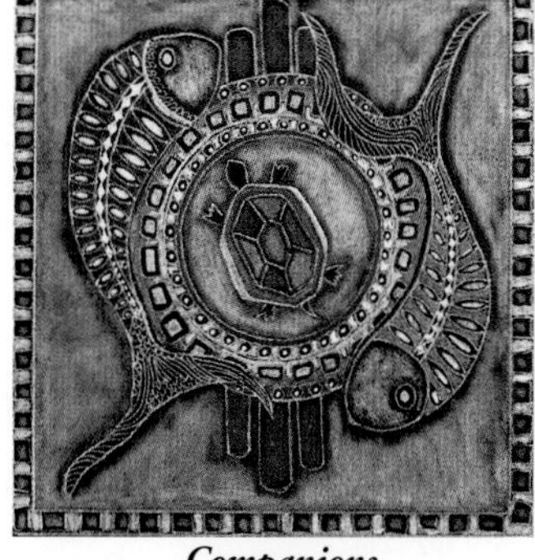

Companions
© Wendy Page 1996

♄♄♄ pō 'aono

♉ Saturday 20

☽□☿ 7:53 am
☉⊼♂ 5:13 pm

☉☉☉ lā pule

♉ ♊ Sunday 21

☽✶♅ 2:06 am
☽□♆ 4:15 am v/c
☽→♊ 10:47 am
☽✶♂ 2:34 pm
21 ☉□☽ 4:42 pm
21 ☽△♄ 4:48 pm
21 ☉⊼♄ 5:56 pm

Waxing Half Moon in ♊ Gemini 4:42 pm PST

February
febrero

☽☽☽ lunes

♊

Monday
22

☽□♃ 1:39 am
☽□♀ 12:06 pm
☽△☿ 9:17 pm

yoga poem
I am the cobra
calm mind floating
on a core of strength
excerpt ¤ Jennifer Shipman 2007

♂♂♂ martes

♊ ♋

Tuesday
23

☽□♅ 7:32 am
☉⚹♇ 8:31 am
☽△♆ 9:29 am v/c
☽→♋ 3:29 pm
☽□♄ 8:54 pm
☽☍♇ 11:53 pm

☿☿☿ miércoles

♋

Wednesday
24

☉△☽ 1:02 am
☽△♃ 6:20 am
☽△♀ 8:06 pm

♃♃♃ jueves

♋ ♌

Thursday
25

Bodies – Susie Orbach
Fat is a Feminist Issue
The Impossibility of Sex
City of Thieves

☽△♅ 9:48 am v/c
☽→♌ 5:08 pm
☽☌♂ 7:14 pm
☽⚹♄ 10:04 pm

♀♀♀ viernes

♌

Friday
26

No Exact Aspects

Animals and People Together

Our mission is to connect humans and animals for mutual healing and growth, knowing that all lives are enriched when trust, dignity, respect, and creativity are shared. Our vision includes a therapy animal program, farm therapy, animal rescue, and a wilderness exposure program, with the shared focus of helping foster animal/people relationships and healing the nature-deficit disorder we see in our culture, especially affecting children. We know, Nature heals.

excerpt © Diane Bergstrom 2008

Animal Wheel ¤ *Dorrie Joy 2008*

♄♄♄ sábado

♌ ♍

Saturday

27

☿☌♆ 6:03 am
☿☌⚷ 11:01 am
☽☍♆ 11:34 am
☽☍☿ 12:15 pm v/c
☽PrG 1:50 pm
☽→♍ 4:52 pm

☉☉☉ domingo

♍

Sunday

28

☽△♇ 12:50 am
☉☌♃ 2:44 am
♃ApG 6:09 am
☽☍♃ 8:20 am
☉☍☽ 8:38 am

Full Moon in ♍ Virgo 8:38 am PST

Machi

☽☽☽ Jumatatu

Peace Frog ¤ Marc Dragiewicz 2003

♍ ♎

Monday
1

☽☍♀ 4:32 am
☿→♓ 5:28 am
☽☍♅ 9:36 am v/c
☿⚻♂ 4:13 pm
☽→♎ 4:31 pm
☽✶♂ 5:45 pm
☽☌♄ 9:01 pm

♂♂♂ Jumanne

♎

Tuesday
2

☽□♇ 12:44 am
☿⚻♄ 7:13 pm

☿☿☿ Jumatano

♎ ♏

Wednesday
3

☽△♆ 12:43 pm v/c
☽→♏ 6:11 pm
☽□♂ 7:09 pm
♀☌♅ 8:07 pm

♃♃♃ Alhamisi

♏

Thursday
4

☽△☿ 2:53 am
☽✶♇ 3:00 am
☿✶♇ 3:54 am
☽△♃ 12:56 pm
☉△☽ 7:21 pm

♀♀♀ Ijumaa

♏ ♐

Friday
5

☽△♅ 4:06 pm
☽□♆ 5:50 pm
☽△♀ 8:31 pm v/c
☽→♐ 11:36 pm

Touching the world of the tumbleweeds has allowed me to feel what it's like to naturally embody change. These wild nomads of the desert readily transform and playfully tumble around in their dance with life and death, all according to their unique, ingenious design. Tumbleweeds know about rooting themselves only when and where it's nourishing. And they intentionally move on from what-has-been when the cycle is complete, when that purpose has been served, honoring it all with their ease, lightness and quirky grace. Tumbleweeds have shown me how to call in the winds to let old attachments go.

I've come to see this aged gathering of browned tumbleweeds as a council of elders who hold and seed sacred ground for the generations to come. The tumbleweeds know it's never too late to remember what's been forgotten. If we've come here to tumble, to love or heal or dream, to build or sing or create, we can start any time, any day.

In the harvesting of the tumbleweeds and their teachings, I've grown aware of the understanding we share. That I'm home and it's time for me to dig in my roots and tenaciously hold my center, to reach out and give and receive in the sharing with a spidery open-armed embrace. And it's time for the tumbleweeds to move on, to uproot and get untangled so they can follow their spirits' callings and flow with the freedom of their quests.

The prickly brown Tumbleweeds easily pull away from the sandy soil and I walk with them toward the open mesas, huge billowy armfuls of sundried plants held over my head. I place them on the ground on the other side of the fence so they're lying now on wilderness lands —free to dance with the elements and join up with the winds and continue on their way.

excerpt from "Tumbleweeds" © JoAnne Dodgson 2008

♄♄♄ Jumamosi

♐

Saturday
6

☽△♂ 12:22 am
☽✶♄ 4:13 am
☽□☿ 5:55 pm
☽□♃ 8:58 pm

☉☉☉ Jumapili

♐

Sunday
7

♀→♈ 4:33 am
☉□☽ 7:42 am
♀△♂ 11:15 am
☿ApG 2:54 pm
☿☌♃ 5:45 pm

Waning Half Moon in ♐ Sagittarius 7:42 am PST

March
Jatunpuquy killa

☽☽☽ Killachaw

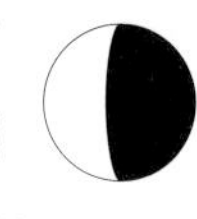

Monday
8

☽□♅ 1:27 am
☽⚹♆ 3:13 am v/c
☽→♑ 9:13 am
☽□♀ 12:30 pm
☽□♄ 1:47 pm
☽☌♇ 7:33 pm

Re-Invent the Wheel
© Sandra Lory 2008

♂♂♂ Atichaw

♑

Tuesday
9

♀☍♄ 12:21 am
☽⚹♃ 9:08 am
☽⚹☿ 3:27 pm

☿☿☿ Quyllurchaw

♑

♒

Wednesday
10

☉⚹☽ 12:41 am
♂D 9:09 am
☽⚹♅ 1:59 pm v/c
☽→♒ 9:42 pm
☽☍♂ 10:18 pm

♃♃♃ Illapachaw

♒

Thursday
11

☽△♄ 2:01 am
☽⚹♀ 8:14 am
♀□♇ 9:35 am

♀♀♀ Ch'askachaw

♒

Friday
12

☽ApG 2:05 am

Letter from Gaia

In your living spaces, watch
for the mirror movements
of global breadth. Respond

as if every small movement
of twig or feather
mattered to every being.

This is the way
of all of my moving:
all effects and constructs,
all destructs and rebuilds:
ant hill, turtle egg,
avalanche.

And what will you birth?
For you, I will open
my deep chasms of fire
and microbial pools, groan
my mothering womb
chorus of species
song to bring the you
of all you are
into Be.

Wear green, spring green
thoughts, eat green at every
meal, bleed green blood,
photosynthesize
the green shift of life
into your deepest cell.

Sleep green in and under
green. Feed your eyes
with green. Breathe
the new of green.
Tell others.

© Kate Rose Bast 2008

© Sandra Lory 2008

♄♄♄ K'uychichaw

♒ ♓

Saturday

13

☽☌♆ 4:57 am v/c
☽→♓ 10:43 am
☽⚹♇ 9:21 pm

☉☉☉ Intichaw

♓

Sunday

14

☉☌☿ 4:16 am
☽☌♃ 12:16 pm

Daylight Saving Time Begins 2:00 am PST

Textures

I am being re-woven
by invisible threads
shifting, flowing,
rattling my core.

Cells flake away, fresh ones stir
replenishing this body
that houses my being.

I am releasing my hold on
time, sequence, expectation,
drifting away from the confines
of daytime doing

immersing into landscapes of
dreams, totems, guides
vibrant and alluring
calling me, nudging me
pulling me into rich textures
of mud and twine,
encircled by firey blossoms,
green spirally shells,
gatherings of rooted feet
igniting the flame
of my imagination.

I am longing
to decipher the code of
eagles and otters,
pods of mermaids
floating to silent melodies
toward the source of
light—wholeness—worlds
below the shimmery
surface of things.

¤ Holly Wilkinson 2007

IV. REINVENT SELF

Moon IV: March 15–April 14

New Moon in ♓ Pisces March 15; Sun in ♈ Aries March 20; Full Moon in ♎ Libra March 29

The Meditation

A snake slithered my way, her eyes like glowing embers. A call that it was time. Earth and air circled, lifting me higher than the canyons, with talons gentle as the breeze. The rawness of me carried lovingly through sky, slow and with purpose. Winds soon ruffled what had grown into feathers. From inside I felt a deep cry, birthing from that whimpering groundling to the full and beauteous feral of my being. Old knowing, wisdom of the ages, life in myriad form beat through my veins. Stories of blood and tears filled me, forgotten struggles of humanness replaced by the thing that is greater.

I've known my place since that Spirit discovery, the wild expanse of possibility and strength that is me. The Creatrix of all things breathes through this little body. Smiling, laughing, playing all the while, in a world crafted by and for our own adventures.

© Anna Rose Renick 2008

March
Malaki

☽☽☽ pō 'akahi

In Control

♓
♈

Monday
15

☉☌☽ 12:01 pm
☿☌♅ 12:39 pm
☽☌♅ 2:38 pm
☽☌☿ 3:01 pm v/c
☽→♈ 9:32 pm
☽△♂ 10:29 pm

New Moon in ♓ Pisces 12:01 pm PDT

♂♂♂ pō 'alua

♈

Tuesday
16

☽☍♄ 12:55 am
☽□♇ 7:54 am
☽☌♀ 9:08 pm
☉☌♅ 9:50 pm

☿☿☿ pō 'akolu

Wednesday
17

☿→♈ 7:12 am
☿△♂ 2:33 pm
♅ApG 8:02 pm

♃♃♃ pō 'aha

♈
♉

Thursday
18

☿☍♄ 2:04 am
☽⚹♆ 2:22 am v/c
☽→♉ 7:29 am
☽□♂ 8:46 am
☽△♇ 5:34 pm

♀♀♀ pō 'alima

♉

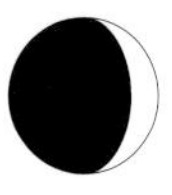

Friday
19

☽⚹♃ 10:36 am
☿□♇ 11:16 am

Year at a Glance for ♈ Aries (Mar. 20–Apr. 19)

You're the perfect warrior, champion of a new world rising. 2010 is a year for polishing armor and weapons, to become lean, fit and ready for anything. Don't go looking for battles yet, though an exercise in preparation appears June–early August. There is more to come.

Your most powerful weapon is desire, the enthusiasm for your unique role in the world. Get clear on an image of what you want; paint it, collage it, sing it or write it out as poetry. Strength fused with desire delivers everything you'll need to step forward.

Important in 2010 is to clear away blocks, anything that drags you down or back into the past. These could be old attitudes, old relationships, outmoded venues or ways of presenting yourself to the world. You may project obstructions onto others, feeling held back by their issues; they are merely holding up mirrors to show you where you need to firm yourself.

Focus on simplifying, freeing yourself of anything that siphons off that pure, fierce Aries force. Your home is a refuge, your place of renewal and rejuvenation; make sure it feels warm, comforting, free of clutter and distractions.

Don't be afraid to ask for help. Call upon your ancestors. There are gifts, talents, passions from past lives or bloodlines lining up to be available for these times. When you've slain your inner monsters and freed your deepest desires, your contagious passion and fearlessness will ignite in you incisive leadership in service to Mother the Earth.

Gretchen Lawlor © Mother Tongue Ink 2009

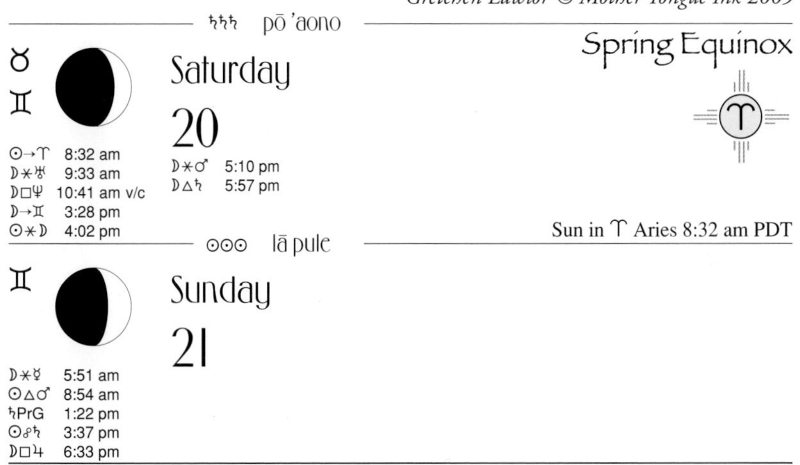

Spring Equinox

On Vernal Equinox, the cosmic scales are balanced in perfect equilibrium: equal day, equal night. With bone cold winter behind, we celebrate the life force, rejoicing in a fresh, clear, bright spring day. Tender stems and shoots push through the fertile soil, buds explode, and the Egg of Spring hatches a living creation! Eostre, Goddess of the divine fertile female, calls to the spirit of youth in each woman.

Come! Join us! Look how we glow! We are Maidens—covered with flowers, dancing wildly through the forest towards the village. Our joyful energy is as high as the sky above. We know there is distress in this world. We have seen the dark smoke from faraway wars. But today is a new day of promise and renewal, when we will be honored as Daughters and claim our womanly strength.

We carry eggs, dyed red for the womb, and for the powers of rebirth. Come, join the band of our mothers, sisters, elders—singing, drumming, making music, holding birch branches with streaming ribbons to honor the Goddess Lada. We are excited as the ceremony begins! We are young, we are growing into our power.

Ffiona Morgan © Mother Tongue Ink, 2008

Burdock Spirit
¤ *Asha Croggon 2005*

She is WIND
The Summoner
who releases
quick-fingered,
fast-flown seeds of change
from her precious
Wellspring Pod.
She is wild exhaustion
lightly transformed into
exhilarating joy.
Hare's egg nested under
a spell of twisted hazel.
Her dance is an
AWAKENING
a great momentous
birthing, calling,
urging new life out
onto the surface
of the land.
She dances through
impulsive freedoms,
small bright leaves,
and the dynamic
early mornings of
SPRING RISE

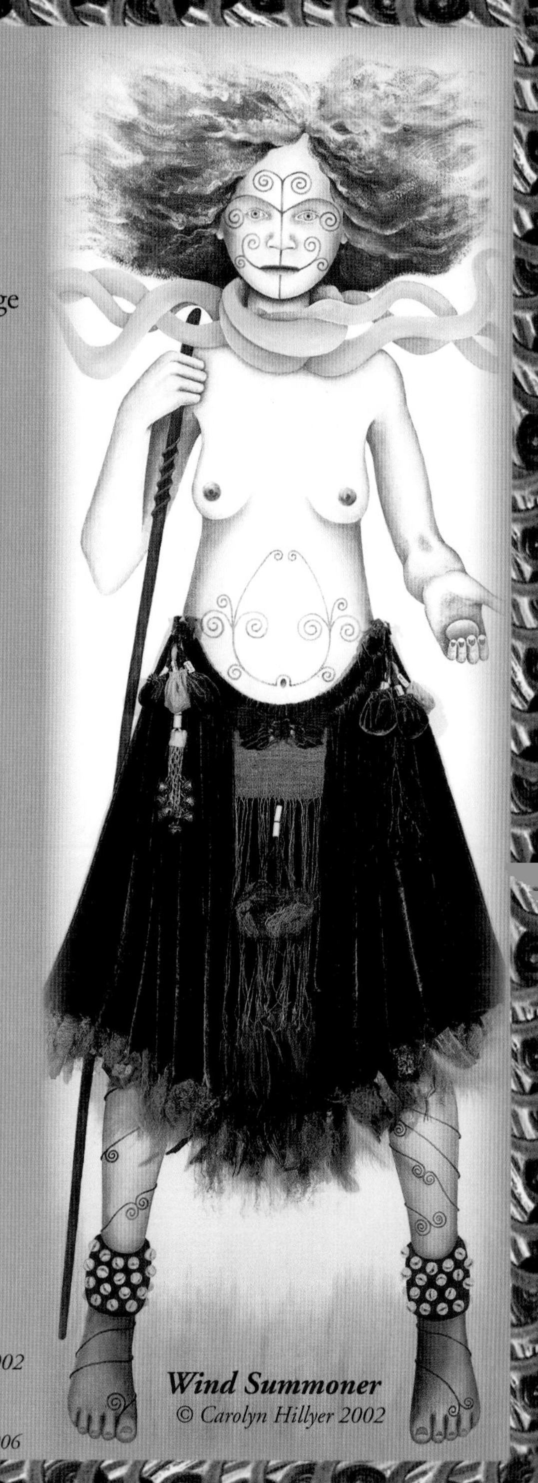

Wind Summoner

March
marzo

☽☽☽ lunes

♊
♋

Monday
22

☽✶♀ 12:54 am
☽□♅ 3:49 pm
☽△♆ 4:49 pm v/c
♂✶♄ 6:53 pm
☽→♋ 9:16 pm
☽□♄ 11:20 pm

♂♂♂ martes

♋

Tuesday
23

☉□☽ 2:00 am
☽☍♇ 6:38 am
☽□☿ 7:55 pm

Waxing Half Moon in ♋ Cancer 2:00 am PDT

☿☿☿ miércoles

♋

Wednesday
24

☽△♃ 12:03 am
☽□♀ 10:14 am
☽△♅ 7:39 pm v/c

♃♃♃ jueves

♋
♌

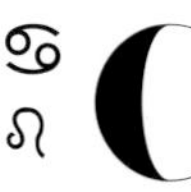

Thursday
25

☽→♌ 12:39 am
☽✶♄ 2:21 am
☽☌♂ 3:15 am
☉△☽ 8:57 am
☉□♇ 6:45 pm

♀♀♀ viernes

♌

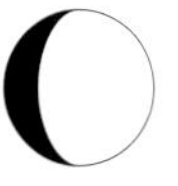

Friday
26

☽△☿ 6:05 am
☽△♀ 4:36 pm
☽☍♆ 10:04 pm v/c

The Limping Goddess: She-Who-Survives

She limps into the room
    bent with the cargo of rape, battering
    single-parent mothering and bureaucratic neglect
    if she is fat or gay or nonwhite or Jewish
    the pains multiply;
she has carried them all.

Her lotus feet have trudged this planet
for aeons; torn tennis shoes tell
how far she's traveled. She hunches
against the winter wind, her second-hand
coat like a blanket she wraps around
her golden body. Occasionally, she flies
over buildings, lands on tree tops,
is mistaken for a fat bird.

And occasionally, she falls,
intensifying her limp. But make no mistake;
that golden skin was mined in the black earth,
her feet, though limping and calloused,
are the lotus feet of She-Who-Survives.
A broken yet shining forgotten deity
returning, and there are millions
like her, multi-colored, limping
Goddesses returning to lay down our cargo
and reclaim our own.

© Pesha Joyce Gertler 1983

Summer Tree
© Jamie Branker 1998

♄♄♄ sábado

♌ ♍

Saturday

27

☽→♍ 1:57 am
☽△♇ 10:40 am
☽PrG 7:50 pm

☉☉☉ domingo

♍

Sunday

28

☽☍♃ 4:30 am
☽☍♅ 9:55 pm v/c

March/April
Machi/ Aprili

Soul Reflection
© Lisa Seed 2006

☽☽☽ Jumatatu

Monday
29

☽→♎ 2:21 am
☽☌♄ 3:29 am
☽⚹♂ 6:05 am
☽□♇ 11:06 am
♀⚹♆ 11:24 am
☉☍☽ 5:25 pm

Full Moon in ♎ Libra 5:25 pm PDT

♂♂♂ Jumanne

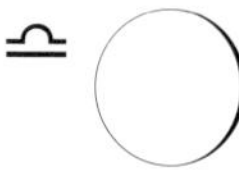

Tuesday
30

♀⚹⚷ 12:44 am
☽☍☿ 9:27 pm
☽△♆ 11:52 pm

☿☿☿ Jumatano

Wednesday
31

☽☍♀ 3:13 am v/c
☽→♏ 3:41 am
☽□♂ 8:19 am
♀→♉ 8:35 am
☽⚹♇ 12:50 pm
♀⚻♄ 6:16 pm
☿⚹♆ 6:21 pm

♃♃♃ Alhamisi

♏

Thursday
1

April

☽△♃ 9:33 am
☿⚹⚷ 2:18 pm

♀♀♀ Ijumaa

♏
♐

Friday
2

☽△♅ 3:22 am
☽□♆ 3:54 am v/c
☿→♉ 4:06 am
☽→♐ 7:53 am
☽⚹♄ 8:33 am
☿⚻♄ 9:53 am
☽△♂ 1:46 pm

All aspects in Pacific Daylight Time; add 3 hours for EDT; add 7 hours for GMT

Shattered Mirrors

i will turn to meet my destiny,
  reflected in shattered mirrors.
heart broken open,
  i will pick up the pieces
no matter how sharp
  to reflect
  what is neglected
  in dark corners.
wounded, light-deprived,
  with prayerful hands i'll
  recycle devastation to
  nourish new life.
art, like gardening,
  is an act of faith and healing,
  shining for the world.
as Mystery's greater
  than the sum of all suffering,
  i will trust to Love.

¤ *Mimi Foyle 2008*

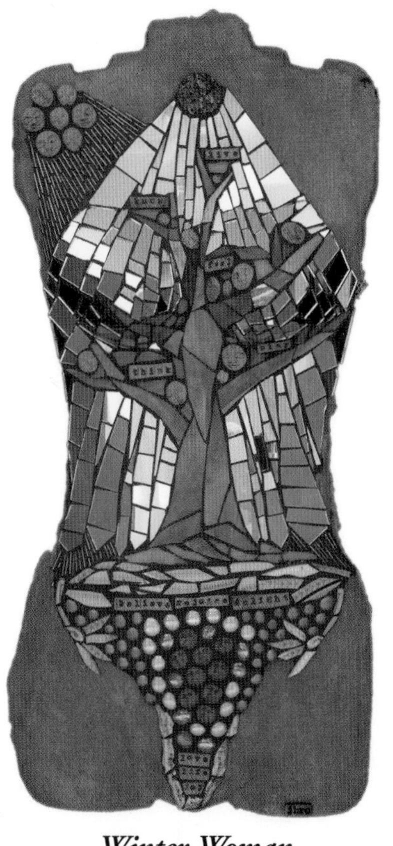

Winter Woman
© *Jeannette Brossart 2008*

♄♄♄ Jumamosi

♐

Saturday

3

♀□♂ 2:25 am
☉△☽ 9:23 am
☽□♃ 5:02 pm

☉☉☉ Jumapili

♐
♑

Sunday

4

☽□♅ 1:30 pm
☽⚹♆ 1:57 pm v/c
☽→♑ 6:07 pm
☽□♄ 6:30 pm
♀△♇ 8:12 pm
☿□♂ 9:16 pm

April
Pachapuquy Killa

☽☽☽ Killachaw

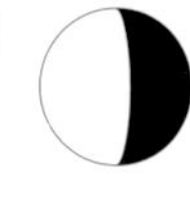
♑
Monday
5

☽△☿ 2:02 am
☽☌♇ 4:42 am
☽△♀ 5:39 am

The Poet's Journey
© Kat Beyer 2008

♂♂♂ Atichaw

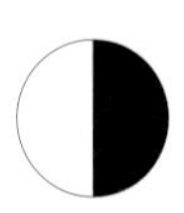
♑
Tuesday
6

☉□☽ 2:37 am
☿△♇ 3:46 am
☽⚹♃ 6:42 am
♇R 7:34 pm

Waning Half Moon in ♑ Capricorn 2:37 am PDT

☿☿☿ Quyllurchaw

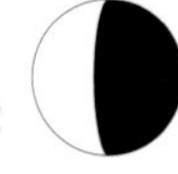
♑
♒
Wednesday
7

☽⚹♅ 1:18 am v/c
☽→♒ 5:51 am
☽△♄ 5:53 am
♄→♍ 11:51 am
☽☍♂ 3:02 pm
☽□☿ 8:47 pm

♃♃♃ Illapachaw

♒
Thursday
8

☽□♀ 12:50 am
☽ApG 7:38 pm
☉⚹☽ 8:53 pm

♀♀♀ Ch'askachaw

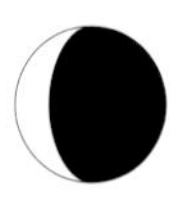
♒
♓
Friday
9

☽☌♆ 2:44 pm v/c
☽→♓ 6:48 pm

Recovering *© Sara Glass 2003*

Request to Pluto

Oh, Precious Pluto,
Planet of Prescribed Burn—
while you are destroying
my old structures,
kicking my butt,
singeing outdated ideas
and illusions to ash,
could you spark a
fire in my heart,
reseed my dreams
like fireweed after
the forest burns, which
returns stronger, fuller,
more resilient, richer,
with greater color, longevity,
fortitude and strength?
With humble caution and
great respect,
Capricorn

© Diane Bergstrom 2008

♄♄♄ K'uychichaw

♓ 

Saturday

10

☽⚹♇ 5:43 am
☽⚹☿ 2:38 pm
♂⚻♇ 5:51 pm
☽⚹♀ 8:32 pm

☉☉☉ Intichaw

♓ 

Sunday

11

☽☌♃ 10:13 am

The Mother Place

With five small bowls that fit neatly together, one inside the other, I am teaching women about the power of the uterus. The largest bowl fits in the palm of my hand, and the smallest is the size of a pencil eraser. These bowls represent the way that the uterus holds energy and passes information from one generation to another. The women watch my hands as I align the bowls, one by one, according to their size.

I point to the smallest bowl, saying, "*This is you.*" Slipping this tiny bowl into the next one I say, "*You were held in your mother's womb.*" Placing the two bowls together into the next bowl I say, "*Your mother's eggs were fully formed while she was held in her mother's body. In this way, you were also held in your grandmother's womb.*" I continue to join the bowls together, until the five are sitting in my palm, one inside the other. "*Because your grandmother carries the energy of her mother's and grandmother's wombs, so you are linked to them as well.*" The bowls rest neatly in my hand. The women sit squarely in front of me. I see each of them wrapped in layers of female energy from the women ancestors who came before them.

I set the bowls down. "*Now, this is you,*" I tell them, pointing to the largest bowl. From the large bowl I lift the next bowl, which still holds three others. "*This is one of your creations.*" One by one, I lift the smaller bowls and place each next to the bowl that served as its container. With each bowl, I tell the women, "*This is the seed of one of your creations.*" I continue until the five bowls, five generations, sit in a line. Each bowl is separate, but the action of lifting one bowl from the next reveals the nature of this shared lineage. "*This is how your womb, and the energy that you carry, influences all that you create. This is your legacy of creation.*" The room is silent, as the women remember their mother place.

from Wild Feminine © *Tami Lynn Kent 2008*

Woman With Pots: Palmares
© *Toni Truesdale 2004*

V. INNER CIRCLES

Moon V: April 14–May 13

New Moon in ♈ Aries April 14; Sun in ♉ Taurus April 19; Full Moon in ♏ Scorpio April 28

Not What I Expected

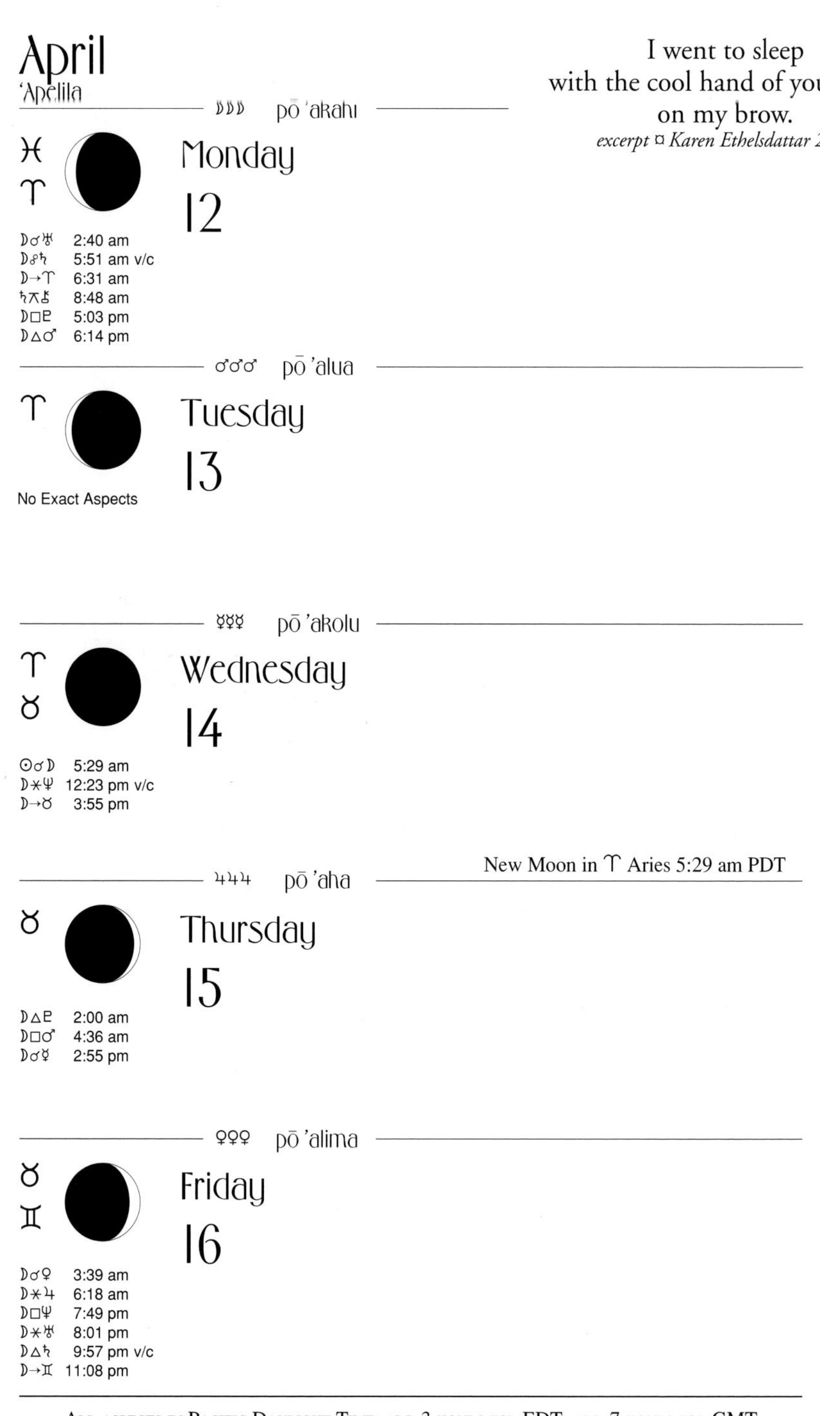

April
'Apelila

I went to sleep
with the cool hand of your
on my brow.
excerpt ¤ Karen Ethelsdattar 200

☽☽☽ pō 'akahi

♓ ♈

Monday 12

☽☌♅ 2:40 am
☽☍♄ 5:51 am v/c
☽→♈ 6:31 am
♄⚻⚷ 8:48 am
☽□♇ 5:03 pm
☽△♂ 6:14 pm

♂♂♂ pō 'alua

♈

Tuesday 13

No Exact Aspects

☿☿☿ pō 'akolu

♈ ♉

Wednesday 14

☉☌☽ 5:29 am
☽⚹♆ 12:23 pm v/c
☽→♉ 3:55 pm

New Moon in ♈ Aries 5:29 am PDT

♃♃♃ pō 'aha

♉

Thursday 15

☽△♇ 2:00 am
☽□♂ 4:36 am
☽☌☿ 2:55 pm

♀♀♀ pō 'alima

♉ ♊

Friday 16

☽☌♀ 3:39 am
☽⚹♃ 6:18 am
☽□♆ 7:49 pm
☽⚹♅ 8:01 pm
☽△♄ 9:57 pm v/c
☽→♊ 11:08 pm

ALL ASPECTS IN PACIFIC DAYLIGHT TIME; ADD 3 HOURS FOR EDT; ADD 7 HOURS FOR GMT

and they do
(yei bi chai trail)

if everyone who ever walked this path before
or went before us, or came after
all walked this

anyone we ever needed, all the ancestors, the progeny
anyone who ever made our life meaningful,
the person who wore the red ski cap on the bus
that led us to that poem about minds on fire,
anyone who ever needed a word shared, a poem,
a hug, anyone who ever
took something we were or created
and folded it belly deep into themselves

if all of them walked with us now
(and they do)
if all of them walked with us now
we would know this path is never lonely
(sometimes even crowded)
and often crowded

if all of them walked with us now
(and they do)
we would never feel lost
never be alone

if all of them walked with us now
(and we do)

¤ *Marna 2008*

Crossing Over
© *Nancy Holley 2002*

♄♄♄ pō 'aono

♊ 

Saturday
17

☽✶♂ 12:48 pm
♀✶♃ 1:43 pm
☿R 9:06 pm

☉☉☉ lā pule

♊ 

Sunday
18

☉✶♆ 1:16 am
☽□♃ 1:11 pm

April

abril

☽☽☽ lunes

Monday 19

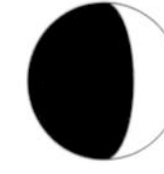

♊ ♋

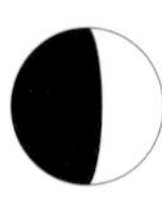

☽△♆ 1:31 am
☽□♅ 1:49 am
☉⊼♄ 2:06 am
☽□♄ 3:15 am
☉✶☽ 3:21 am v/c
☽→♋ 4:39 am
☽☍♇ 2:05 pm
☉✶⚷ 9:24 pm
☉→♉ 9:30 pm
⚷→♓ 11:37 pm

Sun in ♉ Taurus 9:30 pm PDT

♂♂♂ martes

Tuesday 20

♋

☽✶☿ 2:19 am
☽△♃ 6:29 pm

☿☿☿ miércoles

Wednesday 21

♋ ♌

☽✶♀ 12:33 am
☽△♅ 6:08 am
☽✶♄ 7:07 am v/c
☽→♌ 8:42 am
☉□☽ 11:20 am

Waxing Half Moon in ♌ Leo 11:20 am PDT

♃♃♃ jueves

Thursday 22

♌

☽☌♂ 12:18 am
☽□☿ 4:43 am

♀♀♀ viernes

Friday 23

♌ ♍

☽□♀ 8:11 am
☽☍♆ 8:35 am v/c
☽→♍ 11:24 am
♀□♆ 12:54 pm
☉△☽ 5:39 pm
♀✶♅ 7:06 pm
☽△♇ 8:19 pm

All aspects in Pacific Daylight Time; add 3 hours for EDT; add 7 hours for GMT

Year at a Glance for ♉ Taurus (April 19–May 20)

What contributions can Taurus-born bring to the world in 2010? Hold firm to your hopefulness for the future. Compose a wish list for yourself, and for the planet. To maximize potential for success have it ready before Spring Equinox (March 20). Don't fret about how anything will come about, just dream BIG, and don't do your dreaming alone. Your hopefulness and optimism are contagious. Plotting and scheming with others invokes unexpected results and situations not anticipated, intended or even possible if you were doing this alone.

The maps we have all used for navigating life are less accurate for these wildly changing times. When change is necessary, Taurus prefers manageable increments. You have extraordinary talent for accomplishing great things in calm, steady steps, with minimal resources, and you NEVER give up. Cohorts will appreciate this in 2010.

Don't let other people's ideas override your natural responses. If your abilities aren't being appreciated, reach out beyond your personal circle to new friends. Your appreciation for the quirky genius in others brings you into some wild communities this year, changing your perspective suddenly and forever.

Life compels you to get your act together through health stresses or work challenges. Commit to a regular exercise program, gather tools and techniques that amplify your efficiency. Get serious about your diet; jettison destructive habits; learn to accomplish more with less effort to be potently focused, able to respond, ready and resource-filled.

Gretchen Lawlor © Mother Tongue Ink 2009

Sacred Braid *© Christina Hagen 2005*

♄♄♄ sábado

♍

Saturday

24

♀△♄ 12:44 am
☽△☿ 5:27 am
☽PrG 2:04 pm
♀→♊ 10:05 pm

☉☉☉ domingo

♍ ♎

Sunday

25

☽☍♃ 1:02 am
♀□⚷ 2:09 am
☿□♂ 3:41 am
☉△♇ 8:44 am
☽☍♅ 11:08 am

☽☌♄ 11:20 am v/c
☽→♎ 1:16 pm
☽△♀ 2:40 pm
☽□♇ 10:07 pm

April
Aprili

☽☽☽ Jumatatu

♎

Monday
26

☽✶♂ 7:10 am
♄☍♅ 4:23 pm

♂♂♂ Jumanne

♎
♏

Tuesday
27

☽△♆ 12:45 pm v/c
☽→♏ 3:28 pm

☿☿☿ Jumatano

♏

Wednesday
28

Lunar Beltane

☽✶♇ 12:30 am
☉☍☽ 5:18 am
☽☍☿ 5:48 am
☉☌☿ 9:44 am
☽□♂ 11:20 am

Full Moon in ♏ Scorpio 5:18 am PDT

♃♃♃ Alhamisi

♏
♐

Thursday
29

♀⚻♇ 6:32 am
☽△♃ 8:04 am
☽□♆ 4:48 pm
☽✶♄ 5:07 pm
☽△♅ 5:39 pm v/c
☽→♐ 7:36 pm

♀♀♀ Ijumaa

♐

Friday
30

☽☍♀ 7:23 am
☽△♂ 6:17 pm

Beltane

I wake at dawn, anticipating May Day, Feast of Flowers and Cross-Quarter holyday, when the Taurus Power Gate of Earth opens to the streaming tide of summer.

Yesterday we frolicked in lush nature, singing, gathering flowers and greenery for garlands. The tall Maypole tree awaits, its multi-colored ribbons waving as if anticipating the dance. On this bright sumptuous day, we will go a-maying to each home, reviving the tradition of giving gifts to ensure prosperity.

I rise, placing a wreath of roses in my hair, caressing the folds and curves of my voluptuous body with erotic scents. I will see my lover today, and feel the magnetism between us.

As I walk through the blooming earth to join friends, I realize that passionate love takes many forms, and that the earth is my greatest lover. I bless my blue planet, vowing unchanging devotion and care for Her. Seeing Earth as a living, breathing female body has changed me, and become the cornerstone of my commitment to Her.

Magic Carpet Ride *© AmmA 2004*

Today we joyfully dance the Maypole; tonight we celebrate our bodies with sexual abandon, then leap the blazing bonfire flames. Aphrodite's Day, day of the Goddess, day of love.

Ffiona Morgan © Mother Tongue Ink 2008

Relationship Advice

It works really well to see your lover—
new lover or partner of 10, 20, 30 plus years—
as a young deer   or a bandicoot
some animal small and wild but curious enough
to stop and sniff the air in your direction
willing in complete stillness
to come close to your outstretched hand

    DO NOT REACH TO PAT OR PET OR STROKE
stay in unknowing
stay in surrender
stay in the soft rhythm of breathing wonder

It also works well to imagine you have become lost
in a country where no one speaks your language
Be utterly grateful for a smile
for the tender weathered hands
offering you a bowl of something unrecognizable
    that steams scents mysterious and delicious

You will be a child again in this country
    watching all the things you cannot understand
    amazed that you have landed in beginning again
Don't make believe that the story is about you
    that you are chosen to be on a quest
    that there are dragons of which you need to rid this kingdom

No   instead take in the syllables offered to you
    hold them with your tongue   lumpy and awkward
    like stones or pieces of stew
You may gag a little   we all do
Accept kindness and coaxing
and a gentle clean cloth soaking up inevitable tears
Soon   you will speak   whole   words

Prayer

We nourish
One another
In the high dream
Of being

excerpt © Sheila Kay 2008

Infinity
© Lindy Kehoe 2005

♄♄♄ Jumamosi

♐ Saturday

1

May

May Day/Beltane

☿PrG 3:50 am
☽□♃ 3:34 pm

☉☉☉ Jumapili

♐ ♑ Sunday

2

☽⚹♆ 12:05 am
☽□♄ 12:09 am
☽□♅ 1:08 am v/c
☽→♑ 3:00 am
☽☌♇ 1:04 pm
☽△☿ 1:46 pm
♄⚻♆ 3:22 pm

May

Ariwaki killa

☽☽☽ Killachaw

Africa: After War
¤ *Betty LaDuke 2008*

♑

Monday
3

☉△☽ 3:57 am
☿△♇ 5:01 am

♂♂♂ Atichaw

♑
♒

Tuesday
4

☽✶♃ 2:47 am
☉□♂ 6:09 am
☽△♄ 10:39 am
☽✶♅ 12:07 pm v/c
☽→♒ 1:51 pm
☽□☿ 10:35 pm

☿☿☿ Quyllurchaw

♒

Wednesday
5

☽△♀ 4:11 pm
☽☍♂ 7:23 pm
☉□☽ 9:15 pm

Waning Half Moon in ♒ Aquarius 9:15 pm PDT

♃♃♃ Illapachaw

♒

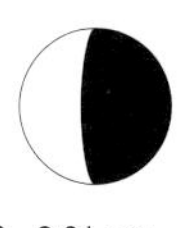

Thursday
6

☽ApG 3:01 pm
☽☌♆ 11:36 pm v/c

♀♀♀ Ch'askachaw

♒
♓

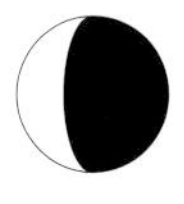

Friday
7

☽→♓ 2:34 am
☽✶☿ 9:21 am
☽✶♇ 1:03 pm
♀✶♂ 2:55 pm

All aspects in Pacific Daylight Time; add 3 hours for EDT; add 7 hours for GMT

I looked at the Okanagan decision-making process in its traditional sense.…when we approach the decision-making process, one component is reserved for the land…we have people who are called "land speakers". We have a word for it in our language. I was fortunate in that I was trained and brought up as a land speaker in my community…We have different people, trained as part of the family system, to be speakers for the children, for the mothers, for the Elders, for the medicine people, for the land, for the water—for all these different components that make up our existence.

My part has been to be trained by my Elders to think about the land and to speak about the land…Each time a decision is made, even the smallest decision, my responsibility is to stand up and ask, How will it impact the land? How is it going to impact our food? How is it going to impact our water? How is it going to impact my children, my grandchildren, my great-grandchildren, what's the land going to look like in their time? So in that process of *en'owkinwiwx*, there's a built-in principle in terms of how we interact.. . .Someone has to ask those questions. That's their responsibility.

When we include the perspective of land and we include the perspective of human relationship, one of the things that happens is that community changes. People in the community change. The realization that people and community are there to sustain you creates the most secure feeling in the world.

Excerpts from An Okanagan Worldview of Society *by Jeannette Armstrong*
from Original Instructions: Indigenous Teachings for a sustainable Future
edited by Melissa K Nelson © 2008 Bear & Company in collaboration with Bioneers

♄♄♄ K'uychichaw

♓

☽□♀ 11:40 am
☉✶☽ 3:10 pm

Saturday 8

☉☉☉ Intichaw

♓
♈

☽☌♃ 5:32 am
☽☍♄ 10:58 am
☽☌♅ 1:12 pm v/c
☽→♈ 2:29 pm

Sunday 9

Gate A-4

Wandering around the Albuquerque Airport Terminal, after learning my flight had been detained four hours, I heard an announcement: "If anyone in the vicinity of Gate A-4 understands any Arabic, please come to the gate immediately." Well—one pauses these days. Gate A-4 was my own gate. I went there. An older woman in full traditional Palestinian embroidered dress, just like my grandma wore, was crumpled to the floor, wailing loudly. "Help," said the Flight Service Person. "Talk to her. What is her problem? We told her the flight was going to be late and she did this." I stooped to put my arm around the woman and spoke to her haltingly. "*Shu dow-a, Shu-bid-uck Habibti? Stani schway, Min fadlick, Shu-bit-se-wee?*" The minute she heard any words she knew, however poorly used, she stopped crying. She thought the flight had been cancelled entirely. She needed to be in El Paso for major medical treatment the next day. I said, "You're fine, you'll get there, who is picking you up? Let's call him." We called her son and I spoke with him in English. I told him I would stay with his mother till we got on the plane and would ride next to her—Southwest.

She talked to him. Then we called her other sons just for fun. Then we called my dad and he and she spoke for a while in Arabic and found out of course they had ten shared friends. Then I thought just for the heck of it why not call some Palestinian poets I know and let them chat with her? This all took up about two hours. She was laughing a lot by then. Telling about her life, patting my knee, answering questions. She had pulled a sack of homemade mamool cookies—little powdered sugar crumbly mounds stuffed with dates and nuts—out of her bag—and was offering them to all the women at the gate. To my amazement, not a single woman declined one. It was like a sacrament. The traveler from Argentina, the mom from California, the lovely woman from Laredo—we were all covered with the same powdered sugar. And smiling. There is no better cookie. And then the airline broke out the free beverages from huge coolers and two little girls from our flight ran around serving us all apple juice and they were covered with powdered sugar too. And I noticed

VI. SPOKES OF COMMUNITY

Moon VI: May 13–June 12

New Moon in ♉ Taurus May 13; Sun in ♊ Gemini May 20; Full Moon in ♐ Sagittarius May 27

Reaching Hands ¤ *Janaia Donaldson 2002*

my new best friend—by now we were holding hands—had a potted plant poking out of her bag, some medicinal thing, with green furry leaves. Such an old country traveling tradition. Always carry a plant. Always stay rooted to somewhere. And I looked around that gate of late and weary ones and thought, this is the world I want to live in. The shared world. Not a single person in this gate—once the crying of confusion stopped—seemed apprehensive about any other person. They took the cookies. I wanted to hug all those other women too. This can still happen anywhere. Not everything is lost.

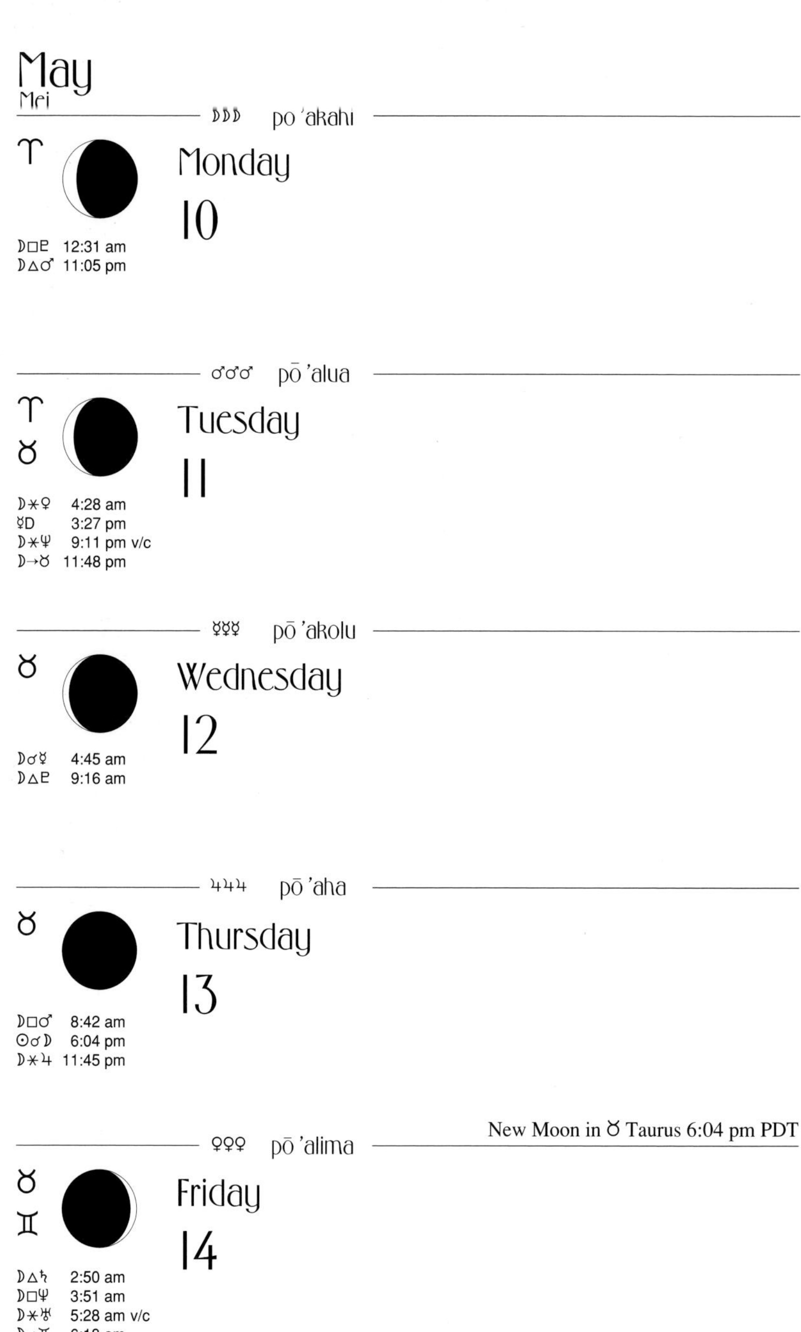

May
Mei

☽☽☽ po 'akahi

♈

Monday
10

☽□♇ 12:31 am
☽△♂ 11:05 pm

♂♂♂ pō 'alua

♈
♉

Tuesday
11

☽⚹♀ 4:28 am
☿D 3:27 pm
☽⚹♆ 9:11 pm v/c
☽→♉ 11:48 pm

☿☿☿ pō 'akolu

♉

Wednesday
12

☽☌☿ 4:45 am
☽△♇ 9:16 am

♃♃♃ pō 'aha

♉

Thursday
13

☽□♂ 8:42 am
☉☌☽ 6:04 pm
☽⚹♃ 11:45 pm

New Moon in ♉ Taurus 6:04 pm PDT

♀♀♀ pō 'alima

♉
♊

Friday
14

☽△♄ 2:50 am
☽□♆ 3:51 am
☽⚹♅ 5:28 am v/c
☽→♊ 6:18 am

Nomads © Gaia Orion 2005

Nomads

These Nomads are carpet weavers. On their carpets they weave pictures of the stories of their lives. They weave as they go and carry all their belongings. All of them, young and old, pregnant, carrying babies, carry everything. They walk all day, day after day, and sleep anywhere. This is their way of life. They have very little, only the necessary. Everyday is a new day. They walk across the plains, through the fields full of rich colours and textures. This beauty is the fabric of their life woven in their carpets. I think I could live like this.

This painting is inspired by an Iranian movie, called *Gabbeh*, which is about those nomads.

© Gaia Orion 2005

♄♄♄ pō 'aono

♊

Saturday

15

☽✶♂ 3:41 pm

☉☉☉ lā pule

♊ ♋

Sunday

16

☽☌♀ 3:15 am
☽□♃ 5:06 am
☽□♄ 7:18 am
☽△♆ 8:25 am

☽□♅ 10:06 am v/c
☽→♋ 10:45 am
☽✶☿ 5:02 pm
☽☍♇ 7:25 pm

May
mayo

La Fortuna
© Luz-Maria López 2007

☽☽☽ lunes

Monday
17

♀□♃ 3:57 am
☉⚹♃ 5:41 pm

♂♂♂ martes

♋ ♌ 

Tuesday
18

♀□♄ 1:18 am
☽△♃ 9:11 am
☉⚹☽ 10:07 am
☽⚹♄ 10:37 am
☽△♅ 1:35 pm v/c
☽→♌ 2:06 pm
♀△♆ 3:12 pm
☉△♄ 5:27 pm
☽□☿ 10:01 pm

☿☿☿ miércoles

♌ 

Wednesday
19

☉□♆ 11:14 am
☿△♇ 11:47 am
♀□♅ 12:41 pm
♀→♋ 6:05 pm

♃♃♃ jueves

♌ ♍ 

Thursday
20

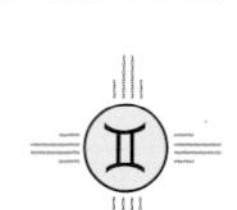

☽PrG 1:48 am
☽☌♂ 1:51 am
♀△⚷ 11:49 am
☽☍♆ 2:43 pm
☉⚹♅ 2:48 pm
☉□☽ 4:43 pm v/c
☽→♍ 4:58 pm
☽⚹♀ 7:05 pm
☉→♊ 8:34 pm

Waxing Half Moon in ♌ Leo 4:43 pm PDT
Sun in ♊ Gemini 8:34 pm PDT

♀♀♀ viernes

♍ 

Friday
21

☽△♇ 1:21 am
☽△☿ 3:09 am
☉□⚷ 7:06 pm

All aspects in Pacific Daylight Time; add 3 hours for EDT; add 7 hours for GMT

Year at a Glance for ♊ Gemini (May 20–June 21)

In 2010 your unconventional approach to public or professional issues is applauded, in particular by those in positions of authority. And of course, with your innate exuberance you'll bring all sorts of companions along for the ride. What may appear disorganized or scattered generally arises from an underlying wisdom/logic in Gemini-born.

If you want to change jobs, lucky winds blow opportunity your way this year. You feel more worthy of recognition, and others feel it. Rebelliousness against authority increases; impulsive decision-making benefits from the perspective of a more earthy (Taurus, Virgo, Capricorn) colleague. Gemini bores more easily than any other sign, perhaps you just need a fresh project. Talent emerges from an unexpected event or circumstance.

Of course, all work and no play makes Jill a dull girl; make sure you write in "Play"—"Love"—"Create" on your calendar. Be deliberate, structure will help all of these flourish in your life in 2010. Re-evaluate your talents—where do you waste your energy or not take your genius seriously? What makes you unique?

Love? Be intentional. Cultivate your lover-self. Older lovers may be the most satisfying, or the focused appreciation of an enduring relationship enriches it. More Gemini will be committing to relationships than any other sign this year.

Time with children reminds you to play; you may rediscover that creative passion you once set aside. Concentration and disciplined efforts in anything fun—be it sport or art—steadies your course, brings calm and focus to all of your endeavors.

Gretchen Lawlor © Mother Tongue Ink 2009

© Leah Marie Dorion 2008

♄♄♄ sábado

♍ ♎

Saturday

22

☽☍♃ 4:09 pm
☽☌♄ 4:14 pm
☽☍♅ 7:34 pm v/c
☽→♎ 7:50 pm

♃☍♄ 10:36 pm
☉△☽ 11:17 pm

☉☉☉ domingo

♎

Sunday

23

☽□♀ 2:40 am
☽□♇ 4:11 am
♀☍♇ 8:15 pm

May
Mei

☽☽☽ Jumatatu

♎ ♏

Monday
24

☽✶♂ 11:30 am
☽△♆ 9:01 pm v/c
☽→♏ 11:17 pm

♂♂♂ Jumanne

♏

Tuesday
25

☽✶♇ 7:44 am
☽△♀ 11:10 am
☽☍☿ 4:15 pm
☉⚻♇ 9:39 pm

☿☿☿ Jumatano

♏

Wednesday
26

☽□♂ 6:02 pm

♃♃♃ Alhamisi

♏ ♐

Thursday
27

☽✶♄ 12:22 am
☽△♃ 1:38 am
☽□♆ 1:55 am
☽△♅ 4:13 am v/c
☽→♐ 4:15 am
☉☍☽ 4:07 pm
♅→♈ 6:44 pm

Full Moon in ♐ Sagittarius 4:07 pm PDT

♀♀♀ Ijumaa

♐

Friday
28

No Exact Aspects

Dancing Women
© Leah Marie Dorion 2007

♄♄♄ Jumamosi

♐ ♑

Saturday
29

☽△♂ 3:12 am
☽□♄ 7:38 am
☽⚹♆ 9:16 am
☽□♃ 9:40 am v/c
☽→♑ 11:44 am
☽□♅ 11:50 am
☽☌♇ 8:49 pm

☉☉☉ Jumapili

♑

Sunday
30

♄D 11:08 am
☽☍♀ 12:23 pm
☽△☿ 4:55 pm

May/June

Aymuray killa/Jawqaykuski killa

Positive Spin
© Jakki Moore 2008

☽☽☽ Killachaw

♑ ♒

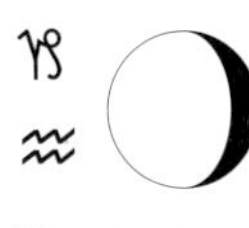

Monday
31

♆R 11:48 am
☽△♄ 5:49 pm
☽⚹♃ 8:41 pm v/c
☽→♒ 10:08 pm
☽⚹♅ 10:22 pm

♂♂♂ Atichaw

June

♒

Tuesday
1

☉△☽ 9:15 pm

☿☿☿ Quyllurchaw

♒

Wednesday
2

☽□☿ 11:44 am

♃♃♃ Illapachaw

♒ ♓

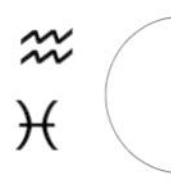

Thursday
3

☽☍♂ 6:42 am
☽☌♆ 7:55 am v/c
☽ApG 9:55 am
☽→♓ 10:33 am
☽⚹♇ 7:58 pm
⚷R 10:05 pm

♀♀♀ Ch'askachaw

♓

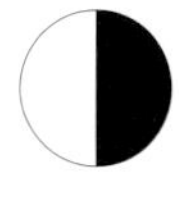

Friday
4

♂☍♆ 10:52 am
☉□☽ 3:13 pm

Waning Half Moon in ♓ Pisces 3:13 pm PDT

All aspects in Pacific Daylight Time; add 3 hours for EDT; add 7 hours for GMT

Women's Laughter

talking the night away
kitchen sink humour
laughing like drains
cackling like crones

hooting like owls
howling like wolves
gut wrenching
belly laughs

filthy jokes
foulmouthed
spitting it out
old bags and bad girls

table thumping
trivial, tribal,
tremendous
the power

of women's laughter

¤ *Cora Greenhill 2005*

Ester © *Sequoia 2007*

♄♄♄ K'uychichaw

♓ ♈

Saturday

5

☽△♀ 1:44 am
☽⚹☿ 8:25 am
☽☍♄ 6:36 pm
☽☌♃ 10:49 pm v/c

☽→♈ 10:50 pm
☽☌♅ 11:19 pm
♃→♈ 11:28 pm

☉☉☉ Intichaw

♈

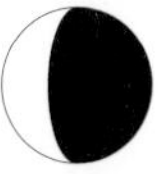

Sunday

6

☽□♇ 7:53 am
♂→♍ 11:11 pm

June
lune

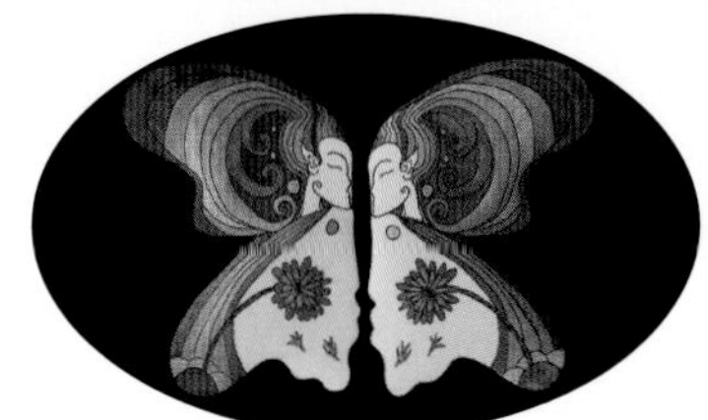

Incubating Wishes
¤ Rosemary Lloyd Freeman 2003

☽☽☽ pō 'akahi

♈

Monday
7

♂⚻♃ 7:26 am
☉⚹☽ 7:31 am
♂⚻♅ 12:03 pm
☽□♀ 6:44 pm

♂♂♂ pō 'alua

♈
♉

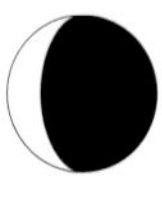

Tuesday
8

♃☌♅ 4:27 am
☽⚹♆ 6:13 am v/c
☽→♉ 8:41 am
☽△♂ 10:06 am
☿△♄ 4:14 pm
☽△♇ 5:08 pm
♂☍⚷ 8:07 pm

☿☿☿ pō 'akolu

♉

Wednesday
9

☿□♆ 3:39 am
☿→♊ 10:41 pm

♃♃♃ pō 'aha

♉
♊

Thursday
10

☿⚹♅ 3:28 am
☿⚹♃ 6:42 am
☽⚹♀ 7:21 am
☽△♄ 11:32 am
☿□⚷ 12:26 pm
☽□♆ 12:50 pm v/c

☽→♊ 3:11 pm
☽⚹♅ 3:47 pm
☽⚹♃ 4:15 pm
☽☌☿ 5:31 pm
☽□♂ 6:42 pm

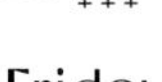

♀♀♀ pō 'alima

♊

Friday
11

☿□♂ 6:27 am

All aspects in Pacific Daylight Time; add 3 hours for EDT; add 7 hours for GMT

Spinning Through Time

As a child I wished my family spoke
English like everyone else.
No accent, no embarrassment, no repetition.

As an adolescent I didn't want to hear my family,
And wished we did not have to make a moral dilemma
of every action, weighing cause and consequence.

As a young woman I began wondering about life,
consequence of actions, about ethical values..

As a mature woman,
I relish accents.

© Susan Byrne 2007

Sisters *© Lisa Seed 2007*

♄♄♄ pō 'aono

♊ ♋

Saturday

12

☉☌☽ 4:14 am
♀✶♄ 8:18 am
☿⊼♇ 12:05 pm
☽□♄ 3:25 pm
☽△♆ 4:35 pm v/c
☽→♋ 6:50 pm
☽□♅ 7:29 pm
☽□♃ 8:19 pm
♀⊼♆ 10:23 pm

New Moon in ♊ Gemini 4:14 am PDT

☉☉☉ lā pule

♋

Sunday

13

☽✶♂ 12:12 am
☽☍♇ 2:17 am

Why I Write

I write to hear my voice,
because there are places of honesty
and beauty that I go in my writing that
I can't always go in my life, and I must.
When I write, I let the parts of me that hold
my breath, breathe. I write to let light into my
being and let darkness out, to own myself, capturing
the rhythms of my cycles: journeys into the abyss,
travels through glory. I write to allow myself to feel,
climb inside my emotions and explore their reaches and
textures, summon my tears, let them wash me hot and
clean then drain me empty and free. I write myself alive and
reborn, whole and holy, to experience myself transformed. I
write because I hurt and because I love, and so I won't lose
anything. And because I am lonely, sensual and spiritual,
and I need to make contact with the divine, and writing
for me is like touching: it is rubbing and rolling my
body against the divine until my boundaries dissolve
and I no longer know where I start and where I stop:
I become part of the universal hum. I write to make
myself eternal, leave a piece of me stained into the
ethers. I write because I believe Goddess listens
for the places where we love and own ourselves.
I write to keep myself company, keep
myself honest, keep from watching TV.
I write to keep my Muse intrigued.
I write because I can't draw.

VII. CREATIVE SPIN

Moon VII: June 12–July 11

New Moon in ♊ Gemini June 12; Sun in ♋ Cancer June 21; Full Moon in ♑ Capricorn June 26

She Changes Everything She Touches *© Jakki Moore 2008*

Come, dip your pen in the language
and write, tonight.
The Muse is standing by with bottles of ink.

excerpt © Marni Norwich 2004

June
junio

☽☽☽ lunes

♋ ♌

Monday 14

♀→♌ 1:50 am
♀△♅ 10:20 am
☽✶♄ 5:38 pm v/c
☽→♌ 8:54 pm
♀⚻⚷ 8:57 pm
☽△♅ 9:36 pm
☽☌♀ 10:35 pm
☽△♃ 10:46 pm

Young Goddess Creates New Toy
© Robyn Waters 2002

♂♂♂ martes

♌

Tuesday 15

♀△♃ 1:07 am
♂△♇ 5:12 am
☽PrG 8:02 am
☽✶☿ 1:41 pm

☿☿☿ miércoles

♌ ♍

Wednesday 16

☉✶☽ 3:27 pm
☽☍♆ 8:24 pm v/c
☽→♍ 10:41 pm

♃♃♃ jueves

♍

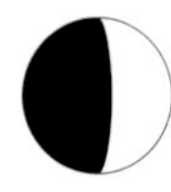

Thursday 17

☽△♇ 5:53 am
☽☌♂ 7:53 am
♀⚻♇ 6:23 pm
☽□☿ 11:35 pm

♀♀♀ viernes

♍

Friday 18

☉□☽ 9:29 pm
☽☌♄ 10:04 pm v/c

Waxing Half Moon in ♍ Virgo 9:29 pm PDT

All aspects in Pacific Daylight Time; add 3 hours for EDT; add 7 hours for GMT

Where Wild Ponies Come From

Along the eastern shore
a Indian spirit chants:
Assateague… Chincoteague…
the sea grasses whisper:
Run so free… run so free…

As the surf breaks behind her,
the little girl squats in the sand
performing
the pony creating ritual.

Carefully she sculpts
the forward reaching head,
the flying mane,
and the galloping legs.

With great solemnity
she pats the final
improvements into place
and nods her head
in affirmation.

As the girl and her guardian
Take their leave,
The little one envisions
The sand horse
running down the beach,

Spirit of the Mustang
© Cathy McClelland 2008

She is very quiet;
content.

Her vision,
consecrated by
the salted holy-water,
breathes life into the sand pony.
The primitive form
is washed away and
far out on the barrier island
a new wild pony is born.

© Janet Ladrach 1998

♄♄♄ sábado

♍

♎

Saturday 19

☽→♎ 1:13 am
☽☍♅ 2:03 am
☽☍♃ 3:55 am
☉□♄ 6:18 am
☽□♇ 8:31 am
☽✶♀ 12:03 pm
☉△♆ 5:21 pm

☉☉☉ domingo

♎
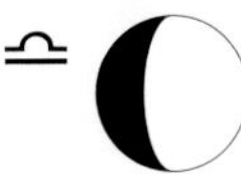

Sunday 20

☽△☿ 11:43 am

Net

a
most
delicate
and
invisible
thread

carefully
spun
to
encircle,

when
woven
in the
proper
way,

becomes
a net
to
cradle
and
sustain.

Celebrating Women's Creative Hands and Spirits

Betty LaDuke © Heifer International 2008

Summer Solstice

Longest day, shortest night, apex of the solar cycle. The fiery Solstice heralds the fullness of the green earth, when Cardea, Goddess of The Hinge, opens the door that shifts our global rhythms from waxing to waning light.

Summer Solstice . . . We met on an incredibly beautiful beach, when Amaterasu, the Sun, was at Her peak. The ocean tide was amazingly strong, and gathering mussels to cook for our supper became an athletic event. We slid in the water, giggled, and tended our meal roasting in the sand. We sat in a circle and wove the Solstice Wheel with wildflowers and roses. We were truly Amazons that day.

After supper when night was falling, we walked slowly down to the water's edge and made a blazing fire. The full moon shone ecstatically bright, and our vibrant drums were definitely alive. We drummed, danced, and chanted spells: O holy Mother Earth, thou art so beauteous! Ocean Water, mighty and strong, stay strong, be healed! Cardea, open the Door, turn the Wheel!

Pele was there, Imanja was there, the Phoenix firebird was there. I was there.

Ffiona Morgan © Mother Tongue Ink 2008

Sarasvati *© Hrana Janto 1992*

June
Iuni

☽☽☽ Jumatatu

Monday 21

Summer Solstice

☽△♆ 2:44 am v/c
☉→♋ 4:28 am
☽→♏ 5:13 am
☉△☽ 5:17 am
☽✶♇ 12:40 pm
☉□♅ 5:27 pm
☽✶♂ 7:20 pm
☽□♀ 9:22 pm

Sun in ♋ Cancer 4:28 am PDT

♂♂♂ Jumanne

♏

Tuesday 22

☉△⚷ 1:20 am

☿☿☿ Jumatano

♏ ♐

Wednesday 23

☉□♃ 6:21 am
☽✶♄ 8:04 am
☽□♆ 8:32 am v/c
☽→♐ 11:10 am
☽△♅ 12:09 pm
☽△♃ 2:52 pm
♇PrG 7:56 pm

♃♃♃ Alhamisi

♐

Thursday 24

☽□♂ 4:17 am
☽△♀ 9:20 am
☿□♄ 9:23 am
☿△♆ 11:33 am

♀♀♀ Ijumaa

♐ ♑

Friday 25

☿→♋ 3:32 am
☿□♅ 9:36 am
☉☍♇ 11:55 am
☿△⚷ 11:56 am
☽□♄ 4:19 pm
☽✶♆ 4:33 pm v/c
☽→♑ 7:21 pm
☽□♅ 8:25 pm
☽☍☿ 10:41 pm
☽□♃ 11:37 pm

All aspects in Pacific Daylight Time; add 3 hours for EDT; add 7 hours for GMT

Year at a Glance for ♋ Cancer (June 21–July 22)

A trip, pilgrimage, workshop or vision quest February–March or late in 2010, exposes you to electrifying aha's that occur best when you are in unfamiliar territory, and your past has less hold on you. Glimpses of a very different future fuel your ambitions, provide unconsidered options and alter your course.

Destiny now calls you to review past loyalties, to approach each relationship as new, full of possibilities. You may find yourself in close contact with unique souls not drawn so much by individual needs but by a sense of a deeper work, a common passion. By sharing you have more resources available, look for win-win situations. You have a heightened capacity to empower each other, though there will be battles. Don't hang onto people who won't share, won't change or won't believe in you.

In the middle of all this fire and excitement, pay close attention to your home and family. Do the circumstances support you and provide a firm base for respite from the stresses of life for years to come? Or do they need attention, time, clarification and stabilization? Do you need to move on? Don't make do out of sentimental attachment to the past.

You're here to put a new spin on your heritage; all your ancestors are waiting spell-bound to see what you'll do for the world. More often you'll find yourself instinctively reaching for just the right tool or being in the right place—in response to need in these swiftly changing times.

Gretchen Lawlor © Mother Tongue Ink 2009

Windflute *© Jana Lamprecht 2006*

♄♄♄ Jumamosi

♑ ○ Saturday 26

☽☌♇ 3:12 am
☿□♃ 4:08 am
☉☍☽ 4:30 am
☽△♂ 3:53 pm

Full Moon in ♑ Capricorn 4:30 am PDT
Partial Lunar Eclipse 4:38 am PDT *

☉☉☉ Jumapili

♑ ☽ Sunday 27

☿☍♇ 12:15 am
♄⚻♆ 7:46 pm

 *Eclipse visible E. Asia, Australia, the Pacific, and the W. Americas

June/July

Aymuray killa/ Jawqaykuski killa

☽☽☽ Killachaw

♑ ♒

Monday

28

☽△♄ 2:56 am v/c
☉☌☿ 5:07 am
☽→♒ 5:52 am
☽✶♅ 7:00 am
☽✶♃ 10:41 am

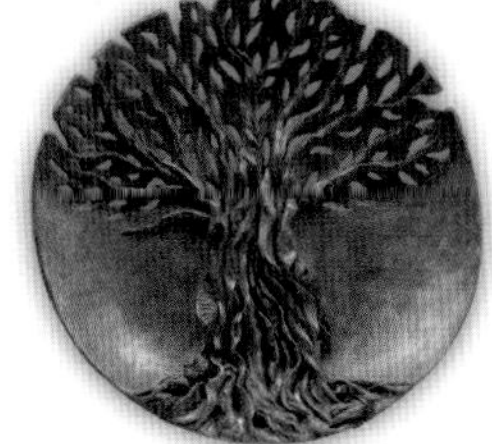

Tree of Life
¤ *Sheila A. Richards 2006*

♂♂♂ Atichaw

♒

Tuesday

29

☿ApG 11:11 am
☽☍♀ 6:14 pm

☿☿☿ Quyllurchaw

♒ ♓

Wednesday

30

☽☌♆ 3:03 pm v/c
☽→♓ 6:09 pm

♃♃♃ Illapachaw

♓

Thursday

1

July

☽✶♇ 2:12 am
☽ApG 3:10 am
☿✶♂ 5:19 am
☉△☽ 2:16 pm
☽☍♂ 9:44 pm

♀♀♀ Ch'askachaw

♓

Friday

2

☽△☿ 12:24 am

Creating our Changes

We find new ways of hardening
hurt into art.
One friend is practising on climbing walls
to strengthen her fingers for sculpture.
She's making an alabaster torso
with a space inside.
Another learnt to forge metal
to cast her own womb in silver.
Suddenly we are all hammering
hot metal into heresies
from our bodies' furnaces.
I find myself carving spirals into stone
laying labyrinths in landscape.

excerpt ¤ Cora Greenhill 2002

Ala
© Cheryl Collins 2007

♄♄♄ K'uychichaw

♓ ♈

Saturday 3

☽☍♄ 4:17 am v/c
☽→♈ 6:44 am
☽☌♅ 7:55 am
☽☌♃ 12:17 pm
☽□♇ 2:31 pm

☉☉☉ Intichaw

♈

Sunday 4

☉□☽ 7:35 am

Waning Half Moon in ♈ Aries 7:35 am PDT

☽☽☽ pō 'akahi

♈
♉

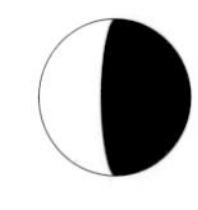

Monday
5

☽□☿ 12:40 am
☽△♀ 6:52 am
♅R 9:49 am
☽✶♆ 2:24 pm v/c
☽→♉ 5:29 pm

♂♂♂ pō 'alua

♉

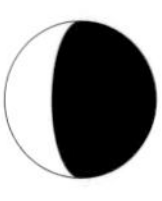

Tuesday
6

☽△♇ 12:47 am
☉✶☽ 9:36 pm

☿☿☿ pō 'akolu

♉

Wednesday
7

☽△♂ 12:28 am
☽✶☿ 7:15 pm
☽□♀ 8:06 pm
☽□♆ 9:53 pm
☽△♄ 11:09 pm v/c

♃♃♃ pō 'aha

♉
♊

Thursday
8

☽→♊ 12:51 am
☽✶♅ 1:53 am
☽✶♃ 6:15 am
☿⚻♆ 12:57 pm
♀☍♆ 4:55 pm
☿✶♄ 10:35 pm

♀♀♀ pō 'alima

♊

Friday
9

☽□♂ 8:06 am
☿→♌ 9:29 am
☿⚻⚷ 2:15 pm
☿△♅ 4:45 pm

Armistice

There is a poem buried
beneath your resistance
to this moment.
I can see the tip
of its shiny head
every time you move
out of the way.
It is your reward for
showing up in this place
despite all the rain.
It is an excerpt
from a conversation
you are having with God.
You thought it needed
to come from you
when all this time
what was really needed
was for it to come
through you.
Imagine:
a circumstance that values your
surrender over your
call to arms.

© Marni Norwich 2006

Night of One Thousand Birds
© Rebecca Guberman-Bloom 2005

♄♄♄ pō 'aono

♊ ♋

Saturday

10

☽△♆ 1:47 am
☽□♄ 3:17 am v/c
♀→♍ 4:31 am
☽→♋ 4:38 am
☽⚹♀ 4:38 am
☽□♅ 5:36 am
☽□♃ 9:52 am
☽☍♇ 10:52 am
♀☍⚷ 12:04 pm
♀⚻♅ 4:55 pm
☉⚹♂ 9:13 pm

☉☉☉ lā pule

♋

Sunday

11

☿△♃ 1:12 am
☿⚻♇ 8:13 am
☽⚹♂ 12:16 pm
☉☌☽ 12:40 pm

Total Solar Eclipse 12:34 pm PDT*
New Moon in ♋ Cancer 12:40 pm PDT

*Eclipse visible S. America, S. Pacific, Easter Is., Chile, Argentina

Legacy'd

for Beverly Brown, 1951-2005

Will you really, finally die
after I use all the Sweetmeat squash seeds
you gave us years ago? Your fat, happy seed children.
I still plant lettuce seeds, Buttercrunch,
that came from your serious saving.
Will you fade when the envelope is empty
of life rattling around in seed form?

There is nothing quite like
putting your seeds in the ground
legacy of trust in tomorrow
despite the end of your today.

How you loved
the science
of the cycles—
the dormant,
the swelling,
the opening
push of tender
miracle sprout
hungry and thirsty

Share the Seeds
© Sandra Lory 2008

the crowded carrots the giant mustard leaves
the hot rank summer of lusty success
    the triumph of Food
Food to share, food to dry, to can
before the shrivel and pucker of pods
where the next generation of seed babies
snuggles down in the cold nursery of winter
to await the next incarnation
while decay enjoys its own feast
and compost works its slow resurrection.

excerpt © Bethroot Gwynn 2008

VIII. CIRCLE OF SUSTENANCE

Moon VIII: July 11–August 9

New Moon in ♋ Cancer July 11; Sun in ♌ Leo July 22; Full Moon in ♒ Aquarius July 25

Saving Seed
© Sequoia 2006

In Sanskrit, *bija*, the seed, means the source of life. Saving seed is our duty; sharing seed is our culture.

Patents on seeds and genetic resources rob us of our birth right and deprive us of our livelihoods by transforming seed saving and seed sharing into intellectual property crimes....

The seed is starting to take shape as the site and symbol of freedom in the age of manipulation and monopoly of life. The seed is not big and powerful, but can become alive as a sign of resistance and creativity in the smallest huts or gardens and the poorest families. In smallness lies power. The seed also embodies diversity...the freedom to stay alive...the freedom of diverse cultures from centralized control. In the seed, ecological issues combine with social justice.

excerpt from Earth Democracy: Justice, Sustainability, and Peace
by Vandana Shiva © 2005 South End Press www.southendpress.org and Zed Books, London and New York www.zedbooks.co.uk

July
julio

Cloud Dance Over Sugarcane
© ScharCbear Freeman 2008

☽☽☽ lunes

♋ ♌

Monday
12

☽✶♄ 4:48 am v/c
☽→♌ 5:53 am
☽△♅ 6:49 am
☽△♃ 11:05 am
☽☌☿ 3:49 pm

♂♂♂ martes

♌

Tuesday
13

♀⚻♃ 1:48 am
☽PrG 4:22 am
♀△♇ 10:55 am

☿☿☿ miércoles

♌ ♍

Wednesday
14

☽☍♆ 3:23 am v/c
☽→♍ 6:15 am
☽△♇ 12:08 pm
☽☌♀ 2:14 pm

♃♃♃ jueves

♍

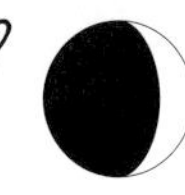

Thursday
15

☽☌♂ 5:30 pm
☉✶☽ 8:39 pm

♀♀♀ viernes

♍

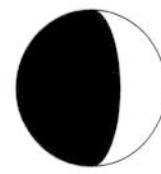

Friday
16

☽☌♄ 6:46 am v/c
☽→♎ 7:24 am
☽☍♅ 8:19 am
☽☍♃ 12:58 pm
☽□♇ 1:24 pm

All aspects in Pacific Daylight Time; add 3 hours for EDT; add 7 hours for GMT

© Linda Erzinger 1994

Soil

Scrape coffee grounds into compost bucket
add eggshell, moldy beans, wilted lettuce
the last potato, sprinkle one handful of night crawlers
top with Demeter's pile of dead leaves.
What dies gives life. Feast and be satisfied.

© Ann Filemyr 2005

♄♄♄ sábado

♎

Saturday 17

☽✶☿ 7:36 am

☉☉☉ domingo

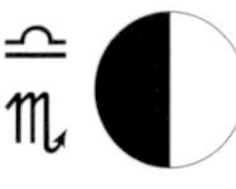

Sunday 18

☉□☽ 3:11 am
☽△♆ 7:26 am v/c
☽→♏ 10:42 am
☽✶♇ 4:55 pm

Waxing Half Moon in ♎ Libra 3:11 am PDT

July
Iulai

ϿϿϿ Jumatatu

♏ 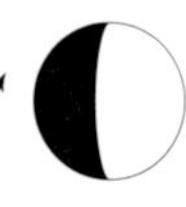

Monday
19

☽✶♀ 4:26 am
☽□☿ 7:39 pm

Harvest

♂♂♂ Jumanne

Tuesday
20

⚷→♒ 2:36 am
☽✶♂ 6:20 am
☉△☽ 1:07 pm
☽□♆ 1:16 pm
☉⚻♆ 3:09 pm
☽✶♄ 4:43 pm v/c
☽→♐ 4:48 pm
☽△♅ 5:44 pm

♄⚻⚷ 10:11 pm
☽△♃ 11:06 pm

☿☿☿ Jumatano

♐ 

Wednesday
21

♄→♎ 8:10 am
☽□♀ 4:42 pm

♃♃♃ Alhamisi

Thursday
22

☽△☿ 11:26 am
☉⚻⚷ 12:52 pm
☉→♌ 3:21 pm
☽□♂ 5:31 pm
☉✶♄ 6:12 pm
☽✶♆ 9:50 pm v/c

Sun in ♌ Leo 3:21 pm PDT

♀♀♀ Ijumaa

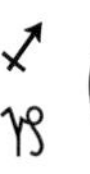 

Friday
23

☽→♑ 1:39 am
☽□♄ 1:55 am
☽□♅ 2:33 am
☉△♅ 3:05 am
♃R 5:03 am
☽□♃ 8:14 am
☽☌♇ 8:18 am

Year at a Glance for ♌ Leo (July 22–August 22)

In your most complex relationships, a puzzle piece is brought to light in 2010. Muddy boundaries that have kept you in vague limbo are the most likely arena. Explosions either inspire a more profound level of commitment, or release so that you both may move forward.

You long for companions who share your creative/spiritual passions; mutual commitment to these interests lifts you out of confusion, lack of trust. For those looking, one met in 2009 becomes more significant.

You long for serious conversations with wise companions. Your agile, inquisitive mind needs to engage its full resources to avoid scattering/worrying. Seek out innovative programs/courses of study, especially ones involving travel to exotic places. You want information you can use to feel more effective in the world. Allow yourself to experience different settings and communities, especially in June and July. More opportunities arise in 2011.

This year an unusual healing technique releases emotional toxins that've held you back for years/lifetimes. Radical or unforeseen changes in circumstances for you, or one close to you, expand your options.

An unexpected inheritance or new funding by mid-July lifts a financial weight that has burdened you in the last couple of years. Keep finances simple, but be open to solutions from diverse sources. Windfalls may allow you to invest in progressive ventures—careful, this is only an infusion, not a steady source. Avoid overextending into projects that tie you into long-term mutual dependence.

Gretchen Lawlor © Mother Tongue Ink 2009

Moon Huntress © *Kat Beyer 2008*

♄♄♄ Jumamosi

♑

Saturday

24

☽△♀ 8:12 am
♃□♇ 9:18 pm

☉☉☉ Jumapili

♑
♒

Sunday

25

Lunar Lammas

☽△♂ 7:20 am v/c
☽→♒ 12:38 pm
☽△♄ 1:19 pm
☽✶♅ 1:29 pm
☉☍☽ 6:36 pm
☽✶♃ 7:24 pm

Full Moon in ♒ Aquarius 6:36 pm PDT

July/August

Jawqaykuski killa/Chakraqunakuy killa

Eve's Apple
© Rebecca Guberman-Bloom 2005

☽☽☽ Killachaw

♒ 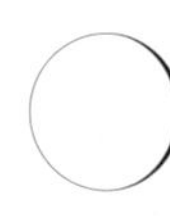

Monday 26

☿☍♆ 3:03 am
☉⊼♇ 4:04 am
☉△♃ 4:30 am
♂⊼♆ 7:41 am
♄☍♅ 10:07 am

♂♂♂ Atichaw

♒ 

Tuesday 27

☿☍⚷ 9:18 am
☿→♍ 2:43 pm
☽☌♆ 8:46 pm v/c
☿⊼♅ 9:42 pm

☿☿☿ Quyllurchaw

♒ ♓

Wednesday 28

☽→♓ 1:00 am
☽☍☿ 2:18 am
☽⚹♇ 7:44 am
☽ApG 4:49 pm

♃♃♃ Illapachaw

♓ 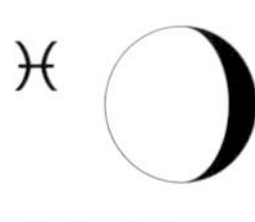

Thursday 29

♂⊼⚷ 1:46 am
♂→♎ 4:46 pm
☽☍♀ 8:44 pm v/c

♀♀♀ Ch'askachaw

♓ ♈ 

Friday 30

☿△♇ 3:04 am
☿⊼♃ 3:44 am
♂☍♅ 6:31 am
☽→♈ 1:42 pm
☽☌♅ 2:23 pm
☽☍♂ 2:49 pm
☽☍♄ 3:16 pm
☽□♇ 8:17 pm
☽☌♃ 8:20 pm

All aspects in Pacific Daylight Time; add 3 hours for EDT; add 7 hours for GMT

Comfort Food

There is a food revolution afoot! Get on the covered wagon with Finisia Medrona as she works to re-wild the Sacred Native American food hoop our ancestors depended on for food in the NW. Our ancestors traveled with the seasons, gathered Camas, Breadroot, and other plants, careful not to take too much, thanking Spirit for abundance, so their children would never hunger. "Civilization" has plowed under and paved over the majority of these early staples.

The average US meal travels 1500 miles to get to your plate. Think global climate imbalance and resource wars. A "locovore" diet is healthier for you and the planet. The processes of refrigeration, transporting, over -tilling, -watering and -fertilizing produce copious greenhouse-trapping gasses. We are eating food without soul—produced in mass volume, heedless of nutritional value, spirit, or care for the next generations.

The solution is in boxes delivered by your local Community Supported Agriculture, at the farmers market, and in your own backyard. A "low carbon" diet travels 17 to 66 times fewer miles than the typical non-local diet. There is a movement to proliferate 2'X2' garden beds and food growing education among urban folks who have limited access to fresh vegetables. *Food-Not-Lawns* is working hard to turn Rhododendrons into Rutabagas. It takes surprisingly little space and time to grow enough food to impact our environmental footprint, our health, our sense of well-being and self-sufficiency.

Re-visioning our diet can help heal the Earth, thwart global warming and resource wars. Reinventing the way we eat is really about remembering our ancestral heritage, and using common sense, permaculture and mutual support to provide for each other's food needs. Maybe it's time we reevaluate what we consider comfort foods.

¤ *Barbara Dickinson 2008*

♄♄♄ K'uychichaw

♈ ◗

Saturday

31

♂☌♄ 1:07 am
☉△☽ 6:13 am

☉☉☉ Intichaw

August

♈ ◗

Sunday

1

☽⚹♆ 8:54 pm v/c

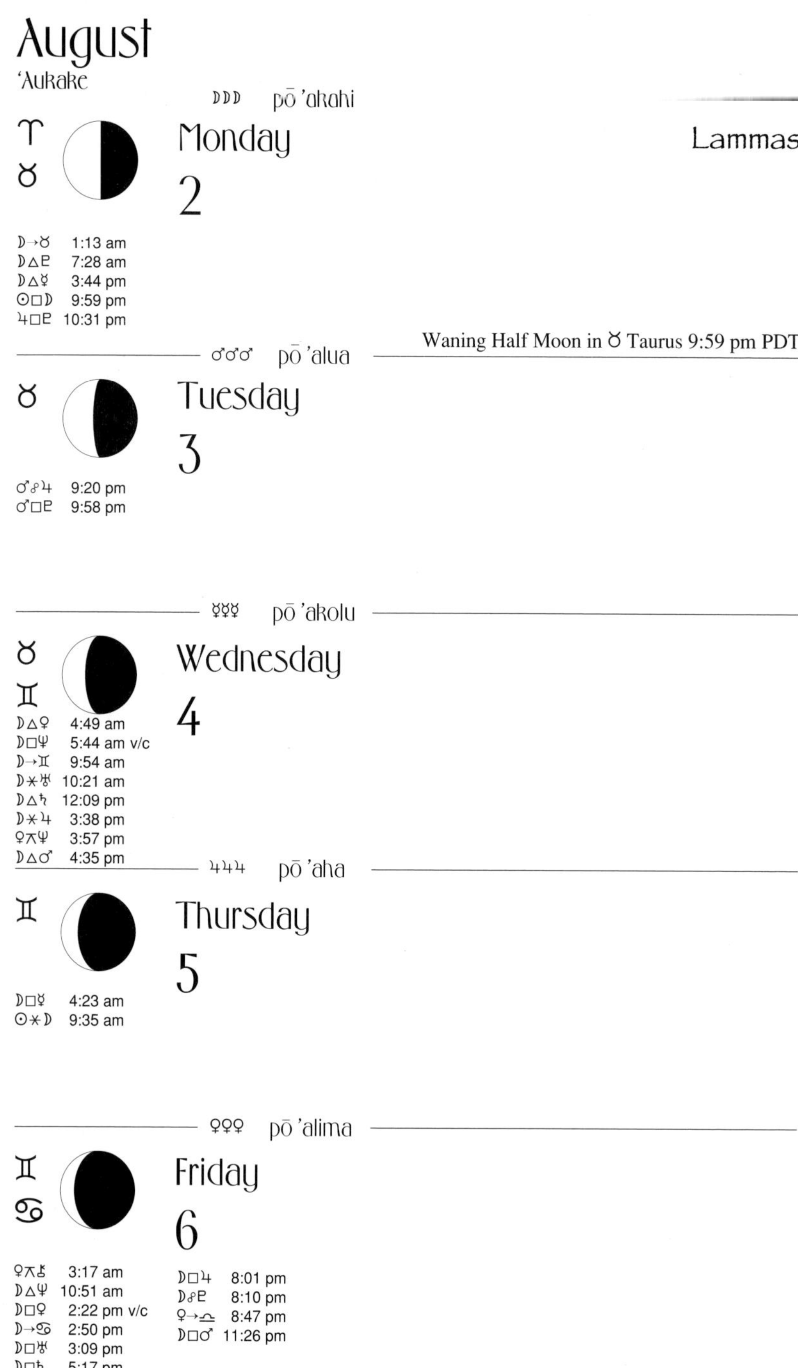

August
'Aukake

☽☽☽ pō 'akahi

Monday 2

Lammas

♈ ♉

☽→♉ 1:13 am
☽△♇ 7:28 am
☽△☿ 3:44 pm
☉□☽ 9:59 pm
♃□♇ 10:31 pm

Waning Half Moon in ♉ Taurus 9:59 pm PDT

♂♂♂ pō 'alua

Tuesday 3

♉

♂☍♃ 9:20 pm
♂□♇ 9:58 pm

☿☿☿ pō 'akolu

Wednesday 4

♉ ♊

☽△♀ 4:49 am
☽□♆ 5:44 am v/c
☽→♊ 9:54 am
☽✶♅ 10:21 am
☽△♄ 12:09 pm
☽✶♃ 3:38 pm
♀⚻♆ 3:57 pm
☽△♂ 4:35 pm

♃♃♃ pō 'aha

Thursday 5

♊

☽□☿ 4:23 am
☉✶☽ 9:35 am

♀♀♀ pō 'alima

Friday 6

♊ ♋

♀⚻⚷ 3:17 am
☽△♆ 10:51 am
☽□♀ 2:22 pm v/c
☽→♋ 2:50 pm
☽□♅ 3:09 pm
☽□♄ 5:17 pm
☽□♃ 8:01 pm
☽☍♇ 8:10 pm
♀→♎ 8:47 pm
☽□♂ 11:26 pm

All aspects in Pacific Daylight Time; add 3 hours for EDT; add 7 hours for GMT

Lammas

Days grow shorter as the sun declines; we harvest golden fields of wheat and first fruits of the trees and gardens. It's Midsummer, the exact half-point between Summer and Fall—time of the Sundance, the Green Corn Ceremony. We hold hands and chant: Habondia, Thank you! We feel the surge of this Cross-Quarter time as the Power Gate of Leo opens and releases the Fire Element, the waning light.

On August Eve, we gathered to sleep in a dream-wheel formation, reflecting the spokes of the Wheel of Fortune. Today we do feel fortunate, blessed by Fortuna, the Corn Mothers, all life-giving Goddesses.

Now in the clear morning, we share dreams and speak of the change. For the first time we have grown our own food, working together with love and the earth to produce fruits, grains and vegetables! We are humbled by the great abundance: our labors have been rewarded. Food is plentiful, no one is hungry. May it be so for all people. Contemplating these gifts, we bless the bread and look forward to a night of feasting. Tomorrow we will plant a new crop. The Wheel turns.

Ffiona Morgan © Mother Tongue Ink 2009

Home Grown Harvest © Sequoia 2008

Harvesting

Skirt soaked with tomato slop
feet caked with mud that
fills the hollows between my toes
and forms a wet brown arch support,
I pick tomatoes.

I step gingerly among pregnant plants
so heavy with round ripening
they no longer even try
to stand up straight —
they lie, legs spread, to be delivered
of their fruit.

Legions of women before me
have fed families
with this food;
my sisters for centuries
bending over squash vines,
my unknown aunties
lifting these fuzzy stems,
carefully closing their hands
around this smooth red fruit.

I want to invoke them
but I do not know their names.
How did they call themselves?
Anonymous mothers
who have no names in his-story books,
still I call upon them:

O, nameless women
who for generations have gathered food
from this continent of corn,
this land of squash, of tomatoes and beans,
today I am blessed to join you.

I stand in this late summer sun
my feet anointed in mud
touched with the blood of these tomatoes
I take my place among you:
American women
harvesting.

Sunflower Days © *Catherine Molland 2008*

♄♄♄ pō ʻaono

♋ 

Saturday

7

♀☍♅ 12:59 am
☽⚹☿ 11:46 am v/c

⊙⊙⊙ lā pule

♋ ♌ 

Sunday

8

♀☌♄ 10:24 am
☽→♌ 4:23 pm
☽△♅ 4:36 pm
☽⚹♄ 7:02 pm
☽⚹♀ 7:36 pm
☽△♃ 9:07 pm

World Trade Organization Protest 1999

As we marched in the streets, drums and whistles pounded with our hearts. Freedom was a melody we sung that floated between the skyscrapers. My breasts were exposed and chilly in the Seattle rain. My sisters and I wrote slogans on our bodies: "100% Organic" and "One Body One Soil." More and more women took off their shirts to join us. Our breasts drew attention to our deep humanity and connection to the earth. Despite the madness of pepper spray and rubber bullets, we returned to the streets each day as a powerful cord of resilience coursed through us. The alchemy of collective action built to a historical crescendo as our voices were heard and the World Trade Organization (WTO) went home. We were part of a greatness that filled us with stories, new friends, and the belief in our ability to bring about change.

Witches Hex

IX. WOMEN AT THE WHEEL

Moon IX: August 9–September 8

New Moon in ♌ Leo Aug. 9; Sun in ♍ Virgo Aug. 22; Full Moon in ♓ Pisces Aug. 24

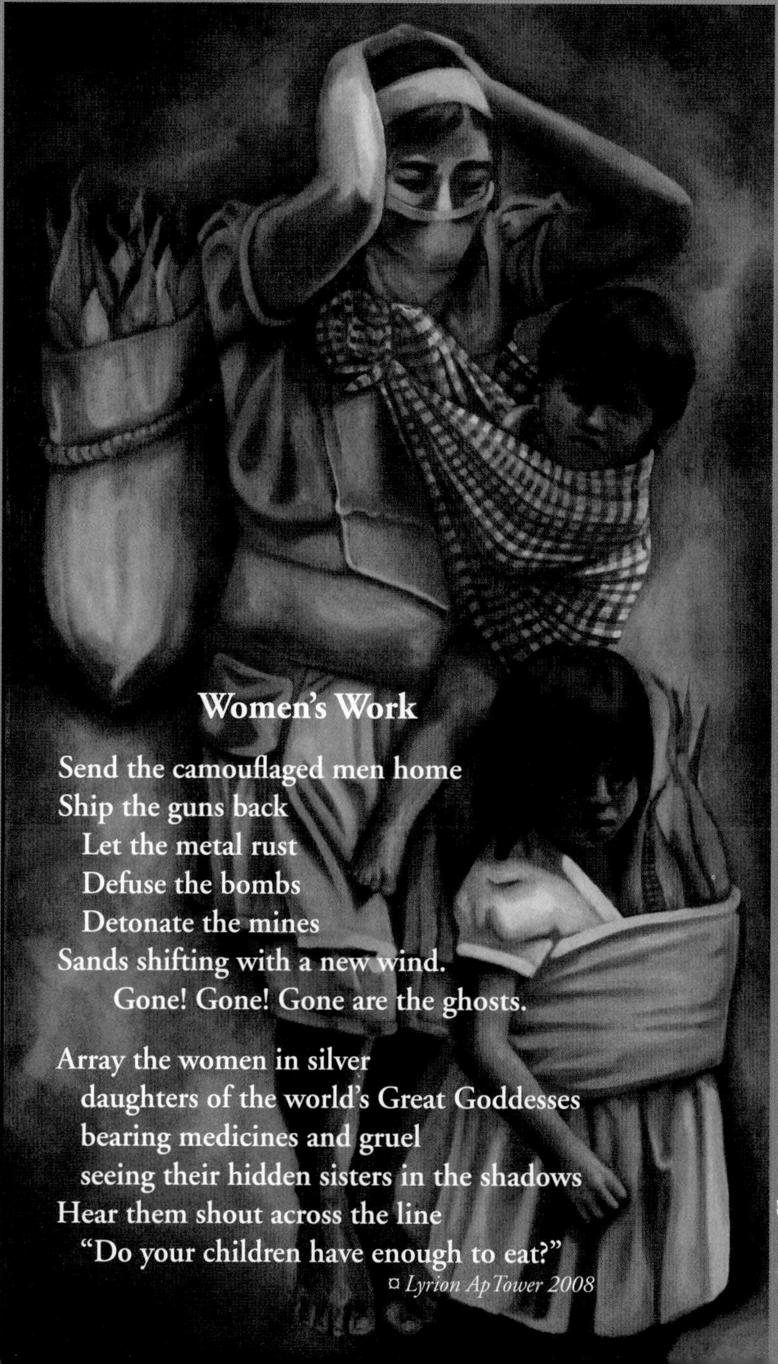

Women's Work

Send the camouflaged men home
Ship the guns back
  Let the metal rust
  Defuse the bombs
  Detonate the mines
Sands shifting with a new wind.
    Gone! Gone! Gone are the ghosts.

Array the women in silver
  daughters of the world's Great Goddesses
  bearing medicines and gruel
  seeing their hidden sisters in the shadows
Hear them shout across the line
  "Do your children have enough to eat?"

¤ *Lyrion ApTower 2008*

Semillas © *Alicia Maria Siu 2006*

Fire Spirit Prayer
© Annie Ocean 2008

August
agosto

☽☽☽ lunes

♌ 

Monday
9

☽⚹♂ 2:40 am
♀☍♃ 4:40 pm
☉☌☽ 8:08 pm
♀□♇ 9:05 pm

New Moon in ♌ Leo 8:08 pm PDT

♂♂♂ martes

♌ ♍ 

Tuesday
10

☽PrG 11:06 am
☽☍♆ 12:10 pm v/c
☽→♍ 4:01 pm
☽△♇ 8:52 pm

☿☿☿ miércoles

♍ 

Wednesday
11

☽☌☿ 5:04 pm v/c

♃♃♃ jueves

♍ ♎ 

Thursday
12

☽→♎ 3:42 pm
☽☍♅ 3:46 pm
☽☌♄ 7:01 pm
☽☍♃ 8:06 pm
☽□♇ 8:38 pm

♀♀♀ viernes

♎ 

Friday
13

☽☌♀ 1:58 am
☽☌♂ 6:21 am
♅→♓ 8:36 pm

To Be a Witch

When I name myself a witch it is a statement of empowerment, claiming my Goddess-given divinity and place in an all-embracing community of believers, but it is also a challenge to myself to fully embody that title, to live up to it and into and with it. To weave magic and honor the Divine in all life, to hold ritual as a sacred way of offering gratitude and love and joy for the gift of existence, this is to be a witch. To find a way to live simply and in harmony with nature, receptive and present in the moment, amidst the chaos and bustle of modern life, this is to be a witch today. To remember our roots, our herstory, our childhood selves and the inner gypsy spirit that beckons us down the shady glittering forest trail … I name myself witch to connect to those who died for their belief. I name myself witch as a free spirited, nature-loving, Faery-seeking, magic-making, daydreaming, hopeful, grateful, playful, sacred, passionate, pagan manifestation of Divine Love. To be a witch is to embrace the all of life, to bend and weave the energies that flow around us for magical, healing, sacred purpose.

Temperance D.O.M. Tarot © Ffiona Morgan 1991

excerpt ¤ Casey Sayre Baikus 2008

♄♄♄ sábado

♎ ♏

Saturday

14

☉✶☽ 3:06 am v/c
☽△♆ 1:06 pm v/c
☽→♏ 5:26 pm
☽✶♇ 10:36 pm

☉☉☉ domingo

♏ 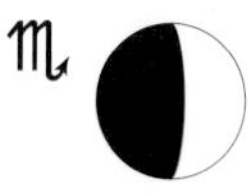

Sunday

15

No Exact Aspects

August
Agosti

ↄↄↄ Jumatatu

Women are collectors
Of splendor in the sun
Where vision meets emotion
We are there with our nets
excerpt © Caressa Mathews 2000

♏ ♐

Monday
16

☽✶☿ 1:10 am
⚷PrG 11:09 am
☉□☽ 11:14 am
♃☍♄ 1:45 pm
☽□♆ 5:48 pm
☽△♅ 10:24 pm v/c
☽→♐ 10:34 pm

Waxing Half Moon in ♏ Scorpio 11:14 am PDT

♂♂♂ Jumanne

♐

Tuesday
17

☽△♃ 2:59 am
☽✶♄ 3:10 am
☽✶♀ 6:56 pm
☽✶♂ 8:42 pm

☿☿☿ Jumatano

♐

Wednesday
18

☽□☿ 9:50 am
☉△☽ 11:57 pm

♃♃♃ Alhamisi

♐ ♑

Thursday
19

☽✶♆ 2:06 am
☽□♅ 6:58 am v/c
☽→♑ 7:17 am
☽□♃ 11:35 am
☽□♄ 12:39 pm
♆PrG 12:41 pm
☽☌♇ 1:02 pm

♀♀♀ Ijumaa

♑

Friday
20

☉☍♆ 3:07 am
☽□♀ 9:45 am
☽□♂ 9:49 am
♀☌♂ 11:49 am
☿R 12:58 pm
☽△☿ 8:45 pm

Year at a Glance for ♍ Virgo (Aug. 22–Sept. 22)

You've grown a sturdier, more streamlined identity in the past few years, a new orientation to life has required introspection. In 2010 give this new self-confidence to the world. Virgo has an innate gift for dealing with other people's problems in simple, practical ways. Allow for trial runs for optimal progress, set incremental, attainable goals, celebrate the small steps—on your relentless journey towards perfection.

What you own may not accurately reflect your new self; pare down to basics, make room for what is soon coming to nourish and support you most effectively in the future. Invest in yourself—spend time/money on new tools or resources that improve your effectiveness.

Unsettling circumstances in the lives of those close to you invite imaginative collaboration; some will be of a short, but highly energizing nature. Be less tolerant of restrictive alliances; stretch the realms of possibility in your close relationships, even though the circumstances may challenge your habitual self-reliance.

Change is supported by pouring attention into play, children, sports, creative works, love affairs. That which obsesses you is a likely agent for regeneration. Superficial experiences won't do, you won't be engaged unless it requires your total focus. Art projects become living healing rituals to clear away old tangles in your lifeline. A sports workout discharges excess energy, soothes your system. Power struggles with children shift when you allow them to introduce their ideas of what is fun, rather than imposing your own.

Gretchen Lawlor © Mother Tongue Ink 2009

© *Kimberly Webber 2008*

♄♄♄ Jumamosi

♑ ♒

Saturday 21

♄□♇ 3:16 am
☉☍⚷ 8:53 am
☽⚹♅ 6:08 pm v/c
☽→♒ 6:37 pm
☽⚹♃ 10:37 pm

☉☉☉ Jumapili

♒

Sunday 22

☽△♄ 12:42 am
☉⚻♅ 3:42 pm
☉→♍ 10:27 pm

Sun in ♍ Virgo 10:27 pm PDT

August

Chakraqunakuy killa

find
the womyn
who goes back
to change
the future
¤ *Patti Sinclair 2007*

☽☽☽ Killachaw

♒

Monday
23

☽△♂ 1:17 am
☽△♀ 3:00 am

♂♂♂ Atichaw

♒ ♓

Tuesday
24

☽☌♆ 1:29 am v/c
☽→♓ 7:11 am
☉☍☽ 10:04 am
☽✶♇ 1:03 pm
☉⚻♃ 5:28 pm
☽ApG 10:54 pm

Full Moon in ♓ Pisces 10:04 am PDT

☿☿☿ Quyllurchaw

♓

Wednesday
25

☽☍☿ 7:04 pm
☉△♇ 10:12 pm

♃♃♃ Illapachaw

♓ ♈

Thursday
26

☽☌♅ 6:59 pm v/c
☽→♈ 7:49 pm
☽☌♃ 10:51 pm

♀♀♀ Ch'askachaw

♈

Friday
27

☽□♇ 1:36 am
☽☍♄ 3:03 am

Pua Mana
© Lisa Seed 2007

♄♄♄ K'uychichaw

♈ ☽

Saturday
28

☽☍♂ 9:09 am
☽☍♀ 1:55 pm

☉☉☉ Intichaw

♈ ♉ ☽

Sunday
29

☽⚹♆ 1:47 am v/c
☽→♉ 7:35 am
☽△♇ 1:11 pm
☉△☽ 8:40 pm

August/September
'Aukake/Kepakemapa

© Anna Oneglia 2001

☽☽☽ pō 'akahi

♉

Monday
30

☽△☿ 11:39 am

♂♂♂ pō 'alua

♉
♊

Tuesday
31

☿PrG 7:46 am
☽□♆ 11:39 am
☽✶♅ 4:13 pm v/c
☽→♊ 5:19 pm
☽✶♃ 7:09 pm

☿☿☿ pō 'akolu

September

♊

Wednesday
1

☽△♄ 1:05 am
☉□☽ 10:22 am
☽□☿ 4:17 pm

Waning Half Moon in ♊ Gemini 10:22 am PDT

♃♃♃ pō 'aha

♊
♋

Thursday
2

☽△♂ 9:30 am
☽△♀ 3:46 pm
☽△♆ 6:26 pm
☽□♅ 10:40 pm v/c
☽→♋ 11:50 pm

♀♀♀ pō 'alima

♋

Friday
3

☽□♃ 1:06 am
☽☍♇ 4:46 am
☉☌☿ 5:35 am
☽□♄ 7:34 am
☽✶☿ 5:55 pm
☉✶☽ 7:44 pm

A Fire in the Belly

When I was 5 years old, a fire was planted in my belly. My dad's mother had brought me a children's book called "Boys Are Doctors, Girls Are Nurses," a volume both slim in width and ideas, in my opinion. When she suggested I become a nurse so I could marry a rich doctor, I thought about my miserable family—my abused mother in particular— and quipped, "Why can't I just BE a doctor? Then I won't have to marry anyone at all, and I can use all that extra money to help people." A small, but bright smile suddenly flashed across her face, just like a shooting star. "Girl," she hooted softly, "you may be onto something there."

Over the past 10 years, I have worked as a heavy equipment operator, a pyro-technician, a construction/rigging journeyman and photographer, all in an effort to support myself.

I realized, during my time spent living and working in a male-dominated culture, that we wimmin need to build a peaceful army of sisters, daughters, and mothers who can both nurture and fight—who live with every bit of our mind, body and soul fully awake—especially as the world becomes more unstable. It is my sincere hope that, in preparing such an army, we can truly bridge the gap between men and wimmin, haves and have-nots, between religions, races, sexes and ways of life—and create a sustainable future for all. Together, we need to hold up the entire sky, not just bits and pieces.

excerpt © Susan M. Barron 2008

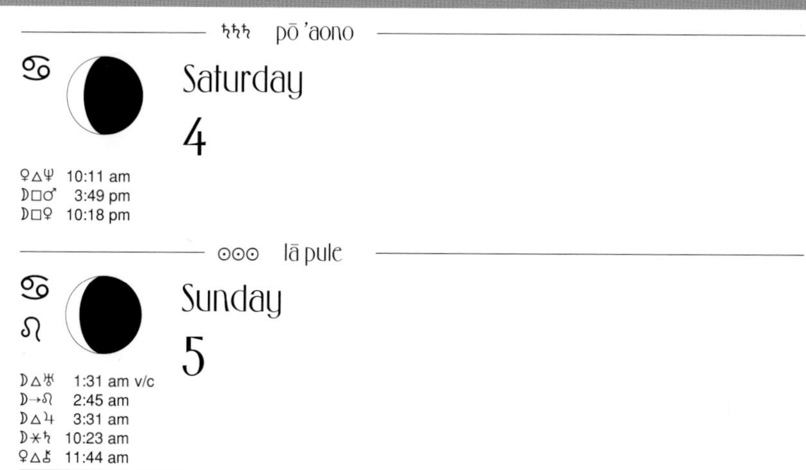

Dark Matter

In the morning
time when light takes hold of the
sky to make air a presence, a wash of
goodspeaking without words,

I come across the deep time, the newness
and I turn away from spinward, toward the place holding
sleep, the still fallow stretches:
I know there is no clearer place than this
nothing deeper than this.

I walk until I become the dark air.
I become the velvet depth of Not Yet,
Of Ever, of Before. I feel the thickening of Life
In me, the essential wholeness.

When we speak of That From Which All Arises
And Returns, we are describing not only
Below, the great abysms of creation—

We are namespeakingsilent our centers into being.

When we describe the great flaring
what we must not miss
is the deepest silence in the midst of the motion, the emanating
darkness.

We must not remake the new human mistake
Of the recent past, the last five or eight thousand full circles of earth,
That is: to focus on light and action at the expense of all else.

Photons are not as alone as we think them, and in a way
they are not moving at all or traveling;

We are.

And also this, we are dancing. And also this: what if there are dark
Photons, anti-photons, are they moving the other way, or being still
For every seeming motion? Then when I look at the galaxies starsinging
Brightly now,

What I notice most,

Is the black.

¤ *Marna 2006*

X. THE CENTER

Moon X: September 8–October 7

New Moon in ♍ Virgo Sept. 8; Sun in ♎ Libra Sept. 22; Full Moon in ♈ Aries Sept. 23

Warrioress *© Melissa Harris 1992*

All you long for will lie curled warm in your palm if you lay yourself open and surrender to the shape of things.

excerpt © DV Trimmer 2006

September

septiembre

☽☽☽ lunes

Crescent Beach *© Lisa Kagan 2006*

♌

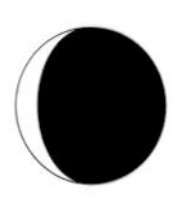

Monday

6

☽✶♂ 6:38 pm
☽☍♆ 9:52 pm

♂♂♂ martes

♌
♍

Tuesday

7

☽✶♀ 1:17 am v/c
☽→♍ 2:53 am
♀⚻♅ 6:49 am
☽△♇ 7:17 am
☽☌☿ 2:13 pm
☽PrG 8:47 pm

☿☿☿ miércoles

♍

Wednesday

8

☉☌☽ 3:30 am
♀→♏ 8:44 am
♀⚻♃ 10:36 am
♃→♓ 9:49 pm

New Moon in ♍ Virgo 3:30 am PDT

♃♃♃ jueves

♍
♎

Thursday

9

☽☍♅ 12:35 am
☽☍♃ 1:59 am v/c
☽→♎ 2:01 am
☽□♇ 6:26 am
☽☌♄ 10:09 am
♂△♆ 6:16 pm

♀♀♀ viernes

♎

Friday

10

☽△♆ 8:57 pm
♂△⚷ 9:17 pm
☽☌♂ 10:16 pm v/c

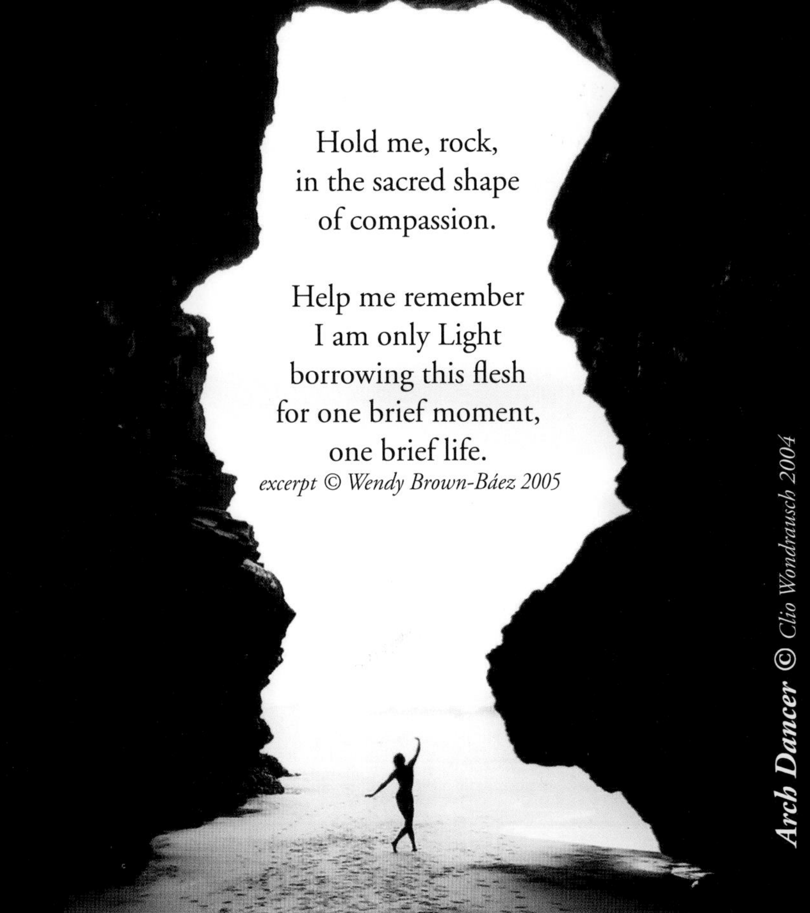

♄♄♄ sábado

♎ ♏

Saturday

11

☽→♏ 2:21 am
☽☌♀ 5:54 am
☽⚹♇ 6:59 am
☽⚹☿ 11:28 am

☉☉☉ domingo

♏

Sunday

12

♀⚹♇ 3:43 am
☉⚹☽ 12:06 pm
☿D 4:09 pm
☽□♆ 11:57 pm

September

Septemba

☽☽☽☽ Jumatatu

Raven Meditation ¤ Shannon "Shakaya Breeze" Leone 2008

Monday 13

♂⊼♅ 1:30 am
☽△♅ 3:58 am
☽△♃ 4:53 am v/c
☽→♐ 5:52 am
☽□☿ 3:38 pm
☽✶♄ 4:01 pm
♂⊼♃ 5:19 pm
♇D 9:36 pm

♂♂♂ Jumanne

♐

Tuesday 14

♂→♏ 3:38 pm
☉□☽ 10:50 pm

Waxing Half Moon in ♐ Sagittarius 10:50 pm PDT

☿☿☿ Jumatano

♐ ♑

Wednesday 15

☽✶♆ 7:01 am
☽□♅ 11:17 am
☽□♃ 11:51 am v/c
☽→♑ 1:30 pm
☽✶♂ 2:44 pm
☽☌♇ 6:52 pm
☽✶♀ 11:53 pm

♃♃♃ Alhamisi

♑

Thursday 16

☽□♄ 12:58 am
☽△☿ 1:35 am

♀♀♀ Ijumaa

♑

Friday 17

☉△☽ 2:19 pm
☽✶♅ 10:04 pm
☽✶♃ 10:13 pm v/c

For Mimi In Jail

Brave as you were, you will only get braver
Just as colors ring and deepen in the dusk
Keep out an ear for the wild voice inside you
As you sit up steeping in the city's musk

Narrow, the walls, the locked walls that surround you
While they're taking your time for breaking their rules
But wide is the sky, and it's all hidden inside you
Like a file in a pie, starry dome of your mind

And don't mind the doubt and keep to your counsel
Don't you worry about all that wasted time
'Cause day in day out with your hands tied behind you
You touch more than you see, you are working our way free

And narrow, the path, it is wished we would follow
Looking neither up nor down
Enlightened horizon or dim bloody hollow
Just swallow, just swallow
But wide is the sky, and it's all hidden inside you
Unexplored, unconfined, starry dome
of your mind

from the CD "Corvidae" © Myshkin 2002

Radar Birds *© Myshkin 2008*

♄♄♄ Jumamosi

♑ ♒

Saturday

18

☽→♒ 12:34 am
☽□♂ 5:23 am
☽△♄ 1:09 pm
☽□♀ 2:37 pm
♃☌♅ 6:03 pm
♂✶♇ 7:48 pm

☉☉☉ Jumapili

♒

Sunday

19

☉⚻♆ 6:43 am
☉⚻⚷ 9:04 pm

September

Chakrayapuy killa

☽☽☽ Killachaw

♒ ♓

Monday 20

☽☌♆ 6:09 am v/c
☽→♓ 1:15 pm
♅PrG 1:27 pm
♃PrG 2:30 pm
☽✶♇ 6:56 pm
☽△♂ 9:45 pm

I would make of myself
a temple
I mean
I would cease pretending
I am something else
¤ *Jane Mara 2006*

♂♂♂ Atichaw

♓

Tuesday 21

☽ApG 1:04 am
☉☍♃ 4:36 am
☽△♀ 6:23 am
☉☍♅ 9:58 am
☽☍☿ 11:42 am

☿☿☿ Quyllurchaw

♓

Wednesday 22

☉→♎ 8:09 pm
☽☌♃ 10:05 pm
☽☌♅ 10:52 pm v/c

Fall Equinox

Sun in ♎ Libra 8:09 pm PDT

♃♃♃ Illapachaw

♓ ♈

Thursday 23

☽→♈ 1:47 am
☉☍☽ 2:17 am
☽□♇ 7:25 am
☽☍♄ 3:31 pm

Full Moon in ♈ Aries 2:17 am PDT

♀♀♀ Ch'askachaw

♈

Friday 24

No Exact Aspects

All aspects in Pacific Daylight Time; add 3 hours for EDT; add 7 hours for GMT

Year at a Glance for ♎ Libra (Sept. 22–Oct.23)

Each person is born in answer to a problem or need that seeks solution; in these extraordinary times, Libra is the channel for collaborations that couldn't even be guessed at before now. Whether creating electrifying atmospheres where others are zapped by the amplified collective genius, or exploring the unique possibilities of unintentional community—you are doing what you are meant to be. It may be simply your turn to lie on the couch, in your stillness holding space so others can process or progress more effectively. It's more about being than doing; there is such power in random events this year.

Focus upon being honest—above all be true to yourself. Your energy levels will plummet if you are distracted by irrelevant commitments. If you feel ignored or unappreciated in your work, explore non-traditional schedules, a less conventional or demanding job. Daydreaming is an excellent yoga this year.

At times this year you may feel as though you are moving through mud. Trust that strong foundations for future success are forming at your core. Be gentle, small indulgences are nourishing. Libra does not thrive in isolation; nothing needs to be difficult in order to be valuable.

Extraordinary encounters accelerate awakening, especially June to early August, and there will be plenty more of this happening in the next few years. Invitations to progressive social engagements/activism ignite and excite you. Your relationships are becoming more spacious, and thrive with experimentation, through changing routines and roles.

Gretchen Lawlor © Mother Tongue Ink 2009

Maat D.O.M. Tarot © Ffiona Morgan 1991

♄♄♄ K'uychichaw

♈ ♉

Saturday

25

☽⚹♆ 6:12 am v/c
☽→♉ 1:17 pm
☉□♇ 5:26 pm
☽△♇ 6:48 pm

☉☉☉ Intichaw

♉

Sunday

26

☽☍♂ 4:27 am
☽☍♀ 10:25 am

Radio-Free Hekate

(written to be read aloud, as a prayer)

Stop a moment, she said, and listen.

Not with your ears. They will lead you astray.
Listen with your feet.
Nestle them naked
    down deep into the tangles of the roots and grass,
    burrow your toes under the warm soil, investigate,
    tune into the right station,
let the ground rise up into your arches, fill up your base
surround your heels with the movement.

Listen with your skin.

Pull the sound up through every muscle in your legs,
the earth is playing you like a harp, you are being strummed,
softly,   strongly,   an insistent tune,
a pinnacle point of pitch and vibration
at the space where all your strings come together

let this sound, this calling from the earth,
fill up the hollows of your sacrum,
course its winding way up your backbone,
chime up each rib like a xylophone,   catch
and keep the rhythm of your beating heart.

    Tha-Bump.   Tha-Bump.
Sound growing
and moving
and expanding
exploding into all its potential
as it blasts from your
fingers and mouth and eyes,
through your every cell

the incredible, undeniable,
untamable sound of living
that your ears, alone,
would never understand.

¤ *Victoria Day 2002*

The Serpent's Path
© Durga Bernhard 2003

Fall Equinox

Equinox, when the scales are again balanced in perfect equilibrium, honors equal day, equal night. The harvest is threshed, darkness lengthens, and Summer is gone. We feast, give thanks, and bless Goddess as Reaper, sharing food and goods with those who don't have enough. The fall air is brisk, leaves blow in the wind, yet I can still feel the waning sun, while the Moon glows orange. The leaves' flaming colors remind me that life burns most intensely just before it dies, and Autumn is the beginning of the season of death, when Kore descends into the underworld.

In Her Hand © *Qahira Lynn 1997*

For me it is a time of introspection and taking stock, similar to Jewish Rosh Hashanah, a day of self-examination. I review mistakes, request forgiveness from anyone I may have offended, and make future resolves. Turning leaves, turning inward: I look deep into my soul. My altar Broom sweeps out internal debris, acknowledging my faults and weaknesses, relinquishing grudges, forgiving others and asking myself: have I shared? Loved enough? Been unkind? Judged others? Adhered to my own standards? Grown as a human being? The personal really *is* political: we change the world when we change ourselves.

Ffiona Morgan © Mother Tongue Ink 2009

September/October

Kepakemapa/'Okakopa

☽☽☽ pō 'ahahi

♉ ♊

Monday

27

☽△☿ 2:39 am
☽□♆ 4:13 pm
☽⚹♃ 6:27 pm
☽⚹♅ 8:03 pm v/c
☽→♊ 11:10 pm

♂♂♂ pō 'alua

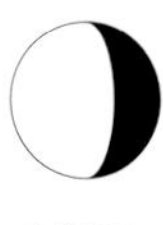

Tuesday

28

☉△☽ 9:27 am
☽△♄ 1:16 pm

☿☿☿ pō 'akolu

♊

Wednesday

29

☽□☿ 7:30 pm

♃♃♃ pō 'aha

♊ ♋

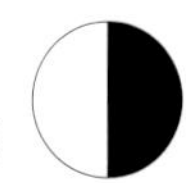

Thursday

30

☽△♆ 12:03 am
☽□♃ 1:43 am
☽□♅ 3:37 am v/c
☽→♋ 6:46 am
☽☍♇ 11:55 am
☉☌♄ 5:42 pm
♄ApG 8:00 pm
☽□♄ 8:40 pm
☉□☽ 8:52 pm

Waning Half Moon in ♋ Cancer 8:52 pm PDT

♀♀♀ pō 'alima

October

♋

Friday

1

☽△♂ 2:39 am
☽△♀ 4:50 am
☿⚻♆ 5:32 am
☿⚻⚷ 11:00 am
☿☍♃ 3:36 pm

Riddler © Nancy Watterson 2008

By now, I've memorized all of the Tarot.
The High Priestess sits quietly, watching us.
She's been writing secrets in her Book of Shadows.
She's lonely. It's lonely being mysterious.

excerpt © Lorraine Schein 2003

♄♄♄ pō 'aono

♋ ♌

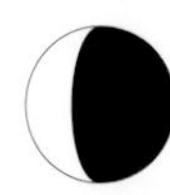

Saturday 2

☽△♃ 6:07 am
☿☍♅ 7:23 am
☽△♅ 8:14 am
☽✶☿ 8:21 am v/c
☽→♌ 11:21 am

☉☉☉ lā pule

♌

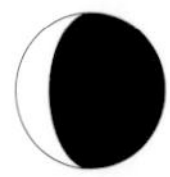

Sunday 3

☽✶♄ 12:53 am
☉✶☽ 4:26 am
☿→♎ 8:04 am
☽□♂ 8:40 am
☽□♀ 8:53 am
♀☌♂ 2:58 pm

Prayer to Changing Woman

Changing Woman—all creatures bow to you, to your eternal wisdom. Like us you change, too. Born infant in the east, you gracefully crawl to the south, become potent maiden. With your first blood, you dance to the west, become adult woman. Slowing down on your journey to the north, hair silvering and body resilient with old age, you become elder in the north. And then with turquoise cane, you walk bent and small, back towards east from whence you came, performing your eternal mystery of renewal and rebirth.

Goddess of many names—Changing Woman, White Shell Woman, Turquoise Woman, grant us your serenity about change, help us see into the dark glass of impermanence, to honor the things that come as well as go, to trust your eternal cycles of birth to death and to know there will be rebirth again. Help us find peace in all things that change, in our bodies that grow old. Grant us your vision to guide our lives through our passages, large and small. Help us trust in the guiding spirit that directs and births all things, from the tiniest seed to the wisdom in our cells. Help see us through the rising and setting of all our suns, the waxing and waning of our many moons. Spread your white shell of protection under our feet and help us walk with turquoise cane into our old age. Grant us the promise of your rebirth. We bow to you, oh Goddess of Change.

© Beth Beurkens 2008

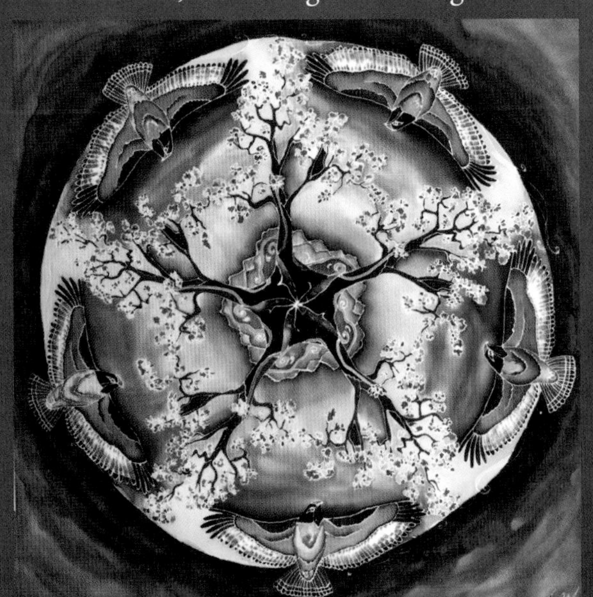

Redtail Mandala ¤ *Jennifer G. Metz 2008*

XI. LIFE CYCLES

Moon XI: October 7–November 5

New Moon in ♎ Libra Oct. 7; Full Moon in ♈ Aries Oct. 22; Sun in ♏ Scorpio Oct. 23

Saronaya Mironiska ¤ *Dorrie Joy 2008*
Knowth Chamber ¤ *Mimi Foyle 2008*
Mama Earth © *Anna Rose Renick 2002*
She Holds The Wheel Now ¤ *Rosemary Lloyd Freeman 2008*

October
octubre

☽☽☽ lunes

♌
♍

Monday
4

☽☍♆ 6:52 am v/c
☽→♍ 1:00 pm
☽△♇ 5:41 pm
☿□♇ 11:08 pm

The Beginning
© Jeannine Chappell 2003

♂♂♂ martes

♍

Tuesday
5

☽⚹♀ 10:01 am
☽⚹♂ 11:42 am

☿☿☿ miércoles

♍
♎

Wednesday
6

☽PrG 6:41 am
☽☍♃ 7:12 am
☽☍♅ 9:43 am v/c
☽→♎ 12:51 pm
☽□♇ 5:30 pm
☽☌☿ 11:08 pm

♃♃♃ jueves

♎

Thursday
7

☽☌♄ 2:24 am
☉☌☽ 11:44 am

♀♀♀ viernes

New Moon in ♎ Libra 11:44 am PDT

♎
♏

Friday
8

♀R 12:05 am
☿☌♄ 4:35 am
☽△♆ 6:37 am v/c
☽→♏ 12:52 pm
☽⚹♇ 5:40 pm

All aspects in Pacific Daylight Time; add 3 hours for EDT; add 7 hours for GMT

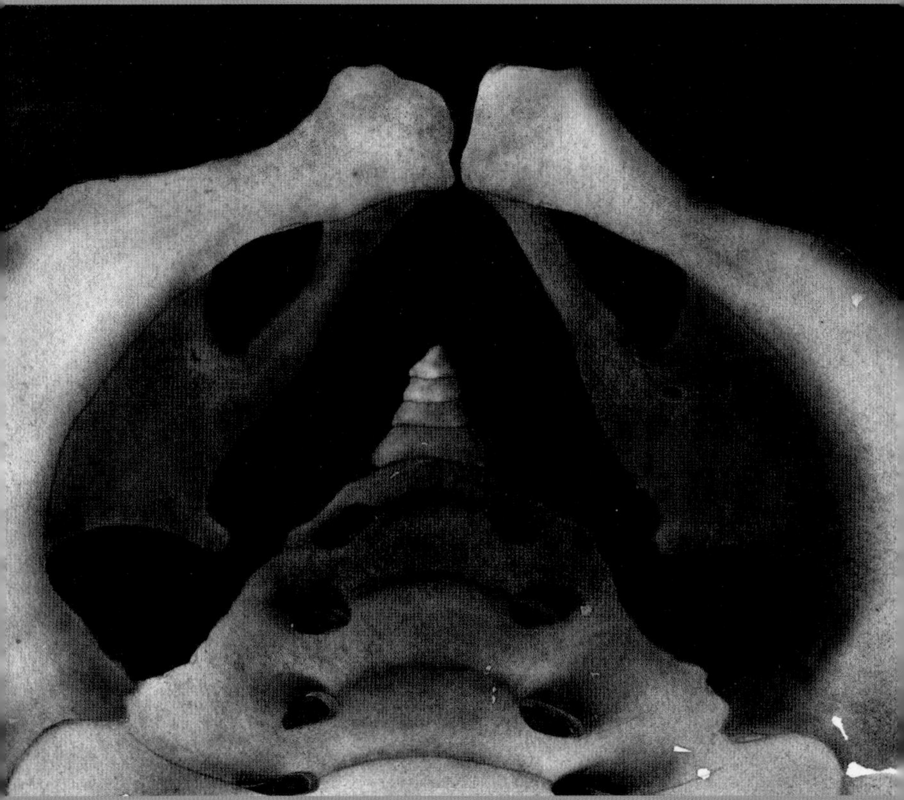

Through the Rabbit Hole

♄♄♄ sábado

♏

Saturday
9

☽☌♀ 10:35 am
☽☌♂ 5:06 pm

☉☉☉ domingo

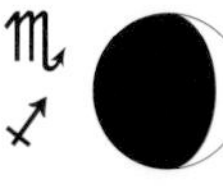

Sunday
10

☽△♃ 8:09 am
☽□♆ 8:27 am
☽△♅ 11:27 am v/c
☽→♐ 3:09 pm

October
Oktoba

☽☽☽ Jumatatu

Monday
11

☽✶♄ 7:01 am
☽✶☿ 5:31 pm

Ker

♂♂♂ Jumanne

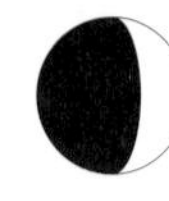

Tuesday
12

☉✶☽ 12:43 am
☽□♃ 1:15 pm
☽✶♆ 1:59 pm
☽□♅ 5:08 pm v/c
☽→♑ 9:17 pm

☿☿☿ Jumatano

♑

Wednesday
13

☽☌♇ 2:57 am
☽□♄ 2:58 pm
☽✶♀ 9:09 pm

♃♃♃ Alhamisi

♑

Thursday
14

☽□☿ 10:57 am
☽✶♂ 12:32 pm
☉□☽ 2:27 pm
☽✶♃ 10:21 pm

♀♀♀ Ijumaa

Waxing Half Moon in ♑ Capricorn 2:27 pm PDT

♑ ♒
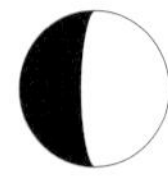

Friday
15

☽✶♅ 2:49 am v/c
☽→♒ 7:24 am

Unassisted Childbirth

The decision to birth my babies at home was quite a lot for my family to handle. But when we made the decision to birth unassisted, people were down right frightened. Birth in their eyes is an illness. Something for a doctor to "fix." Not something to "toy" with by one's self. But nothing the family said could make me wish for anything but birthing unassisted.

Our first child was born just after midnight in a small desert apartment in the middle of the summer. The coyotes sang her into the warm birthing pool after 24 hours of peaceful labor, just her father and I.

Our second child was welcomed by bats into the Midwestern summer night. He too slid from his warm womb home into a pool of body temperature water. His three year-old sister watching and supporting his entrance into our world.

Each of my pregnancies have been Spirit-led. My children have told me where and when they wish to be born. No doctors have compared this pregnancy to that, or this child to that. They are both strong and healthy beings who have been blessed with not only a healthy home birth, but unassisted births. As they were conceived, so they were born. Surrounded in the privacy and deep love and connection their parents have created.

© Heidi Eich-Dittberner 2007

♄♄♄ Jumamosi

♒

Saturday

16

☽△♄ 2:40 am
☽□♀ 7:09 am
☉☌☿ 6:04 pm

☉☉☉ Jumapili

♒
♓

Sunday

17

☽□♂ 4:17 am
☉△☽ 7:58 am
☽△☿ 8:56 am
☽☌♆ 11:49 am v/c
☿⚻♃ 4:42 pm
☽→♓ 7:52 pm

October
Tarpuy killa

☽☽☽ Killachaw

♓

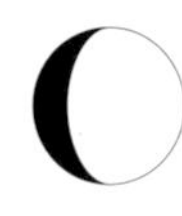

Monday
18

☽⚹♇ 2:08 am
☿△♆ 5:03 am
☉⚻♃ 7:12 am
☿△⚷ 8:07 am
☽ApG 11:21 am
☽△♀ 6:02 pm

Snake Dancer ¤ *Lorrie Joy 2008*

♂♂♂ Atichaw

♓

Tuesday
19

☿⚻♅ 3:00 am
☉△♆ 5:18 am
☉△⚷ 10:16 am
☽△♂ 8:48 pm
☽☌♃ 10:15 pm

☿☿☿ Quyllurchaw

♓
♈

Wednesday
20

☽☌♅ 3:25 am v/c
☽→♈ 8:23 am
☿→♏ 2:19 pm
☽□♇ 2:39 pm
☉⚻♅ 5:17 pm
♂△♃ 6:42 pm

♃♃♃ Illapachaw

♈

Thursday
21

☽☍♄ 4:46 am

♀♀♀ Ch'askachaw

♈
♉

Friday
22

♂□♆ 8:35 am
☽⚹♆ 11:41 am
☿⚹♇ 12:38 pm
♂□⚷ 2:50 pm
☉☍☽ 6:36 pm v/c
☽→♉ 7:29 pm

Full Moon in ♈ Aries 6:36 pm PDT

All aspects in Pacific Daylight Time; add 3 hours for EDT; add 7 hours for GMT

Year at a Glance for ♏ Scorpio (Oct. 23–Nov. 22)

Indignation with flair is a great political strategy and may be your best evolutionary contribution to these changing times. ("If I can't dance—I don't want to be part of your revolution." Emma Goldman.) Deep play is your specialty; your bold strokes inspire art, children, us all, to be more outrageous.

Revision of your long-range plans during the last two years benefits from one last shakeup/wakeup in the first half of 2010. Don't assume you have it all figured out; an unexpected conversation may provide a critical piece to the puzzle. By August, your course should be set.

Near year's end you may be offered a position of power, or you may be called to make an irrevocable decision. Make sure you understand the deeper implications. If possible, try out the position or situation and decide from your visceral response.

Scorpio is a natural detective/psychologist, further training in progressive healing techniques may increase your effectiveness and well-being this year or next.

You demand devotion and offer the same to your close companions. Bid farewell to those whose direction in life runs contrary to yours. There is more shedding to come, you'll be saying "no thanks" more often than "yes please" in 2010.

Love must never be bland for Scorpio, and this year presents intriguing twists and turns. Shed some personal inhibition/reserve to attract someone new or reawaken delicious child-play between long-term companions. Scorpio thrives on intensity, is known to throw tantrums just to liven things up.

Gretchen Lawlor © Mother Tongue Ink 2009

♄♄♄ K'uychichaw

♉

Saturday

23

☽△♇ 1:40 am
☽☍☿ 3:36 am
☉→♏ 5:35 am
☽☍♀ 12:07 pm
☿ApG 6:29 pm

Sun in ♏ Scorpio 5:35 am PDT

☉☉☉ Intichaw

♉

Sunday

24

♂△♅ 7:56 am
☽⚹♃ 6:27 pm
☽□♆ 9:11 pm
☽⚹♅ 11:50 pm

October
Okakopa

Respect Death
the Great Relaxer
Nothing is
denied Her succor.
excerpt ¤ Jane Mara 2008

☽☽☽ pō 'akahi

♉ ♊

Monday 25

☽☍♂ 12:49 am v/c
☽→♊ 4:47 am
☿☌♀ 6:17 am

♂♂♂ pō 'alua

♊

Tuesday 26

☽△♄ 1:00 am
☉⚹♇ 12:01 pm

☿☿☿ pō 'akolu

♊ ♋

Wednesday 27

☽□♃ 1:56 am
☽△♆ 4:52 am
☽□♅ 7:19 am v/c
☽→♋ 12:14 pm
☽☍♇ 6:11 pm
☉△☽ 8:35 pm
☽△♀ 11:05 pm
♂→♐ 11:47 pm

♃♃♃ pō 'aha

♋

Thursday 28

☽□♄ 8:14 am
☽△☿ 11:08 am
☉☌♀ 6:10 pm

♀♀♀ pō 'alima

♋ ♌

Friday 29

☽△♃ 7:27 am
☽△♅ 12:48 pm v/c
♀PrG 2:22 pm
☽→♌ 5:38 pm
☽△♂ 7:56 pm

Samhain/Hallowmas

She parts the thin, fragile veils that stretch into eternity, between life and death, on this Cross-Quarter when the intense Scorpio Power Gate opens, releasing the potent Water element that signals the dying of the solar year.

She sees the arching bridge to the spirit world where three intense Hags guard the intersection of all crossroads: Hathor, Hecate, and Baba Yaga, keepers of the scrolls of the dead and of the key to other worlds. She hears their low, whistling, voices in the wind, "Everything that dies is reborn." With an awesome power they shift—Maiden to Mother, to Crone, and back again.

Hecate reaches for her hand—in times past she would have been terrified. Now she touches and embraces Her wisdom, protection and acceptance.

"The year is dying," she asks, "am I?" The Hags say it is not her time. She is led to the Altar of the Dead to light candles for her ancestors. She glances beyond the Old Ones and sees her beloved dead gathered on the bridge. They offer gifts: acceptance of her Crone-self, and the slow death of her physical body. She embraces death as a delicious reunion. She weeps with gratitude.

Ffiona Morgan © Mother Tongue Ink 2009

Do you ever feel spirits of the dead
as they come brushing past on their way to the light?

excerpt from "Gypsy" © Lilly Coyote 2003

West Kennet Long Barrow *© Monica Sjöö 1989*

Earth-Laden Idol

My mother shuffles now with broken arches and bony bunions that rub raw the edges of her fuzzy, black woolen slippers—slippers so tattered that they barely contain her nylon-enshrouded feet. Dementia dotes on her brain and cancer ravages the one sagging breast and beyond.

Does she see the memories of sophisticated style, sassy spirit and radiant posture reflected in my glistening eyes? Does she realize how high she rises above her stooped form in my heart, towering above me in poise and gentle dignity? Does she even notice that she is as graceful and sensuous as the drooping willow that softly shades our narrow, woodland stream out back?

Earth-laden idol, do you have a sense of those things long past?

I remind her of lovely memories, memories that won't outlast the sweep of the minute hand swiftly circling the dusty face of the grandfather clock in the hall. I allow her to cradle against the recesses of my perspiring body—the rounded hump hugging my bulging belly—as we snuggle on my parent's worn-out, double bed. Frightened and with feeble effort, she tries to tighten my already firm grip around her.

As we look out over the meadow, her gaze sets on the swallow standing guard over her young brood at the top of the rough-hewn feeder, just beyond the fence line. She whistles their song. My mouth turns upward into a soft smile piercing her fragrant hair, and tears begin to quietly escape unnoticed.

As I hold her, we are one again. We've journeyed full circle—she and I—so how can I let her go? But the appointed time will arrive when I must release her from my maternal embrace, as she did for me almost fifty years ago, to experience the full freedom of life once again.

excerpt © MC Torinus 2008

Shades of Autumn ¤ *Michelle Wilkinson 2007*

Psyche's Harvest

If the peaches have gone bad,
the apples long since fallen,
the blackberries
already turned to vinegar
I say, leave presentation
to the young.
We are done with blooming.
Let's go out
in an autumn blaze.
Rotten to the core will be
our rallying cry.
It takes courage to decay,
a keen nose to find
gold beneath the bruise,
and calm to wither
while the worms
churn us
to sweetest earth.

© Joanne Rocky Delaplaine 2004

Jungle Path
© Mimi Foyle 2007

♄♄♄ pō 'aono

♌

Saturday
30

☽□♀ 1:49 am
☉□☽ 5:46 am
☽✶♄ 1:15 pm
☽□☿ 10:12 pm

Waning Half Moon in ♌ Leo 5:46 am PDT

☉☉☉ lā pule

♌ ♍

Sunday
31

Samhain/Hallowmas

☽☍♆ 2:01 pm v/c
☽→♍ 8:51 pm

Crediti and the Local Economy

I live in a cooperative, ecological community of spirit in Italy, and we have coined our own currency called the *crediti*. This complimentary currency comes in many denominations, from heavy 20 *crediti* coins, silver and ringed with brass, to tiny 20 *cali* pieces, which parallel cents or *centesimi*. The coins of the *crediti* are imprinted with spirals and sacred language, leaves and flowers, crabs and conch shells, sacred dancers in motion, flags of Damanhur, chalices, fire altars, pyramids and butterflies.

I receive *crediti* for my productive efforts and I give them back through my contribution to the community. This contribution includes the collective ownership of property, the *nucleo* or cooperative houses we share, the expenses of food and water, improvements and utilities. We each contribute *crediti* to a safety net for citizens in need. We contribute collectively to the expenses of raising children and offering their education, and we also share in their care and nurturing. We contribute our resources and energy to the projects of the *nucleo*, which range from organic agriculture to care for the elderly. We organize our human resources to construct homes and infrastructure, plant gardens and greenhouses, prepare food, organize and clean, to make our homes viable, beautiful, and lively.

Our economic system is a model of local sustainability. As worldwide banking situations fluctuate, we use *crediti* to continue compensating our teachers and purchasing organic peaches. As stock markets ebb and dive, we remain steady in our everyday exchanges. By cutting through credit cards and coining complimentary currency, instead of discarding money along pathways of excessive profit and sending it overseas, we buy and trade, live and thrive within the intimate exchange of a local economy.

¤ *juliett jade chi 2008*

Bottle Wall © *Annie Ocean 2007*

XII. RESTORE BALANCE

Moon XII: November 5–December 5

New Moon in ♏ Scorpio Nov.5; Full Moon in ♉ Taurus Nov. 21; Sun in ♐ Sagittarius Nov. 22

MudGirls Natural Building Collective

Sam Barlow ¤ MudGirls Collective 2008

November
noviembre

☽☽☽ lunes

♍ 

Monday
1

☽□♂ 1:45 am
☽△♇ 2:30 am
☽⚹♀ 2:40 am
♀⚹♇ 6:37 am
☉⚹☽ 12:16 pm

♂♂♂ martes

♍ ♎  

Tuesday
2

☽⚹☿ 6:18 am
☽☍♃ 12:23 am
☽☍♅ 5:36 pm v/c
☽→♎ 10:19 pm

☿☿☿ miércoles

♎  

Wednesday
3

☽□♇ 3:54 am
☽⚹♂ 5:38 am
☽PrG 10:31 am
☽☌♄ 5:34 pm

♃♃♃ jueves

♎ ♏ 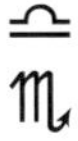 

Thursday
4

☿△♃ 2:46 pm
☽△♆ 4:34 pm v/c
☽→♏ 11:15 pm

♀♀♀ viernes

Lunar Samhain

♏ 

Friday
5

☽☌♀ 1:24 am
☽⚹♇ 4:59 am
⚷D 9:20 am
☉☌☽ 9:52 pm
☿□♆ 11:44 pm

New Moon in ♏ Scorpio 9:52 pm PST

Precious Threads

EcoFashion Show

Lights flash in shadow, music growls
models prowl the catwalk
and the crowd howls
for family and friends,
all sizes, shapes, and ages—
Here's Mary vamping up
  in crimson retro satin,
and Claudine, 65, a fairy
  in a frock with glowing wings.
Sian is strutting out
  in 70's orange velvet trousers
  with a sharp 90's jacket
  newly collared cherry red.
Teenage sister dances like a dervish
  in blue jeans, tutu,
  crafted sequin-slogan T-shirt
  and Granny's highheel,
  anklestrap, sparkly green shoes.

Into the Mystery

Drama-divas, punky warriors, pixies trailing worn lace and petals, celebrating beauty that's joyous, creative, wild—And no big corporations, no landgrab, no sweatshops, no toxins in the water—this is pre-loved, ethical, organic, re-made, old gold braid, all for sale, spinning out of clever shops up Catherine Hill.

This town is making choices, taking precious threads from the past to weave a future dressed in glory: cut-down, turned round, jazzed up, hand-made embroidery, fake-furs and serious fair trade.

♄♄♄ sábado

Saturday

6

☿□⚷ 2:10 am
☽△♃ 2:47 pm
☿△♅ 5:14 pm
☽□♆ 6:29 pm
☽△♅ 8:21 pm

☽☌☿ 8:44 pm v/c
♆D 11:04 pm

☉☉☉ domingo

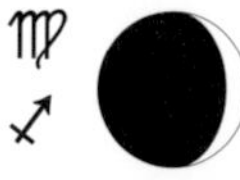

Sunday

7

☽→♐ 12:27 am
☽☌♂ 1:42 pm
♀→♎ 7:05 pm
☽✶♄ 9:48 pm

Daylight Savings Time ends 2:00 am PDT

November

Novemba

☽☽☽ Jumatatu

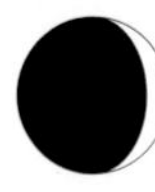

Monday

8

☿→♐ 3:43 pm
☽□♃ 6:03 pm
☽✶♆ 10:09 pm

♂♂♂ Jumanne

♐ ♑

Tuesday

9

☽□♅ 12:04 am
☽✶♀ 4:35 am v/c
☽→♑ 5:37 am
☽☌♇ 12:14 pm

☿☿☿ Jumatano

♑

Wednesday

10

☽□♄ 4:57 am
☉✶☽ 4:16 pm

♃♃♃ Alhamisi

♑ ♒

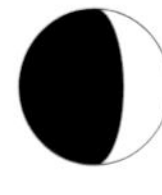

Thursday

11

☽✶♃ 2:03 am
☽✶♅ 8:31 am
☽□♀ 11:57 am v/c
☽→♒ 2:32 pm

♀♀♀ Ijumaa

♒

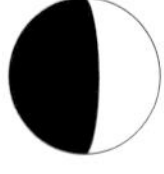

Friday

12

☽✶☿ 12:21 am
☽✶♂ 12:49 pm
☽△♄ 3:50 pm

All aspects in Pacific Standard Time; add 3 hours for EST; add 8 hours for GMT

Estrella at Home ¤ *Dolphin 2008*

Searching for My Source

The woman I am searching for
has long left the steel tap of convention
to drink from the mouth of the spring.

excerpt © Elizabeth Kampouris 1997

♄♄♄ Jumamosi

♒

Saturday

13

☉□☽ 8:39 am
☽☌♆ 6:10 pm
☽△♀ 10:33 pm v/c

Waxing Half Moon in ♒ Aquarius 8:39 am PST

☉☉☉ Jumapili

♒
♓

Sunday

14

☽→♓ 2:24 am
☽⚹♇ 9:57 am
☽□☿ 9:00 pm
♂⚹♄ 9:58 pm

November
Pawqarwara Killa

☽☽☽ Killachaw

Fountain of the Goddess *© Josslyn Meyeres 2007*

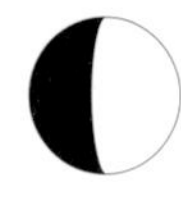

Monday
15

☽ApG 3:45 am
☽□♂ 5:15 am
☉△♃ 3:44 pm

♂♂♂ Atichaw

♓ ♈

Tuesday
16

☽☌♃ 1:55 am
☉△☽ 2:52 am
☽☌♅ 8:37 am v/c
☽→♈ 2:59 pm
☽□♇ 10:35 pm

☿☿☿ Quyllurchaw

♈

Wednesday
17

☽△☿ 5:25 pm
☽☍♄ 5:30 pm
☿✶♄ 6:09 pm
☽△♂ 9:15 pm

♃♃♃ Illapachaw

♈

Thursday
18

☉□♆ 1:54 am
☉□⚷ 6:46 am
♃D 8:53 am
♀D 1:18 pm
☽✶♆ 6:14 pm
☽☍♀ 9:33 pm v/c
☉△♅ 9:57 pm

♀♀♀ Ch'askachaw

♈ ♉

Friday
19

☽→♉ 2:04 am
☽△♇ 9:32 am

Biomimicry

"How would Nature do it?" is the question Biomimicry asks in seeking to design viable solutions for survival of life on Earth. Nature is the Mother of invention, whose handiwork includes all of creation and provides everything needed to sustain life. After 3.8 billion years of evolution, what works is alive to reveal Her secrets.

What can a leaf teach us about capturing the energy of the sun to create a molecular-sized solar cell? Discovering how gecko's feet stick to the wall without goop helps develop a glue-free adhesive to facilitate recycling paper products. The tensile strength of spider's thread is greater than steel, and may provide a template for manufacturing strong fibers without the use of heat or toxins. The red algae sea purse protects itself by jamming bacterial communication signals with a non-toxic compound that humans can apply for healing. Nature provides a veritable witch's brew of snake venom, butterfly wings, spiral seashells, whale song, bat sonar—to conjure creative problem-solving for restoring sustainability.

The human niche in current eco-systems needs to shift from a colonizing survival strategy (quickly exploiting all the resources in an environment and moving on) toward a sustainable mature eco-systems approach. Organisms capable of living together in one place over time recycle wastes, diversify and cooperate, using the habitat without bankrupting it.

Based on the premise that Nature knows best and that what is good for Mother Earth is good for us all, Biomimicry is reinventing technology to re-balance the wheel of life.

© *Musawa 2009 (adapted from* Biomimicry: Innovation Inspired by Nature, *by Janine Benyus, www.biomimicryinstitute.org)*

♄♄♄ K'uychichaw

♉ Saturday 20

☿☌♂ 10:53 am
☽⚹♃ 10:42 pm

☉☉☉ Intichaw

♉ ♊ Sunday 21

☽□♆ 3:17 am
☽⚹♅ 4:45 am
☉☍☽ 9:27 am v/c
☽→♊ 10:46 am

Full Moon in ♉ Taurus 9:27 am PST

November

Nowemapa

☽☽☽ pō ʻakahi

♊ 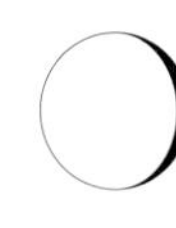

Monday

22

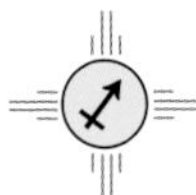

☉→♐ 2:14 am
☽△♄ 12:04 pm
☽☍♂ 9:22 pm

Sun in ♐ Sagittarius 2:14 am PST

♂♂♂ pō ʻalua

♊ ♋

Tuesday

23

☽☍☿ 12:25 am
☽□♃ 5:39 am
☽△♆ 10:04 am
☽□♅ 11:24 am
☽△♀ 1:56 pm v/c
☽→♋ 5:14 pm

☿☿☿ pō ʻakolu

♋

Wednesday

24

☽☍♇ 12:24 am
☽□♄ 6:05 pm

♃♃♃ pō ʻaha

♋ ♌

Thursday

25

☿□♃ 6:18 am
☽△♃ 10:50 am
☽△♅ 4:18 pm
☽□♀ 7:44 pm v/c
☽→♌ 10:01 pm

♀♀♀ pō ʻalima

♌

Friday

26

☉△☽ 5:15 am
☽✶♄ 10:36 pm

Year at a Glance for ♐ Sagittarius (Nov. 22–Dec. 21)

A sudden decision to move adds to the chaos of the times; wisest choices come from considering long-term implications. If possible, temper your natural impulsiveness enough to be suspect of the advice of long-standing friends. Don't jump for an old dream you think is finally coming true, it may be a very stale old dream. You may choose to perch rather than to build, while you sort out just where you want to be going and with whom.

Sagittarius, fond of bold strokes and great leaps of faith, may instead decide to knock out a wall or start a community garden. New playmates appear, children bring joy, fertility increases this year and next. Pick up an instrument, write poetry or science fiction. Old loves and new loves mingle, making mayhem of plans, while launching unexpected adventures.

Current economic crisis demands a deeper resourcefulness. Resurrect skills, reinvest old assets, become a specialist in a particular niche. Recycling, selling off possessions free you of the tyranny of stuff. Poetry slams or community singalongs are perfect venues for your ability to inspire and uplift, though even morning yoga sessions in some living room bring out the teacher or wise mentor in you.

Loyalty and longing play tug-of-war, requiring you to review your dreams and aspirations. This may leave you rudderless for a while. Simple acts of appreciation, and gratitude for the good things in your life, help you define what's truly important, and find new ways to live according to those values.

Gretchen Lawlor © Mother Tongue Ink 2009

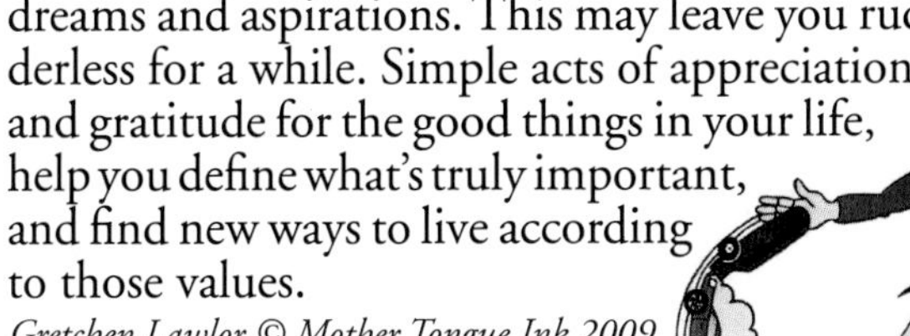

Bicycle Solutionary © *Emily Butterfly 2008*

♄♄♄ pō 'aono

♌

Saturday 27

☿✶♆ 5:13 am
☿✶⚷ 10:53 am
☽△♂ 12:34 pm
☿□♅ 6:27 pm
☽☍♆ 6:49 pm
☽△☿ 8:05 pm

☉☉☉ lā pule

♌
♍

Sunday 28

☽✶♀ 12:30 am v/c
☽→♍ 1:34 am
☽△♇ 8:38 am
☉□☽ 12:36 pm

Waning Half Moon in ♍ Virgo 12:36 pm PST

November/December

noviembre/diciembre

☽☽☽ lunes

♍ 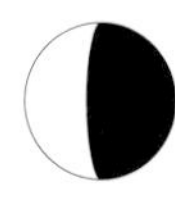

Monday

29

♂□♃ 6:51 am
♀→♏ 4:33 pm
☽☍♃ 5:41 pm
☽□♂ 6:15 pm
☽☍♅ 10:41 pm

♂♂♂ martes

 ♎ 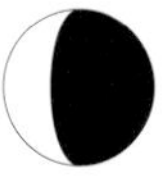

Tuesday

30

☽□☿ 3:17 am v/c
☽→♎ 4:15 am
☽PrG 10:54 am
☽□♇ 11:22 am
☿→♑ 4:10 pm
☉✶☽ 7:03 pm

☿☿☿ miércoles

December

Wednesday

1

☽☌♄ 4:48 am
☿✶♀ 8:35 am
☽✶♂ 11:30 pm

♃♃♃ jueves

Thursday

2

☽△♆ 12:08 am v/c
☽→♏ 6:43 am
☽☌♀ 8:43 am
☽✶☿ 9:40 am
♂✶♆ 11:39 am
☽✶♇ 2:00 pm
♂✶⚷ 11:06 pm

♀♀♀ viernes

♏ 

Friday

3

♂□♅ 6:00 am
☽△♃ 11:27 pm

Make Light of It

Put your shoulder to the wheel
your ped to the pedal, your tread to the treadle.

Gaviotas! Revolutionary eco-village in Ecuador:
kids on the see-saws pump water from the aquifer.

Club Watt! The first Sustainable Dance Club: people moving
on the dance floor generate electricity for lights.

Coming soon: Nanofiber clothes produce current as you move.
Strap-on-the-leg generator charges your phone as you walk.

Put your shoulder to the wheel
your ped to the pedal, your tread to the treadle.

What else can we imagine?

If it moves, hook it up. If it spins, attach wires.

What else can we remember?

My friend Julienne has a 1905 photo
of her great-great-great grandmother showing off
her patented invention: a fan run by her treadle sewing machine.

What else can we power?

Gyrate! Stomp! Jump! Swing! Dance the Revolution!
Work your play! Go wild! Make whir! Make juice!

New Moon in ♐ Sagittarius 9:36 am PST

Nā kūpuna a me nā ʻānela
Ancestors and guardian angels
are always whispering
manaʻo kahiko / ancient wisdom
through my *puʻuwai* / heart into my *noʻonoʻo* /thoughts
During those *mālie* / still moments of quiet
when I can hear them
They are always there
Nānā ʻana / watching over me
protecting and keeping my *ʻuhane* / spirit safe
waiting for me to *hōʻala* / wake up
to ask for *kōkua* / guidance
They have always been around
since before time and beyond
Sometimes
I block them out
I won't listen
I struggle on my own
They always wait patiently for me
to ask for their *mālama* / support
They don't persist when I won't *hoʻolohe* / listen
They wait until I am ready to hear
Then they keep me up
till all hours with their inspirations
Even in my dreamtime
They are always there
In those moments when I listen to them
They come to me in the *makani* / wind and the *ua* / rain
in the sunrises and sunsets
They come to me through the *aloha* / love in my heart
They help me *ʻike* / see what is real and tangible
They are always there
I *ʻike* / know no matter what happens to me
I am not alone on this journey
They are holding my hands all the way home

¤ *Melina Keawe 2007*

XIII. COMING FULL CIRCLE

Moon XIII: December 5–January 4

New Moon in ♐ Sagittarius Dec. 5; Full Moon in ♊ Gemini Dec. 21; Sun in ♑ Capricorn Dec. 21

Pele

December

Desemba

☽☽☽ Jumatatu

Wise Ravens *© Lori Cohen 2006*

Monday

6

☽□♃ 4:27 am
☽⚹♆ 8:17 am
☽□♅ 9:13 am
☽☌♂ 1:46 pm v/c
☽→♑ 3:16 pm
☽⚹♀ 9:53 pm
☽☌♇ 11:24 pm

♂♂♂ Jumanne

Tuesday

7

☉⚹♄ 12:00 am
☽☌☿ 12:41 am
♂→♑ 3:49 pm
☽□♄ 7:17 pm

☿☿☿ Jumatano

Wednesday

8

♀⚹♇ 8:19 am
☽⚹♃ 12:21 pm
☽⚹♅ 5:07 pm v/c
☽→♒ 11:30 pm

♃♃♃ Alhamisi

Thursday

9

☽□♀ 9:31 am

♀♀♀ Ijumaa

Friday

10

☿R 4:04 am
☽△♄ 5:29 am
☉⚹☽ 12:02 pm
☿⚹♀ 1:04 pm

Evocation

goat's rue calendula bergamot chaste
Wisdom.
Words emanate from the earth
Echoes of lives, long dead
to me, not yet born.
Strong are the women
who walk with me through these woods
unseen and unremembered but still known.
Their knowledge,
once used to ease, to uplift, to bind
the pains and the dreams of
the women around them,
now only remembered by history
in the pointing accusations
Witchcraft.
Their extinguished lives folded into themselves,
into the flames,
leaving only their remains,
dense nuggets, dust to dust,
to forever influence the cycles of the earth.
Healing.
cypress raspberry leaf chamomile sage
The soil is the medium to understanding. Listen to the words.
Strive to secure power from the Earth. Struggle to bear life to insight.

¤ *Victoria Day 1992*

Sunset at Ancient Spirals © *Josslyn Meyeres1997*

♄♄♄ Jumamosi

♒ ♓

Saturday

11

☽☌♆ 3:09 am v/c
☽→♓ 10:40 am
☽⚹♂ 4:50 pm
☽⚹♇ 7:58 pm
☽⚹☿ 10:04 pm

☉☉☉ Jumapili

♓

Sunday

12

☽△♀ 12:39 am

December

Ayamarq'ay Killa

☽☽☽ Killachaw

♓ ♈

Monday 13

☽ApG 12:31 am
☉□☽ 5:59 am
☽☌♃ 12:16 pm
☽☌♅ 4:35 pm v/c
☿☌♇ 8:03 pm
☿☌♂ 8:09 pm
♂☌♇ 8:15 pm
☽→♈ 11:14 pm

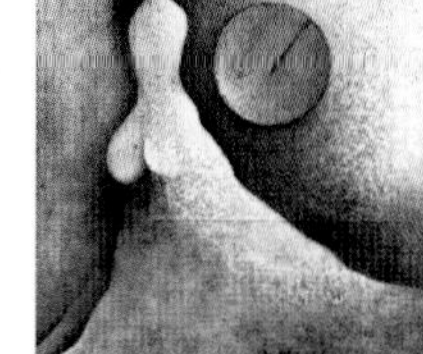

Holy Bath
© Stephanie Clifton 2002

Waxing Half Moon in ♓ Pisces 5:59 am PST

♂♂♂ Atichaw

♈

Tuesday 14

☽□☿ 7:57 am
☽□♇ 8:43 am
☽□♂ 9:32 am

☿☿☿ Quyllurchaw

♈

Wednesday 15

☽☍♄ 6:44 am
☉△☽ 11:32 pm

♃♃♃ Illapachaw

♈ ♉

Thursday 16

☽⚹♆ 3:41 am v/c
☽→♉ 10:49 am
☉□♃ 1:47 pm
☽△☿ 2:52 pm
☽△♇ 8:06 pm

♀♀♀ Ch'askachaw

♉

Friday 17

☽△♂ 12:34 am
☽☍♀ 7:49 am

at the Muse-eum remember to dance

Take the arms from clocks and invent games of chance
Use the face as a sundial—or better yet, just look up
And instead use that clock wheel
for the museum of the future that
demonstrates our past cults, along with the cell phone
and the keyboard, the aluminum foil, a plastic toothbrush,
orthodontia, a car lighter, a can of coke.
Surgery scalpels, airplane parts, a hoe.

Create an oratory for the muses who will visit the museum
about mining and smelting and how we've surpassed them.
They know our history is the crucible
On which our post-metal, post-mining liberation is forged.

Now we lean into history
like the edge of a bluff
against which
goating down red rubble
is a dance.

A game of chance decorated by
arrows that no longer tell time
but point to places on a map
we feel with our hands and heels.

Prefer space to time, place to line
And as at the center of the museum
Remember to dance.

¤ *Marna 2008*

Cappadoccian Wagon, Turkey
© *Myshkin 2007*

♄♄♄ K'uychichaw

♉ ♊ ☾

Saturday

18

☉⚹♆ 2:29 am
☿→♐ 6:53 am
☽⚹♃ 10:24 am
☉□♅ 10:48 am
☽□♆ 12:58 pm
☽⚹♅ 1:36 pm v/c
☉⚹⚷ 5:10 pm
☽→♊ 7:37 pm

☉☉☉ Intichaw

♊ ☾

Sunday

19

☉☌☿ 5:23 pm
☿PrG 11:04 pm

The New Archaic

¤ *Mimi Foyle 2004*

In the beating of my heart I hear
the beating of your drums.
In the whirring of my brain I hear
The shaking of your rattles and
the jingle of your dusty steps.
I myself take up the rhythm;
I myself take up the dance.

In the beating of the drum,
I lay down my hours,
lay down my time,
lay down these thick
and heavy ways.
I lay down this kind of time
and take up the ancient ways,
recalling the not-forgotten
I lay my self down in long-ago trance.

In the beating of the drum, I hear
your feet come near to me, hear your
hearts in my own body, your thoughts
in my own mind, strong and clear as
shining stars, deep and long as rivers run.

Nearer now celestial wheels, your spirits
awake my ears; beaming faces full of hope,
you know and claim me as your own.
My own beloveds, yes, and look behind you!
Back and back spirals are turning,
eternally beating, beaming, whirring.

On the double helix road, walking
the heartbeat way, out of time and space
and into re-membering of bonds never broken.
Face to face, you reach in deep and pull a
still-life snake from inside the guts of me
Wake this sleeping snake, you say,
And begin the new archaic.

Winter Solstice

It's dark—roomful of wemoon—the steady drumbeat sends me into trance. I am warm and safe, knowing I am loved by those with whom I commune in the dark. The woodstove's pine and oak fill the air with sweet incense. The drumbeat will not cease until morning.

I let go, and journey into the dream-time, to the underworld, traveling through a cave-tunnel, with only a small candle for light, but I am not afraid. Soft bells ring and a crystal bowl sings. While Mother Sun returns and Earth renews, I tread this sacred path, realizing I am now rebirthing myself and re-lighting my inner flame.

The tunnel opens into a cave, where circles of Bears, the Wise Ones, raise their arms, forming a birth canal. I joyfully enter.

Drums draw me back, they speak of the pulsing web-thread that is being connected to the hub of the wheel. In the stillness of winter, when daybreak arrives, we will light the blessed Solstice fire, then travel to the sea. It will be good to know that I can start over.

Ffiona Morgan © Mother Tongue Ink 2009

Echoes of Our Ancestors *© Mara Berendt Friedman 2000*

December
Kēkēmapa

☽☽☽ pō 'akahi

♊

Monday
20

☽△♄ 12:42 am
☿⚹⚷ 9:58 am
☿□♅ 3:30 pm
☽□♃ 5:01 pm
☽△♆ 7:09 pm
☽☍☿ 7:19 pm
☽□♅ 7:42 pm
☿⚹♆ 9:02 pm

Hawthorn Shield
© Sheila Broun 1988

♂♂♂ pō 'alua

♊
♋

Tuesday
21

☉☍☽ 12:13 am v/c
☽→♋ 1:22 am
☽☍♇ 10:00 am
☉→♑ 3:38 pm
☿□♃ 4:59 pm
☽☍♂ 8:06 pm

Winter Solstice

Full Moon in ♊ Gemini 12:13 am PST
Total Lunar Eclipse 12:13 am PST*
Sun in ♑ Capricorn 3:38 pm PST

☿☿☿ pō 'akolu

♋

Wednesday
22

☽△♀ 3:05 am
☽□♄ 5:19 am
☽△♃ 9:11 pm
☽△♅ 11:25 pm v/c

♃♃♃ pō 'aha

♋
♌

Thursday
23

☽→♌ 4:50 am

♀♀♀ pō 'alima

♌

Friday
24

☽⚹♄ 8:16 am
☽□♀ 9:10 am
☽△☿ 5:45 pm

*Eclipse visible E. Asia, Australasia, Pacific, Americas, Europe

Year at a Glance for ♑ Capricorn (Dec. 21–Jan. 20)

In this roller coaster ride of being human in a metamorphosizing world, Capricorns are experiencing personally what we are all witnessing in our political, spiritual and economic leaders and systems. Crises reveal rot, misappropriation, dark underbellies—demanding major clearing and reconstruction. You have the opportunity, wherever you hold influence, to be a model of wise change and compassionate administration. Show us self-mastery and devotion to healthy systems rather than oppressive control and manipulation; the world is watching.

Our whole archetype of authority is in crisis. Everyone is being challenged to reconsider where we give away personal authority. Making choices that restore some sense of personal autonomy is wise.

Rumblings of change deep within you wrestle with obligations out in the world. Profound restructuring requires that you disappear periodically. Take personal retreat time. Restless, submerged or misplaced parts of yourself are waking up, clamoring to be more present in your life. Experiment. Perhaps it's time to climb out from under an oppressive mortgage or let go of a home that no longer fits you; you may acquire housemates.

2011 is optimal for a move; go exploring in 2010. Put yourself in learning communities for possibilities that you would not come to on your own. Carve out a niche specialty in a bigger market. Network, let people know about your talents and progressive ambitions.

Love is affected by all of this. Capricorns are earth signs with rich sensuality. Dedicate some necessary retreat time to romancing the right one.

Gretchen Lawlor © Mother Tongue Ink 2009

Neeram Salem
¤ Eve-Marie Roy 2007

♄♄♄ pō 'aono

♌ ♍

Saturday

25

☽☍♆ 1:28 am v/c
☽PrG 4:16 am
☽→♍ 7:14 am
☉△☽ 1:56 pm
☽△♇ 3:48 pm

☉☉☉ lā pule

♍

Sunday

26

☽△♂ 7:04 am
☽✶♀ 2:49 pm
☉☌♇ 5:04 pm
☽□☿ 5:36 pm

December/January 2011

diciembre/enero

☽☽☽ lunes

♍ ♎

Monday

27

☽☍♃ 2:49 am
☽☍♅ 4:20 am v/c
☽→♎ 9:38 am
☽□♇ 6:25 pm
☉□☽ 8:18 pm

♂♂♂ martes

Waning Half Moon in ♎ Libra 8:18 pm PST

♎

Tuesday

28

♇ApG 10:38 am
☽□♂ 12:42 pm
☽☌♄ 1:40 pm
☽⚹☿ 7:11 pm

☿☿☿ miércoles

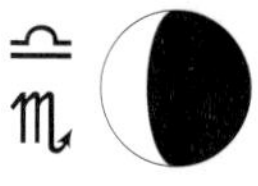

♎ ♏

Wednesday

29

☽△♆ 7:05 am v/c
♂□♄ 7:29 am
☽→♏ 12:49 pm
☽⚹♇ 9:56 pm
☿D 11:21 pm

♃♃♃ jueves

♏

Thursday

30

☉⚹☽ 3:51 am
☽⚹♂ 7:39 pm

♀♀♀ viernes

♏ ♐

Friday

31

☽☌♀ 5:11 am
☽△♃ 11:11 am
☽□♆ 11:33 am
☽△♅ 11:57 am v/c
☽→♐ 5:21 pm

Raven Reflection © Cathy McClelland 2008

Speak to me, Raven
in the oral tradition
through the shuffling of wings
of stories primeval.

excerpt ¤ *Kersten Christianson 2008*

♄♄♄ sábado

January 2011

Saturday
1

☽✶♄ 11:21 pm

☉☉☉ domingo

♐

Sunday
2

☽☌☿ 6:02 am
☽✶♆ 5:45 pm
☽□♃ 5:49 pm
☽□♅ 6:08 pm v/c
☽→♑ 11:39 pm

☽☽☽ Jumatatu

♑

Monday 3

☽☌♇ 9:42 am

Creation D.O.M. Tarot © Ffiona Morgan 1991

♂♂♂ Jumanne

♑

Tuesday 4

♀□♆ 12:27 am
☉☌☽ 1:03 am
♃☌♅ 4:53 am
♀△♅ 5:33 am
♀△♃ 5:39 am
☽□♄ 7:00 am
☽☌♂ 3:49 pm

Partial Solar Eclipse 12:51am*
New Moon in ♑ Capricorn 1:03 am PST

☿☿☿ Jumatano

♑
♒

Wednesday 5

♀□⚷ 1:07 am
☽⚹♅ 2:30 am
☽⚹♃ 2:42 am
☽⚹♀ 4:15 am v/c
☽→♒ 8:08 am

♃♃♃ Alhamisi

♒

Thursday 6

☽△♄ 4:59 pm

♀♀♀ Ijumaa

♒
♓

Friday 7

♀→♐ 4:30 am
☉□♄ 6:00 am
☽⚹☿ 6:43 am
☽☌♆ 12:51 pm v/c
♂ApG 4:01 pm
☽→♓ 6:57 pm
☽□♀ 8:16 pm

*Visible over Europe, Africa and Central Asia

The Sun

© Maria Silmon 2000

Creating We'Moon: A Community Endeavour

We'Moon is the creation of a vast web of we'moon—starting with the "Call for Contributions," an open invitation to thousands of wemoon to contribute their art and writing on the theme each year (see p. 232, "Become a **We'Moon** Contributor!"). What you see on these pages is the creative outpouring of womyn all over the world, responding to the **We'Moon 2010** theme. All the submitted art and writing are reviewed in "**We'Moon** Weaving Circles" where local area womyn participate in the preliminary selection process. Next, the "Creatrix" editing collective digests, designs and weaves the material together in alignment with the natural cycles of Moon, Sun, Earth and stars. The process of "production" continues the crafting of the chosen images, words, signs and symbols that are input, scanned, cropped, edited, laid out, designed on the page and proofed to perfection, before being sent off to the printer. All the activity that goes into creating **We'Moon** is her *inbreath*; everything else we do to get it out into the world and into your hands is the *outbreath* in our annual cycle of weaving **We'Moon**.

Origins of We'Moon: We have been producing **We'Moon** for 29 years. The idea of **We'Moon** originated at Kvindelandet, an international women's land in Denmark where 50 to 60 lesbians from different countries lived together in the late 1970s. It was inspired by our learnings about living together as womyn in a creative and magical way, in harmony with the Earth and her cycles. Our astrological charts, hanging on the living room wall, gave us better understanding of each other despite language barriers. In 1980, we were literally "undermined" by a multinational corporation that expropriated our land. Faced with loss of our home base, we turned to the Moon, Sun and stars to keep us in touch with ourselves, each other and the Earth's cycles.

We'Moon was conceived as a handbook in natural rhythms, letting us know when to celebrate the New Moon or Solstice: we could continue circling together even if not in the same place! We wanted to stay in touch through the "Mother Tongue" (the universal native tongue: the language of Mother Nature) across time and space and man-made borders. **We'Moon** continues to be inspired by we'moon all over the world living our visions; expressing the Spirit that moves us in our art and writing; sharing love, lore and lessons learned; grounded in the common roots of international women's culture and Earth-based spirituality.

Musawa © Mother Tongue Ink 2007

We'Moon on the Web

Our website has been updated to include some of the gorgeous art from our contributors and a more user-friendly layout. At www.wemoon.ws, you can window shop our products, make purchases, read and submit raves and reviews, and sign up to receive We'News: a periodic update about specials and new products. See what **We'Moon** astrologers are saying now, and browse our links page, which includes links to websites of many **We'Moon** artists and writers. Find information on We'Moon Land and We'Mooniversity, and how you can become a contributor to **We'Moon**. We also now have a myspace page (www.myspace.com/wemoonspace) and facebook group—add us and share **We'Moon** with your friends!

Myshkin ¤ *Mother Tongue Ink 2009*

We'Moon/ We'Moon Land / We'Mooniversity

Since **We'Moon** Company (dba Mother Tongue Ink) has branched out from We'Moon Land in Estacada to new home offices in Portland and Southern Oregon, We'Moon Land community is currently reinventing itself. We are open to we'moon of all ages visiting and possibly joining us to help steward this womyn's land (practicing earth-based spirituality, consensus, natural healing, organic gardening, permaculture, eco-foresty, earth-friendly building. . .).

We'Moon Land is also the home of We'Mooniversity, an "experiential School of Life for womyn and children in community with Mother Earth," dedicated to bringing the outpouring of **We'Moon** creativity down to earth, where artists, writers, astrologers, healers, priestesses can meet one another, share what we are learning, and gather for spiritual retreats, workshops, ceremonies, and celebrations. If you are interested in being part of any of these activities, visit our web page (www.wemoon.ws), email us (wemoonland@wemoon.ws), and network with our growing web of "Friends of **We'Moon.**" Check out our facebook and myspace pages and pass it on!

Musawa ¤ *Mother Tongue Ink 2009*

30 Years of We'Moon: An Anthology

We are in the process of putting together an Anthology of treasured art and writing distilled from 30 years of **We'Moon**! At last: a **We'Moon** that will not run out at the end of the year!!

Contributors: If you have ever had your work published in **We'Moon**, please send us your current contact information so we can be sure to reach you about the Anthology! anthology@wemoon.ws. Check it out on our web page: www.wemoon.ws/anthology to suggest your favorite **We'Moon** "Oldies but Goodies," ask about the Anthology pre-sale, and help us re-connect with the web of **We'Moon** contributors and friends of the past three decades. Thank you!

Musawa ¤ *Mother Tongue Ink 2009*

From left to right: Top: Eagle and Sequoia. Middle: Sue, Myshkin, Lou and Bethroot. On the floor: Zia, Musawa and Barb

Staff Appreciation

We'Moon has been blessed with a beautiful, competent, conscientious and gifted team during the creation of **We'Moon 2010**.

Lou, Promo and Shipping Deva, is our newest edition to the **We'Moon** Matrix. She swept into our lives with a host of talents and fresh insights. **Sue** is a woman of many gifts, not the least of which she shares with us as Co-Moonager, Accounts Manager and Creatrix Teammate. **Renée** graciously helps out with production needs, lending us her skills as researcher, networker and typist extraodinaire. **Bethroot** is our brilliant Special Editor. We owe much of the beauty and flow of **We'Moon 2010** to her keen eye and mind. **Eagle** is our steadfast Astro Proofer, Creatrix Teammate and Production Assistant for **We'Moon's** 30 year Anthology. Her warm spirit and contageous laughter brighten our workspace. **Myshkin** shares many of her skills with us, as proficient and friendly Sales Deva and sharp, creative Production Assistant. It's a joy working alongside **Sequoia**, our clever Web Mistress and patient, inspired Graphic Designer. **Musawa**, **We'Moon**'s Founder and Crone Editor (29 years and counting!), generously shares her long-time experience and expertise in the grounded business aspects as well as the magical elements of **We'Moon**. **Barb**, We'Moonager and Production Coordinator, continues to keep us all on-task through the ebb and flow of the yearly work cycle. We wish **Tina, Haelan** and **Jennifer** great Abundance, Joy and Love as they move on to other ventures.

Barbara Dickinson © Mother Tongue Ink 2009

© Copyrights and Contacting Contributors

Contributor Bylines and Index

See page 232 for: **How to Become a Contributor**

Becky Bee (Azalea, OR) Woman of many incarnations, cob goddess, mother, vegetable grower, horse trainer, author, traveler, and homemaker. Visit her website at www.beckybee.com **p. 4**

Beth Beurkens, M.A. (Mount Shasta, CA) is the author of *By the Light of Our Dreams*, is on the faculty of College of the Siskiyous and Foundation for Shamanic Studies, and is a poet-teacher for California Poets in the Schools. She is currently publishing her first collection of poetry. www.shamanicuniverse.com **p. 41, 150**

Beth Lenco (Portuguese Cove, Nova Scotia, Canada) is a wild and playful artist, singer, shamanic healer, and teacher living with the forest and the sea. She holds workshops in creativity, ritual, art, and nature connection. www.bethlenco.com **p. 19**

Bethroot Gwynn (Myrtle Creek, OR) is blessed to be Special Editor for We'Moon. She lives at Fly Away Home women's land (33 years now): writing, growing food, making theater and ritual. FFI about spiritual gatherings, working visits, possible residency, send SASE to POB 593, Myrtle Creek, OR 97457 **p. 33, 116, 173**

Betty LaDuke (Ashland, OR) Through my publications, art, and work in the academic world, I honor and give visibility to international women artists who've inspired my work. *Celebrating Women's Creative Hands and Spirits* is one such homage. This 6'x 4' mural will be featured in *Dreaming Cows*, a book celebrating my work from '03–'08, in collaboration with **Heifer International**, text by Sue Bumagin. In *Africa: After War*, children symbolize our collective need for peace. www.bettyladuke.com **p. 90, 108**

Caressa Mathews (Westlake, OH) draws her inspiration from the beauty found in her natural surroundings, the grace of the human form, and the strength of her experiences as a woman. She can be reached at cdmathe1@kent.edu **p. 132**

Caroline GullyLir (Avebury, Wiltshire, UK) is a priestess of Avalon, living in the sacred vale of Avebury. She is the resident artist of the Glastonbury Goddess Temple, ceremonialist and melissa holding sacred space. She is living spiral dreams amongst the silent circles of stone and Lammas crops. www.spinningthewheel.com **p. 154**

Carolyn Hillyer (Dartmoor, Devon, UK) is a musician, artist and writer who lives and works on the wild moorlands of southwest England. She performs and exhibits her work internationally including Europe, Japan, Russia and the Arctic as well as guiding workshop journeys for women. Details of her work on www.seventhwavemusic.co.uk **p. 73**

Casey Sayre Baikus (Siasconset, MA) is a wife, mother, witch, masseuse, dancer and priestess in training, weaving women's moon circles and building earth-based and goddess-aware community through celebration, nature and art. **p. 131**

Catherine Molland (Santa Fe, NM) I love the Great Mother. Being in nature is my passion and painting is my expression of that joy. I create beauty in my art, at my shop, and in my organic garden. Contact: www.catherinemolland.com **p. 127**

Cathy McClelland (Kings Beach, CA) paints from her heart and imagination. Her artwork reflects her love for nature, cross-cultural mythical subjects, magical and sacred places and symbhols. Her hope is that her work inspires the viewer to see and feel the magic that life offers. www.cathymcclelland.com **p. 51, 107, 185**

Cheryl Collins (Kayenta, UT) is an artist, sculptor and author who loves living in the Mojave desert. Her work can be viewed at www.CollinsArt.net **p. 113**

Christina Hagen (Palo Alto, CA) I live in Palo Alto studying my passions; photography, the mind, our paths, our pleasures, our pain. I play with children to stay curious and honor our elderly to stay reverent. Blessings to us all. www.myspace.com/hagendaaz77 —Visit me! **p. 85**

Christina Smith (Nelson, British Columbia, Canada) I am honored and grateful for the opportunity to share my work for healing and truth with the We'Moon community. Namaste. www.earthlyimages.ca **p. 58**

Clio Wondrausch (Totnes, S. Devon, UK) I sing the songs, dance the dance, paint the paintings, gather the wild food She gives me—following my thread. All to celebrate and strengthen the web of wonder so we may live as one. www.wildhearth.co.uk **p. 141**

Colleen (Wheaton, IL) www.MysticalWillow.com My garden, my life, and especially my art—these things are my voice. Prints and originals available, specializing in Magical Portraiture and other commissioned works. Call or email: 630-668-0850, mysticalwillow@comcast.net **p. 43**

Compago Creative (Marlboro, MA) Sandra Pirie-St. Amour is a freelance graphic designer and illustrator. She loves to paint with watercolor but is just as comfortable drawing and painting with a mouse. Images of peace, unity and environmental issues abound in her work. **p. 42**

Cora Greenhill (Hope Valley, UK) lives and works in the UK and Crete, as writer, artist, dance teacher and environmental protectress. www.thirteenthmoon.co.uk **p. 101, 113**

D.J. Webb (Estero, FL) is an illustrator, designer and fine artist, pagan/Buddhist. Her art is inspired by feminist spirituality, deep ecology, mythology and experiences with wildlife, water, stars and sky. View WomenSpirit gallery and contact her at www.djwebbimages.com **p. 47**

DV Trimmer (Houston, TX) is a philosopher, mother, spiritual counselor, and pragmatic idealist. As a female poet she is immensely grateful to have outlived her suicidal impulses to stand today, dazzled by the beauty of the cosmos, fully committed to life. Ich_traum@hotmail.com **p. 139**

Diane Bergstrom (Louisville, CO) is a mask maker, artist, poet, writer, and on the board of APT: Animals and People Together. More information can be found at www.animalsandpeopletogether.org. **p. 63, 79**

Diane Melanie (Totnes, Devon, UK) In love, working whole-heartedly with words, images and materials, I try to reflect my intimate experiences of Earth-Spirit-uality, and offer them in the hope that you, too may become enchanted. dianemelanie@hotmail.co.uk **p. 53**

Dolphin (Ava, MO) Heyho from the Ozark Heartland—Where you can live Wild. **p. 167**

Dorrie Joy (Glastonbury, Somerset, UK) 29, is a self-taught and self-employed artist, dancer, sculptor and craftswoman. She holds workshop journeys for women and girls, and welcomes inspired personal commissions for painting spirit and the deeply feminine. See www.dorriejoy.co.uk **p. 17, 63, 151, 156**

Durga Bernhard (Shandaken, NY) is an artist , illustrator, musician and mother living in the Catskill Mountains. She is the author/illustrator of over twenty picture books for children.To see more of Durga's art, please visit www.durgabernhard.com **p. 146, 204**

Elisa Rosenberg (Chicago, IL) a.k.a. Rose Mountain Art, is an artist of many mediums, including: mask making, drawing, painting, henna, and natural culinary. Check her works out at www.rosemountainart.com and www.myspace.com/elisarosenberg **p. 35**

Elissa Malcohn (Beverly Hills, Florida) *Deviations: Covenant* is available from Aisling Press. Info on the series and more at home.earthlink.net/~emalcohn. I continue a blessed journey with my partner, Mary, our cat, Daisy, and the benevolent spirit of Daisy's buddy, Red. **p. 73**

Elizabeth Fontanella (Salt Lake City, UT) is embracing life with her heart open. She has grown through teaching and community activism. She honors the lineage of women before and after her. **p. 128**

Elizabeth Kampouris (Sedona, AZ) lives and dreams in the beautifully surreal red rocks of Sedona, where she frequently skinny dips in local creeks with her loving partner and their beautiful Goddess daughter, whom she counts as her greatest gift and teacher. **p. 167**

Elizabeth Page Roberts (Brooklyn, NY) is an anti-imperialist activist who works with the War Resisters League (www.warresisters.org). She lives in Brooklyn with her partner and their kindle of spectacular cats. **p. 50**

Emily Butterfly (Oakland, CA) is a creatress of many genres, including illustration, story and song writing and performing, puppeteer, muralist, and custom commissioned work including puppets, drawings and pregnant belly-casts. www.emilybutterfly.com **p. 171**

Eve-Marie Roy (Montréal, Québec, Canada) My paintings are a result of a spiritual quest where the paintbrush attempts to capture the essence behind and within the subject. The human archetype, nature spirits, ethereal landscapes from which we take form. nisantra@yahoo.ca **p. 183**

Ffiona Morgan (Eugene, OR) is a Dianic High Priestess, Author, Artist and Teacher. She is an avid traveler and her work is known around the globe. Ffiona blends political feminism and a deep spirituality in all she teaches. www.daughtersofthemoon.com
p. 28, 29, 53, 72, 87, 109, 125, 131, 145, 147, 159, 181, 186

Gaia Orion (Sebright, Ontario, Canada) explores healing and spiritual themes that manifest in symbolic and archetypal images. These images arise from her quest to understand life and her interest in sacred and ancient forms of art. Originally from Paris, France, she now lives in Canada. www.artbygaia.com **p. 95**

Gretchen Lawlor (Seattle, WA) A passionate astrologer of nearly 40 years! I enjoy assisting We'Mooners in navigating opportunities and challenges with grace and right timing. Emotional, relational, health, creativity and professional issues. Consultations, Lifemaps, classes, workshops: 206-391-8681 light@whidbey.com • www.GretchenLawlor.com
p. 19, 21, 49, 61, 71, 85, 97, 111, 121, 133, 145, 157, 171, 183

Heather Roan Robbins (Rolla, ND) is priestess/reverend of the Turtle Mountain Interfaith circle, and an astrologer (for 30 yrs) who is fascinated by how astrology maps strengths and challenges within a soul, partnership, family, work situation or culture. www.RoanRobbins.com **p. 12, 15, 22**

Heidi Eich-Dittberner (Parkers Prairie, MN) First I am a mother, trying to teach and guide my children through their lives peacefully and confidently. After that I'm a farmer, lover, chef, writer, photographer, artist, healer and dreamer. www.heidilogic.wordpress.com **p. 155**

Holly Wilkinson (Richmond, VT) is a writer, artist, and "midwife for adults," facilitating conversations and circles to deepen a sense of belonging, spirit and vibrancy through imagery, reflection and expression. **p. 68**

Hrana Janto (Tillson, NY) I have long been inspired by mythology, history, fantasy, the natural world and the sacred. Works include: "The Goddess Oracle" (US Games), book covers, Goddess calendars, children's books and more. Visit my website: www.hranajanto.com to see more! **p. 2, 109**

J. Stauber (St. Louis, MO) is a practicing urban/architectural designer, artist, and knitter. Her intention is to honor the uniqueness of the environment, no matter who we are or where we are. Contact her at jenstaub@hotmail.com **p. 56**

Jacqueline Young (Tempe, AZ) is a writer and photographer. She is currently creating a Tarot deck of tiger photos and an image card deck of her photography. **p. 25**

Jakki Moore (Oslo, Norway) is currently living in Norway, illustrating and painting what she is passionate about. She also conducts workshops in Ireland and Bulgaria. Please contact her at: jakkimooreart@yahoo.com www.jakkiart.com Blessed Be… **p. 15, 100, 105**

Jamie Branker (Northridge, CA) My artistic journey began some eighteen years ago when I was pregnant with my fourth daughter. I didn't know at the time that it would be a spiritual journey as well. I surrender to the light and color, the images emerge. **p. 75**

Jana Lamprecht (Otschönwalde-Dorf, Germany) I am living in Portugal in nature on a yoga-tai chi retreat place. I am giving courses and painting murals and canvas. I love to honour our great mother with my paintings. www.paintedvisions.de **p. 111**

Janaia Donaldson (Nevada City, CA) is host of Peak Moment TV. Conversations on communities going local and sustainable (online). She and her partner Robyn live in the Sierra Nevada foothills, where they are protecting 60 acres of forest as wildlife habitat. **p. 93**

Jane Mara (Ashland, OR) I live at the edge of the watershed in Ashland, where I write prose and poetry whenever I can. As a dedicated practitioner of Compassion and Mindfulness, I continue to be astonished and grateful for the insight and release from suffering they bring. **p. 144, 158**

Janet Ladrach (Sugarcreek, Ontario, Canada) I'm now into my second year of retirement and last year I really fell in love with the farm I've lived on for 20 years. I'm still writing poetry and walking the goat. **p. 107**

Jeannette Armstrong (Pendicton Indian Reservation, Canada) Award winning Artist, Author, Activist, Educator. **p. 57, 91**

Jeannette Brossart (Durham, NC) is a self-taught mosaic artist. She loves emphasizing the "pieces" which make up our natural world, often using reclaimed /repurposed materials in her work. **p. 77**

Jeannine Chappell (Richmond, CA) I am a painter, dancer, architectural designer and mother. I live with my husband, my garden and my computer in the San Francisco bay area. www.east-bay.com/jeannine **p. 3, 48, 152, 153, 172, 228**

Jennifer G. Metz (Garberville, CA) Blessed I am to share my art with the world. To have the opportunity to be artist, healer, gardener, traveler, mother of two incredible boys, and lover and partner to the best husband possible. **p. 150**

Jennifer Shipman (Miranda CA) I am an aspiring poet and mother living on a small homestead in Northern California. I could not live without the circle of women who guide me, which includes my mother and grandmothers, my moon group, and my baby daughter. **p. 62**

Joan Watterson (Bend, OR) is a great-grandmother and member of the Association of Traditional Rug Hooking Artists and the High Desert Rug Hookers. She has been hooking for over 20 years, specializing in animal portraits. She spent many years demonstrating her craft at the High Desert Museum in Bend. **p. 39**

JoAnne Dodgson (Abiquiu, NM) is a healer, writer and teacher in ancient Peruvian medicine ways KaTaSee, "living in balance from the heart." www.pathwaysforhealing.net **p. 65**

Joanne Rocky Delaplaine (Bethesda, MD) is a daughter of the night and chaos, and a mother of astonishment. She is guided by 3 fates and her circle of women. Oaks and poplars surround her. All blessings to the ancestors, Peace is her prayer. **p. 45, 161**

Josslyn Meyeres (Saskatoon, Saskatchewan, Canada) Musician, Artist, Teacher, Oma, and life-long learner who aspires to become a children's book author and illustrator. meyjoy@sasktel.net **p. 168, 177**

Joyce Ketterman – (Boynton Beach, FL) Poet, painter, potter, teacher and most recently a counselor using holistic approaches and therapeutic art. Mother of four daughters with four granddaughters and one grandson. Sister of the Universe. Driven by my vision to be a catalyst for positive change. lajoy0703@peoplepc.com **p. 108**

juliett jade chi (Damahur, Italy) called "giada" in Italy, lives in the cooperative ecovillage and spiritual nexus of Damahur, where she crafts organic raw vegan cuisine, dances with fire and writes constantly. jade@jadecreation.org www.jadecreation.org **p. 162**

Karen Ethelsdattar (Union City, NJ) has published 3 books of poetry: *Earthwalking and Other Poems, Thou Art a Woman and Other Poems,* and most recently *Steam Rising Up from the Soul.* Many of her individual poems have appeared in journals, magazines and anthologies. She is a liturgist/ritual maker, especially in rituals affirming women and the feminine presence of God. **p. 51, 82**

Kat Beyer (Madison, WI) is an artist and writer who earned her strength by recovering from a hand injury. She loves her work and the family and forests it comes from. www.katspaw.com **p. 49, 78, 121**

Kate Rose Bast (Colton, OR) is an MFA candidate in Poetry at Antioch University, Los Angeles. She is also a web solutions consultant for We'Moon. www.BastkatWeb.com **p. 67**

Katya (Nina) Sabaroff Taylor (Tallahassee, FL) is happy that the images of women that she "immortalized" in the '70s haven't lost their power and beauty in this new century. Katya is currently compiling her literary works for "posterity". Visit her website at www.creativeartsandhealing.com **p. 128**

Kersten Christianson (Sitka, AK) is a raven-watching, moon-gazing Alaskan who teaches high school English and composes rough draft poetry. She lives with her partner Bruce, daughter Rie, and retrievers Olie, Lena and Uffda on an island in the rainforest of Southeast Alaska. **p. 185**

Kimberly Webber (Rancho de Taos, NM) Painter of the divine feminine archetypes, intergalactic traveler finding nourishment, hope and inspiration in my family, friends, community, and the loving, giving land. Gratitude is the prevalent energy in my life. Blessed Be!! **p. 133**

Laura Amazzone (Venice, CA) is a writer, artist, teacher, yogini and devotee of Goddess Durga in all her fierce and benevolent forms. Visit Laura's temple of goddess jewelry on myspace or www.amazzonejewelry.com She is also collaborating on a documentary on Durga: www.durgarising.com JAI MAA! **p. 44**

Leah Marie Dorion (Prince Albert, Saskatchewan, Canada) is a Métis artist from Saskatchewan. Her website provides insight into Indigenous Women's wisdom www.leahdorion.com **p. 33, 97, 99**

Lilly Coyote (Irving, TX) I am an aging hippie, who recently quit my big fat job in order to stay home, sleep late, garden and learn to rehabilitate urban wildlife. Each day I try to nap during rush hour. **p. 159**

Linda Erzinger (Louisville, KY) I am a part time art therapist, working on being a full time artist. I love creating art from discarded objects. Please visit me with a comment on my blog at: linda_erzinger.livejournal.com **p. 119**

Lindy Kehoe (Ashland, OR) is a painter of magical realms and playful characters. Her art echoes the remembrance of the child heart. She lives and loves in Southern Oregon, dreaming of new earth visions. She is a fairy tale writer, creating stories that weave myths of all time. www.Lindykehoe.com **p. 89**

Lisa Aerianna Tayerle (Wheaton, MD) is a professional gardener and witch, living in an oasis of nature in the suburban Washington, DC area. Her work is a manifestation of magic; its intent is to speak for a renewed relationship with nature and to celebrate the sacredness of our Earth. **p. 41**

Lisa Kagan (Portland, OR) is an artist, writer and educator. She believes in the transformative nature of the creative process to heal, empower, challenge, inform and awaken the human spirit. Contact: lisakagandesigns@hotmail.com **p. 140**

Lisa Noble (Burien, WA) who also writes under the pen name of Lisa Greenstone, loves to make art about magic and loves to write about art. She lives in the Northwest with her husband Bran, three magical cats and Willow the precious beagle. To view more of her work: www.cafepress.com/lisanoble. **p. 4, back cover**

Lisa Seed (Kauai, HI) Vibrantly living and loving life with gratitude. www.LisaSeed.com **p. 76, 103, 135**

Lori Cohen (Dugald, Manitoba, Canada) is an artist, tile maker, spiritual life coach, and BodyTalk and AnimalTalk practitioner. Her deep affinity for nature inspires her artwork and spiritual pursuits. She works to help people embrace their divine potential. www.creativelife.ca **p. 176**

Lorraine Schein (Sunnyside, NY) is a New York writer and poet. Her work has recently appeared in *Gargoyle* and the story anthology *Alice Redux*. The *Futurist's Mistress*, her poetry book, is available from Mayapple Press. **p.149**

Luz Maria López (Covington, LA) paints images inspired by her Latin American/ Mayan ancestry, her childhood memories and stories from everywhere. She is a Magna Cum Laude graduate with a BA in Fine Art. Her work is exhibited nationally and has won a number of awards. **p. 96**

Lyrion ApTower, HPS (Wilton, NH) is actively involved in raising awareness of the ethics of Wicca, mentoring university students, writing and performing all life passages, serving on regional interfaith councils, leading wildcrafting walks, and counseling the Southern New England Pagan community. **p. 129**

Mama Donna Henes (Brooklyn, NY) is an internationally acclaimed spiritual teacher, popular speaker, and award winning author of four books and a CD. She lectures, consults, and produces private and public ceremonial events worldwide. www.DonnaHenes.net **p. 58**

Mara Berendt Friedman (Lorane, OR) has been creating paintings that honor the feminine aspect of spirit for almost two decades. Her work is an expression of her passionate path to "know heart." For a free catalogue of her work: www.newmoonvisions.com **p. 181**

Marc Dragiewicz (Astoria, OR) is a biologist currently living in Astoria. musiclovenature@gmail.com **p. 64**

Maria Silmon (Kirbymoorside, North Yorkshire, UK) I am an artist and natural therapist, living on the North Yorkshire Moors, creating digital imagery and video expressing my continual inspiration from Mother Nature, her awesome plants, trees and creatures. Me, my camera and the undergrowth=BLISS!! Check out my divination pack at www.starseeddivination.com and other work at www.mariasilmon.co.uk **p. 24, 34, 187**

Marianna Crawford (Portland, OR) Ceramist, graphic designer, meditater, doubter, seeker. **p. 81**

Marline W. Koch (Azalea, OR) I live in Oregon amongst the tall timbers. The outhouse angel lives in a forest not far from the back door, surrounded by rhodies, orchids and wildflowers in season. **p. 166**

Marna (Portland, OR) stretches, nipples, and eddies in the slip streams of time, tide, and ancestral shealing with the Pacific Cascadian bioregion, building snake gardens and food forests, laughing astro-blessings while circling with womyn celebrating earth regeneration at www.deeperharmony.com **p. 83, 138, 179**

Marni Norwich (Vancouver, British Columbia, Canada) is delighted to announce the publication of her first book of poetry, *Wildflowers at my Doorstep* (Karma Press, 2008). To read excerpts from *Wildflowers*, please see www.inkcatmedia.com/wildflowers/ Marni is a writer, editor and writing workshop facilitator. **p. 105, 115**

Max Dashu (Oakland, CA) is a feminist history sibyl and Goddess artist. Her first DVD, *Women of Power*, shows our full protency across time and place. See video excerpts on www.supressedhistories.cet, www.MaxDashu.net Peace, Sat Maat Allat. **p. 27**

MC Torinus (Oconomowoc, WI) I am a wife and mother of three grown children. I hold a bachelors degree in music and a masters in Theology. I have taught in both fields for 20 years. I love to kayak, ski, draw, play music, volunteer, and snuggle with my grandson. **p. 160**

Melanie Livengood (Mentor OH) has been writing poetry for a number of years. Her inspiration comes from nature, the Divine, and pure, raw emotion. **p. 43**

Melina Keawe (Kalapana, HI) Artist, poet, native Hawaiian Political / Environmentalist and Feminist. Creative artistic endeavors help me know, heal and express the deeper journeys of the soul. **p. 174**

Melissa Harris (West Hurley, NY) artist and intuitive, offers prints, cards, card decks and other gift items, as well as individual spirit essence portraits. www.melissaharris.com **p. 23, 70, 139**

Meredith Heller (Fairfax, CA) makes life and love in Fairfax. She is a poet, dancer, body-worker, nature lover, and performing singer/songwriter. Listen to her siren-song at www.myspace.com/meredithheller or contact mermaidmh9@gmail.com **p. 104**

Michelle Wilkinson (Exmouth, Devon, UK) My words and digital images evolve from "yogadance", inspired movement in the ever-changing environments of Devon seascapes and trees. Here I am exploring my human relationship with nature. **p. 160**

Mimi Foyle (Quito, Ecuador) practices wild arts and crafts in native tropical forests. She sings, drums, and works for their defense and conservation, especially versus metal mining interests. Email: holywell19@yahoo.com **p. 77, 151, 161, 180**

Miriam Dyak (Seattle, WA) I am a social artist. All my life is poetry—the 40+ years of writing poems, my work as a Voice Dialogue facilitator and teacher, and my work as an unpaid citizen lobbyist in Washington state. miriam@thevoicedialogueinstitute.org **p. 88**

Monica Sjöö (1938-2005, Sweden, Wales, and UK) Prolific artist, writer and activist, devotee of the Great Mother and Her sacred sites and long time beloved We'Moon contributor. View her works at www.MonicaSjoo.org **p. 159**

Motherpeace: Karen Vogel and Vicki Noble For more information and to purchase Tarot cards, visit www.motherpeace.com **p. 30**

MudGirls Natural Building Collective (British Columbia, Canada) is a collective of women natural builders, building beautiful, strong, healthy homes all over the west coast of Canada. www.mudgirls.ca **p. 163**

Musawa (Estacada, OR and Tesuque, NM) I was 36 when I started **We'Moon** and now I'm 65! This 29th edition of **We'Moon** marks the Saturn Return in its life cycle: a lot of water under the bridge. Time to pass it on in a sustainable way that will lay the foundation for the next generation of **We'Moon** for years to come. Am working on the *Anthology: 30 Years of We'Moon* that will be out with the upcoming **We'Moon 2011**—Check it out! **p. 6, 9, 20, 29, 169, 188, 189**

Myshkin (Wolf Creek, OR) is a composer, touring musician, and recording artist, sometimes a visual artist, and recently a natural builder. She's inspired by travel, love, courage, art and mystery. Hear music at: www.myshkinsrubywarblers.com or www.myspace.com/rubywarblers **p. 4, 143, 179, 189**

Nancy Holley (Ashland, OR) is living, laughing, crying, and trying to practice happiness, right work and realistic recycling—happily addicted to new artistic processes and constantly humbled by her own subjectivity. **p. 83**

Nancy Watterson (Oakland, OR) artist. I explore the mysteries of life in my studio along the Umpqua River, where nature teaches, heals, and gives me hope. See more of my work at www.nwattersonscharf.com **p. 149, 165**

Naomi Shihab Nye (San Antonio, TX) is an award winning poet, songwriter and a novelist. She was born to a Palestinian father and American mother. She regards herself as a "wandering poet." **p. 92**

Nevas (Turner, ME) is a lifelong artist and translator of universal vibrations. Using guidance from our ancestral elements, she creates paintings, sculpture and felt images to celebrate the essence of life. Living on Root Star Farm Sanctuary with my Tiger-Femme Starhand, we bring focus to Women in Agriculture and the Arts. contact Nevas at: navas@megalink.net **p. 8**

Patti Sinclair (Stratford, PEI, Canada) has written *Out of the Witches Mouth* and *Motherhood as a Spiritual Practice.* She loves performing poetry and sharing ceremony. See: poet-at-large.blogspirit.com She is honored to be part of We'Moon's wheel. **p. 134**

Pesha Joyce Gertler (Seattle, WA) leads women's writing circles at N. Seattle Community College, The University of Washington's Women's Center, parks and living rooms. Themes include all aspects of women's lives, with a focus on myth and legend. The poem here is dedicated to her students. **p. 75**

Qahira Lynn (Yachats, OR) Quietly visioning and living the Dream on a hill overlooking the ocean with two very magical cats. www.qahiralynn.com **p. 147**

Rebecca Guberman-Bloom (Portland, OR) I work with the creative flow, capturing beauty and divine essence. I paint from my heart and spirit awareness and am working on a fantastical children's story. I hope to inspire God awareness and the Divine energy through my work. Praises to LIFE and to PACHA MAMA, Jai! **p. 115, 122**

Robyn Waters (Scholls, OR) is immersed in writing and illustrating Children's Books in her studio amidst a Cedar Forest. She is nearly finished illustrating *Toes Aren't Just For Piggies,* and then it's off to find a publisher! Check her progress at www.robynwaters.com **p. 59, 106**

Rose Flint (Corsley, Wiltshire, UK) is a poet and art therapist. She is a Priestess-Poet for the Goddess Conference in Glastonbury, England, and works as a writer in healthcare. Her new book is *Mother of Pearl,* available from roseflint9@tiscali.co.uk **p. 54, 165**

Rosemary Lloyd Freeman (Sebastopol, CA) is expanding and taking flight with the wild birds. She is a seductress of honeybees, a dancing High Priestess. She creates hedgehog stories for her daughters. And she paints! **p. 102, 151**

S. Grace Mantle (Ashland, OR) Artist, writer, designer, dancer. Grace lives and works with the cycles of the awakening earth and collective consciousness. She uses her multiple skills to dance "new earth" into being. Enjoy the artwork! **p. 12, 60**

Sandra Lory (Barre, VT) is a founder of Mandala Botanicals, folk herbalist, educator and artist. She is creating bio-diverse gardens in her little industrial city and is co-founder of www.vermonthealers.org. She is dedicated to strengthening the grassroots healthcare system. **p. 66, 67, 116**

Sandra Patorius aka Laughing Giraffe (Ashland, OR) I am enjoying small town life with my partner. I continue to teach and write, and offer astrological consultations in person and on the phone (mention We'Moon for a special discount). I would love to speak to your group on Astrology. Send me your email address for announcements on upcoming workshops and retreats. Call 541-482-0529 or email: laughinggiraffe2001@yahoo.com. Peace Be! **p. 18**

Sandra Stanton (Farmington, ME) Images of the Eternal Goddess. www.goddessmyths.com **p. 45, 54, 175**

Sara Glass (Roseburg, OR) Inspired by nature in her many brilliant forms, I find myself in an Artists Playground nestled in the green lushness of Southern Oregon. Please go to www.indigenousspirit.net **p. 79**

ScharCbear Freeman (Eleele, HI) Artist and poet, living, loving life on this island making my way through art. My passion is oil painting, my purpose is to create. www.scharart.etsy.com • www.scharcbear.8k.com • scharbear@yahoo.com **p.118**

Selina Maria di Girolamo (Ninfield, East Sussex, UK) [Royal Society British Artists] Artist, writer, priestess of the Goddess, witch. Makes unique altar Goddesses and shamanic landscape paintings. Believes in love. selinawitch@darkmother.co.uk, www.myspace.com/selinadigirolamorba **p. 37**

Sequoia (Azalea, OR) Enjoying the beautiful mountains and streams where I live. My partner, dog, and horses keep my life interesting. A potter, teacher and a seeker, I marvel at the wonders of life. **p. 101, 117, 125**

Shannon 'Shakaya Breeze' Leone (Barrie, Ontario, Canada) is a mom and raw foodist whose work expresses the sacred beauty of woman as Goddess, Creator (Mother Nature) and Spiritual Enlightenment on the planet. **p. 142**

Sheila Broun (Bath, UK) relates very closely to Goddess, trees, to the turn of the seasons and weather; aiming to reconnect and realign people to Nature. She can be contacted at sheilabroun.blogspot.com/ **p. 182**

Sheila Kay (Leavenworth, WA) Nested up in the Cascade Mountains, journeying from nurse midwifery to family planning work. ¡Oh Daughters! ah mate, who play and tolerate—my frolic of resonance, footsteps in healing Awake. conoleyfam@aol.com **p. 89**

Sheila A. Richards (Elkins, AR) I live in the Ozarks, surrounded by woods, rocks, cliffs and flowing water. Forms in nature speak to me, the clay becomes the medium, the translation, the bridge, the connection. sheilarichards@prodigy.net or www.sheilarichards.com **p. 112**

Silvie Jensen (Bronx, NY) is a singer, poet, gardener and traveler. She rides her bike along the mighty Hudson River, makes quilts, and practices music, poetry, and yoga. silviejensen@yahoo.com **p. 36**

Stacy Anne Murphy (Portland, OR) lives with her husband Jef at Columbia Ecovillage. She has two, wonderful, grown-up children, Ariel and Sky. She teaches visual and performing arts to kindergarten–8th graders for Portland Public Schools. **p. 55**

Stephanie Clifton (Makawao, HI) is a mixed artist living in Maui. Her varied palette reflects her awakening consciousness in life. Through play and experimentation, weaving together paints, salvaged materials, and personal imagery, she allows the art to create itself, and invites a symbolic story to unfold, revealing a multi-dimensional world. **p. 178**

Susan Baylies (Durham, NC) puts her artwork on T-shirts and also makes a lunar phase card available from www.snakeandsnake.com **p. 224**

Susan Byrne (Enniscorthy, Wexford, Ireland) Dreamer, believer in positive possibilities. **p. 103**

Susan Levitt (San Francisco, CA) is a Tarot Reader, Astrologer, and Feng Shui Consultant. She is the author of five books that are published in eight languages, including the best-selling *The Complete Tarot Kit.* www.SusanLevitt.com **p. 7, 25**

Susan M. Barron (Oakland, CA) is a photographer and writer in Northern California. Her work can be found at www.eightyfeettall.com **p. 137**

Tami Lynn Kent (Portland, OR) Mother, healer, writer—I have spent the past decade translating the healing wisdom and root medicine of the female form into a book for us to know our beauty—*Wild Feminine: Finding Power, Spirit and Joy in the Root of the Female Body.* www.wildfeminine.com **p. 80**

Teresa Wild (Cumberland, British Columbia, Canada) We are all born with a lifeline to the Divine Ocean of Creativity. I was fortunately given guides who told me early on that I was "talented", and I believed them! It is vital to humanity's future that we become elders who inspire our children to express their Divine Nature. www.sunmakerarts.com **p. 4, front cover**

Toni Truesdale (Pecos, NM) Artist / teacher / illustrator / muralist / writer / scholar. www.truesdaleart.com **p. 52, 80, 120, 202**

Vandana Shiva (Dehli, India) is a physicist, environmental activist and author. She has authored over 300 papers in leading scientific and technical journals. She is one of the leaders of the International Forum on Globalization, and a figure of the global solidarity movement known as the alter-globalization movement. **p. 117**

Victoria Christian (Ashland, OR) is a self-taught oil painter whose mission is to create images that deeply move her audience on emotional and spiritual levels.Her book and DVD *Feminine Mysticism in Art: Artists Envisioning the Divine Goddess,* features the work of over 75 artists. www.victoriachristian.com **p. 69**

Victoria Day (Columbia, MO) is a priestess, dancer, and activist who creates from her deep connection with the Divine and her belief that it is essentially important to work for peace. **p. 146, 177**

Wendy Brown-Báez (Minneapolis, MN) believes that creativity is transformative and writing is a spiritual practice. She is the creator of Writing Circles for Healing, a writing support group, and her collection of love poems, sensual and spiritual, *Ceremonies of the Spirit,* is available by her website, www.wendybrownbaez.com **p. 141**

Wendy Page (Victoria, British Columbia, Canada) To heal the planet we need to begin with ourselves and what the soul needs to be happy—nature and creativity—so try to bring more of that into your life. **p. 61**

Errata/Apologies

Even with so many skilled eyes and hands proofing the pages of **We'Moon**, we sometimes overlook some details. In the tradition of the Navajo, some mistakes ensure that unwanted spirits have a venue for escape. So, in the 2009 edition of **We'Moon**, the website listed for Betty LaDuke should be www.bettyladuke.com, and in the 2010 year at a glance, the month of December should start on a Wednesday, not on Tuesday...We appreciate hearing about mistakes that we've made, so if you find one, please email us at mothertongue@wemoon.ws.

We'Moon Ancestors Page

We honor we'moon who have gone between the worlds of life and death recently, beloved contributors to we'moon culture who continue to bless us from the other side. We appreciate receiving notice of their passing.

Del Martin (1921–2008) instigated and inspired the modern lesbian, gay and feminist movements. She was a co-founder in 1955 of Daughters of Bilitis, the first public lesbian rights organization in the US. Editor, writer, advocate, she and her activist colleague and life partner of 55 years, Phyllis Lyon, are revered icons of the struggle for justice for all people.

Eartha Kitt (1927–2008) rose from poverty to fame with her distinctive singing voice and her flamboyant style. She was an outspoken advocate for peace and equal rights, especially for gay people.

Miriam Makeba (1932–2008), honored as "Mama Afrika," took the music of her South African homeland and her gifts as a singer around the world. She was a fierce opponent of apartheid and was exiled from South Africa for 30 years.

Nancy Kassell (1944–2008) was a beloved member of the New Mexico land dyke community. She saved and raised horses, rescued countless dogs, devoted herself to the Earth and all creatures. She served on the non-profit Board for Outland lesbian land and was a strong supporter of the women's land community.

Odetta (1930–2008), folk/blues singer and human rights activist, inspired generations of musicians and music lovers. She was often called "the Voice of the Civil Rights Movement."

Ties that Bind *© Toni Truesdale 1998*

Paula Gunn Allen (1939–2008) American Indian writer, activist, scholar, Paula made important contributions to the women's spirituality movement, especially with her controversial studies about the centrality of "the Feminine" in Native American traditions. A respected poet and novelist, she anthologized writings by Native American women and chronicled contemporary Native American literature.

Please send info to help keep us updated on ones who have recently joined the ranks of We'Moon Ansisters!

Ceres, Pallas, Juno and Vesta: Emerging Planets for Cooperation in 2010

"Asteroids" are small planets, located between the inner, personal planets (Sun to Mars) that move more swiftly through the zodiac, and the outer, social and collective planets (Jupiter to Pluto) whose slower movements mark generational shifts. Among thousands of celestial bodies discovered in the "asteroid belt," Ceres, Pallas, Juno and Vesta are the largest—bridging personal and transpersonal aspects, as well as encouraging qualities that can move us past limiting patriarchal patterns into a more cooperative and sustainable future.

The asteroids/small planets are currently in the process of being redefined by the International Astronomical Union—which declassified Pluto as a planet in 2006, and in 2008 declassified it further from a dwarf planet to a "plutoid." Meanwhile, Ceres has been promoted to the status of a dwarf planet, and that may soon happen to other major asteroids, as well. What does this mean for us? Since the asteroids are generally seen to reflect "female qualities," this reclassification signifies a shift in consciousness towards a more feminist future. The asteroids function as trainers of a new vocabulary in astrology, providing language not only to transcend boundaries between the sexes, but also to overcome the split between mind and matter, between above and below, reconciling body/mind/heart and spirit. This is a time for coming back to earth, seeing things with fresh eyes, a kinder heart, opening space for new forms of partnership with more compassion and freedom. Ceres, Pallas, Juno and Vesta are faces of the Great Goddess who is reawakening in our consciousness now, quickening abilities so urgently needed to solve our many personal, social, ecological and political problems. With these small planets as symbols for diversity, we deepen our power of discernment.

Ceres (Goddess of corn and harvest) symbolizes our ability to nourish ourselves and others in a substantial and metaphoric way. As in the Greek myth of Demeter and Persephone, she helps us to let go and die, to understand mother-daughter dynamics, to re-parent ourselves and to educate by our senses.

Juno (partner of Jupiter) shows us what kind of committed partnership we long for, our own individual way to find fulfillment in personal and professional partnering. She wants partners to be team-workers, with equal rights and responsibilities.

Pallas (Athena) is a symbol for our creative intelligence and often hints at the sacrifice of women's own creativity or the lack of respect for it. She brings to the fore father-daughter issues, and points to difficulties in linking head, heart and womb.

Vesta (Vestal Virgin/fire priestess) reminds us first and foremost that we belong to ourselves and are allowed to do so! She shows us how to regenerate, to activate our passion, and how to carefully watch over our inner fire in the storms of everyday life.

With Pluto in Capricorn until 2024, the preservation of natural resources has top priority. Now is the time to challenge the devastating practices of global corporate agriculture and biotechnology that are de-constructing nature—from climate change to genetically modified foods and patents on traditional foods, medicines and seeds. The fundamental elements that support life on earth have to be reclaimed (clean air/water/earth/fire), providing renewable energy and food for body and soul (crop diversity, small rural and urban farming, organic/local/slow food). We can draw on the nourishing sign of Cancer (opposite Capricorn) to restore healthy, egalitarian, mutually supportive relationships, using Capricorn's focus on structure to maintain personal practices for well-being and hold clear boundaries for ourselves—as well as between corporations/church/and state—even as the structures of life-as-we-know-it dissolve in Pluto's process of deep transformation.

In 2010, Ceres, Palla, Vesta and Juno are all well aspected to help approach the challenging aspects between the social and collective planets. Ceres moves from Sagittarius into Capricorn back and forth between March and October, when she settles into Capricorn, meeting Pluto and the northern moon node head on. A serious food crisis, and continuing natural and man-made disasters are likely, along with rising respect for the earth and nature's awesome powers. Juno and Ceres stand in strong partnership, with a trine until the end of the year, offering the promise of real cooperation, and new forms of teamwork and parenting. Pluto and Saturn square off, calling people to responsibility to create and commit to new rules and structures. Towards the end of the year, Juno, Ceres and Pallas all side with Saturn in opposing Jupiter/Uranus whose conjunction is a freewheeling wild card. Challenges and opportunities abound for quantum leaps towards freedom, especially in the use of media, sharing knowledge and skills worldwide. Vesta, well-centered in herself, backs up Ceres and Juno through supportive sextiles, encouraging each to be who she is amidst the dangers and possibilities of new birth.

Spiral Dance
© Durga Bernhard 1988

Beate Metz © Mother Tongue Ink 2009

2010 Asteroid Ephemeris

2010	Ceres * 1	Pallas 2	Juno ** 3	Vesta * 4
JAN 1	4♐33.7	7♏46.9	4♈25.7	6♍37.5
11	8 31.7	11 10.7	8 34.1	6R28.2
21	12 21.3	14 16.8	13 03.9	5 31.7
31	16 00.6	17 01.8	17 51.6	3 50.9
FEB 10	19 27.9	19 21.8	22 53.7	1 34.7
20	22 41.2	21 11.7	28 07.9	28♌58.9
MAR 2	25 37.9	22 26.4	3♉31.9	26 24.2
12	28 15.4	23 00.4	9 03.4	24 10.8
22	0♑30.5	22R48.5	14 41.0	22 34.4
APR 1	2 19.8	21 47.9	20 22.8	21 44.0
11	3 39.7	19 59.5	26 07.6	21D41.4
21	4 26.5	17 30.2	1♊54.1	22 24.9
MAY 1	4R37.4	14 34.7	7 41.2	23 49.9
11	4 10.8	11 32.5	13 28.0	25 50.8
21	3 07.3	8 44.9	19 13.6	28 22.8
31	1 31.4	6 29.9	24 57.2	1♍21.0
JUN 10	29♐31.6	4 57.9	0♋38.1	4 41.2
20	27 19.9	4 13.2	6 15.8	8 20.2
30	25 10.8	4D14.8	11 49.6	12 15.1
JUL 10	23 17.5	4 58.2	17 19.0	16 23.5
20	21 51.0	6 18.7	22 43.8	20 43.7
30	20 58.0	8 10.5	28 03.1	25 13.8
AUG 9	20D40.7	10 28.7	3♌16.7	29 52.8
19	20 59.2	13 09.0	8 24.1	4♎39.5
29	21 51.1	16 07.6	13 24.6	9 32.7
SEP 8	23 12.9	19 21.3	18 17.7	14 31.9
18	25 01.3	22 47.7	23 02.6	19 36.3
28	27 12.7	26 24.3	27 38.4	24 44.9
OCT 8	29 43.7	0♐09.4	2♍04.1	29 57.5
18	2♑31.8	4 01.4	6 18.5	5♏13.3
28	5 34.2	7 58.6	10 19.9	10 31.6
NOV 7	8 48.6	11 59.9	14 06.6	15 52.0
17	12 13.4	16 04.2	17 36.3	21 13.8
27	15 46.6	20 10.1	20 46.5	26 36.4
DEC 7	19 26.7	24 16.9	23 33.9	1♐59.1
17	23 12.5	28 23.4	25 54.9	7 21.2
27	27 02.6	2♑28.5	27 45.6	12 41.9
JAN 6	0♒56.0	6♑31.3	29♍01.6	18♐00.7
JAN 1	17S07.9	01S01.5	07S12.6	14N06.8
21	18 42.0	00N51.4	03 57.7	15 53.4
FEB 10	19 49.6	03 59.9	00 18.4	18 35.7
MAR 2	20 36.8	08 24.7	03N26.2	21 10.4
22	21 13.0	13 48.2	06 59.0	22 32.1
APR 11	21 50.0	19 22.0	10 05.1	22 25.1
MAY 1	22 38.9	23 51.0	12 32.0	21 07.3
21	23 44.4	26 10.0	14 11.2	18 57.9
JUN 10	24 57.3	26 05.3	14 57.9	16 09.6
30	25 59.6	24 11.0	14 52.3	12 50.6
JUL 20	26 43.0	21 14.0	13 58.4	09 08.1
AUG 9	27 14.6	17 51.2	12 23.5	05 09.2
29	27 42.5	14 26.6	10 17.2	01 01.2
SEP 18	28 07.2	11 15.8	07 49.9	03S07.9
OCT 8	28 23.9	08 29.0	05 13.1	07 09.3
28	28 25.9	06 13.7	02 38.5	10 54.0
NOV 17	28 07.5	04 35.0	00 19.0	14 12.7
DEC 7	27 25.1	03 36.5	01S31.2	16 56.7
27	26S17.7	03N19.8	02S35.4	18S58.9

2010	Psyche 16	Eros ** 433	Lilith 1181	Toro ** 1685
JAN 1	2♓05.9	25♓02.8	27♍47.0	7♏23.1
11	6 13.7	1♈30.8	28 47.1	11 40.8
21	10 30.0	8 24.1	29R07.6	15 34.7
31	14 53.2	15 40.3	28 46.3	19 01.5
FEB 10	19 21.9	23 17.4	27 43.6	21 57.2
20	23 55.1	1♉14.0	26 03.5	24 15.7
MAR 2	28 31.6	9 28.0	23 55.6	25 49.8
12	3♈10.5	17 57.6	21 33.7	26 31.3
22	7 50.9	26 41.1	19 13.9	26R10.1
APR 1	12 31.9	5♊36.1	17 11.9	24 38.4
11	17 12.8	14 40.4	15 38.8	21 52.9
21	21 52.9	23 52.1	14 41.4	18 00.4
MAY 1	26 31.5	3♋08.3	14 21.9	13 23.8
11	1♉07.8	12 26.5	14D38.8	8 38.1
21	5 41.3	21 44.7	15 29.2	4 21.4
31	10 11.0	1♌00.0	16 49.0	1 02.9
JUN 10	14 36.2	10 10.0	18 34.1	28♎54.8
20	18 56.0	19 13.1	20 40.8	27 58.1
30	23 09.3	28 06.8	23 05.5	28D06.0
JUL 10	27 15.1	6♍49.9	25 45.4	29 09.1
20	1♊11.9	15 21.4	28 38.1	0♏58.9
30	4 58.1	23 40.3	1♎41.3	3 27.8
AUG 9	8 31.9	1♎46.5	4 53.2	6 29.5
19	11 50.8	9 40.2	8 12.4	9 59.8
29	14 52.2	17 21.3	11 37.5	13 55.1
SEP 8	17 33.1	24 50.7	15 07.4	18 12.9
18	19 49.6	2♏09.2	18 41.0	22 52.0
28	21 37.6	9 17.1	22 17.2	27 51.3
OCT 8	22 52.7	16 15.7	25 55.3	3♐10.7
18	23 30.7	23 05.7	29 34.4	8 50.8
28	23R28.5	29 47.7	3♏13.5	14 52.2
NOV 7	22 44.9	6♐22.8	6 51.7	21 16.6
17	21 22.8	12 51.5	10 28.1	28 05.9
27	19 30.1	19 14.4	14 01.5	5♑22.8
DEC 7	17 19.5	25 32.2	17 31.0	13 10.5
17	15 07.5	1♑45.3	20 55.2	21 32.8
27	13 10.6	7 54.2	24 12.7	0♒33.6
JAN 6	11♊41.9	13♑59.3	27♏22.1	10♒17.3
JAN 1	11S31.7	09N02.1	04S58.3	21S53.6
21	08 33.9	12 46.0	06 19.6	25 29.5
FEB 10	05 16.2	16 45.5	06 32.5	28 30.0
MAR 2	01 46.3	20 21.4	05 31.0	30 55.7
22	01N47.8	22 46.1	03 39.0	32 34.8
APR 11	05 18.2	23 14.7	01 45.5	32 43.9
MAY 1	08 37.1	21 23.3	00 31.3	30 17.1
21	11 37.8	17 20.7	00 11.0	25 37.9
JUN 10	14 14.0	11 41.8	00 41.6	21 08.8
30	16 21.1	05 10.8	01 53.8	18 23.1
JUL 20	17 56.1	01S32.9	03 37.8	17 22.4
AUG 9	18 58.2	07 59.8	05 44.5	17 36.4
29	19 29.3	13 49.0	08 06.2	18 34.7
SEP 18	19 34.4	18 46.2	10 35.9	19 51.0
OCT 8	19 20.8	22 40.8	13 07.0	21 01.7
28	18 57.1	25 25.4	15 33.7	21 42.4
NOV 17	18 31.0	26 55.2	17 50.5	21 26.3
DEC 7	18 08.6	27 08.9	19 52.7	19 43.0
27	17N58.2	26S09.4	21S36.6	16S01.6

2010	Sappho 80	Amor ** 1221	Pandora 55	Icarus 1566
JAN 1	9♏58.1	5♒38.0	11♓35.5	9♑55.3
11	13 12.5	11 08.2	15 49.7	15 02.9
21	16 12.9	16 28.3	20 13.9	19 55.0
31	18 56.5	21 38.9	24 46.2	24 33.9
FEB 10	21 19.9	26 40.6	29 25.0	29 01.5
20	23 19.1	1♓33.7	4♈09.0	3♒18.9
MAR 2	24 49.7	6 18.3	8 57.0	7 26.6
12	25 47.1	10 54.6	13 47.8	11 25.3
22	26R06.5	15 22.4	18 40.7	15 14.7
APR 1	25 44.5	19 41.5	23 34.7	18 54.5
11	24 39.6	23 51.7	28 29.0	22 24.2
21	22 54.0	27 52.5	3♉23.1	25 42.4
MAY 1	20 36.2	1♈43.1	8 16.2	28 47.5
11	17 59.7	5 22.9	13 07.7	1♓37.3
21	15 22.1	8 50.7	17 57.0	4 08.1
31	13 02.2	12 05.2	22 43.5	6 15.0
JUN 10	11 14.3	15 04.8	27 26.6	7 50.9
20	10 07.8	17 47.3	2♊05.7	8 44.3
30	9D46.7	20 10.2	6 39.9	8R39.0
JUL 10	10 09.8	22 10.6	11 08.5	7 08.7
20	11 14.6	23 44.6	15 30.5	3 32.5
30	12 56.5	24 48.1	19 44.9	26♒53.1
AUG 9	15 11.0	25 16.8	23 50.4	16 07.9
19	17 54.2	25R06.1	27 45.5	1 21.4
29	21 02.1	24 12.8	1♋28.2	15♑15.9
SEP 8	24 31.8	22 35.8	4 56.7	1 31.5
18	28 20.6	20 18.4	8 08.0	21♐27.8
28	2♐26.1	17 29.6	10 59.1	14 08.3
OCT 8	6 46.6	14 23.8	13 26.6	7 57.3
18	11 20.6	11 19.4	15 25.9	1 05.7
28	16 06.5	8 34.6	16 52.9	21♏09.6
NOV 7	21 03.5	6 23.4	17 42.8	8 27.7
17	26 10.6	4 54.4	17R51.6	17D00.6
27	1♑26.7	4 10.3	17 17.6	1♐12.1
DEC 7	6 51.1	4D09.5	16 01.8	12 48.1
17	12 23.2	4 48.6	14 10.6	21 53.5
27	18 02.1	6 02.8	11 56.2	29 31.9
JAN 6	23♑47.3	7♈47.2	9♋34.4	6♑12.4
JAN 1	17S00.2	14S20.7	08S00.3	25S58.9
21	18 34.2	12 13.0	04 03.2	26 00.4
FEB 10	19 34.3	09 39.5	00N06.6	25 28.4
MAR 2	19 54.9	06 51.9	04 21.9	24 38.9
22	19 29.5	04 00.2	08 35.2	23 45.9
APR 11	18 11.7	01 12.9	12 38.7	23 04.8
MAY 1	16 02.9	01N22.1	16 25.4	22 54.2
21	13 30.8	03 37.6	19 48.7	23 40.9
JUN 10	11 26.5	05 25.7	22 43.1	26 07.4
30	10 26.8	06 38.2	25 05.3	31 25.7
JUL 20	10 34.3	07 05.2	26 53.8	41 26.7
AUG 9	11 32.0	06 34.9	28 10.8	57 03.3
29	12 59.0	04 56.8	29 01.7	69 10.2
SEP 18	14 36.0	02 12.2	29 36.0	63 04.4
OCT 8	16 06.1	01S06.2	30 06.9	51 25.3
28	17 14.5	03 55.6	30 49.0	33 52.9
NOV 17	17 48.1	05 27.1	31 52.4	12 34.0
DEC 7	17 36.6	05 33.7	33 10.2	19 13.4
27	16S33.2	04S33.4	34N10.0	22S35.1

2010	Diana (78	Hidalgo 944	Urania 30	Chiron 2060
JAN 1	7♓17.8	0♐04.6	25♏45.1	23♒06.9
11	10 29.8	1 04.8	29 32.2	23 42.7
21	13 53.8	1 57.3	3♐10.1	24 21.4
31	17 27.8	2 40.9	6 36.8	25 02.1
FEB 10	21 10.3	3 14.2	9 50.4	25 44.1
20	25 00.0	3 36.2	12 47.9	26 26.5
MAR 2	28 55.6	3 45.9	15 26.5	27 08.3
12	2♈56.1	3R42.7	17 42.8	27 48.8
22	7 00.7	3 26.3	19 32.6	28 27.2
APR 1	11 08.5	2 57.1	20 51.9	29 02.6
11	15 18.7	2 15.8	21 36.3	29 34.4
21	19 30.8	1 24.0	21R41.8	0♓01.8
MAY 1	23 43.9	0 23.7	21 06.3	0 24.4
11	27 57.7	29♏17.6	19 50.1	0 41.7
21	2♉11.5	28 08.8	17 58.0	0 53.3
31	6 24.5	27 00.6	15 40.6	0 58.9
JUN 10	10 36.2	25 55.9	13 12.2	0R58.5
20	14 45.8	24 57.8	10 50.3	0 52.1
30	18 52.3	24 08.7	8 50.9	0 40.0
JUL 10	22 55.0	23 30.1	7 25.4	0 22.8
20	26 52.5	23 03.5	6 40.7	0 00.9
30	0♊43.3	22 49.3	6D38.5	29♒35.4
AUG 9	4 25.8	22D47.7	7 17.0	29 07.3
19	7 57.6	22 58.3	8 33.1	28 37.5
29	11 16.2	23 20.5	10 22.5	28 07.6
SEP 8	14 18.3	23 53.4	12 41.0	27 38.5
18	16 59.8	24 36.1	15 24.9	27 11.7
28	19 16.1	25 27.3	18 30.5	26 48.2
OCT 8	21 01.6	26 25.9	21 54.9	26 29.0
18	22 10.1	27 30.7	25 35.7	26 14.9
28	22 36.2	28 40.4	29 30.6	26 06.5
NOV 7	22R15.2	29 53.9	3♑37.7	26D04.1
17	21 06.6	1♐09.6	7 55.7	26 08.0
27	19 16.3	2 26.5	12 22.9	26 18.1
DEC 7	16 57.5	3 43.1	16 58.3	26 34.1
17	14 31.2	4 58.0	21 40.8	26 55.6
27	12 20.7	6 10.0	26 29.4	27 22.2
JAN 6	10♊45.6	7♐17.7	1♒23.3	27♒53.1
JAN 1	06S22.9	44S31.1	20S51.3	08S09.8
21	03 39.6	45 51.3	22 34.3	07 50.3
FEB 10	00 35.8	47 13.6	23 51.3	07 25.6
MAR 2	02N43.5	48 32.7	24 45.0	06 57.9
22	06 13.2	49 41.1	25 20.2	06 29.5
APR 11	09 47.8	50 29.6	25 42.1	06 03.0
MAY 1	13 22.1	50 49.9	25 51.9	05 40.7
21	16 51.3	50 38.7	25 42.7	05 24.6
JUN 10	20 10.5	50 00.1	25 06.1	05 16.5
30	23 15.9	49 05.2	24 12.0	05 17.2
JUL 20	26 04.4	48 07.0	23 27.5	05 26.4
AUG 9	28 34.7	47 17.0	23 10.4	05 42.7
29	30 47.9	46 42.3	23 18.7	06 03.6
SEP 18	32 47.8	46 26.2	23 39.7	06 25.7
OCT 8	34 39.9	46 29.3	23 58.3	06 45.7
28	36 24.8	46 50.3	24 00.5	07 00.4
NOV 17	37 44.2	47 27.4	23 35.2	07 07.8
DEC 7	37 54.3	48 18.2	22 34.8	07 06.9
27	36N31.1	49S20.8	20S55.2	06S57.4

Giving the positions of asteroids every ten days in LONGITUDE at 00:00 GMT

2010 Planetary Ephemeris (Noon GMT*)

LONGITUDE — JANUARY 2010

Day	Sid.Time	☉	0 hr ☽	Noon ☽	True ☊	☿	♀	♂	♃	♄	♅	♆	♇
1 F	18 44 8	10♑57 35	13♋13 58	20♋45 44	21♑ 5.0	18♑28.2	8♑28.7	18♌44.3	26♒27.6	4♎31.1	23♓ 6.2	24♒35.8	3♑19.6
2 Sa	18 48 5	11 58 43	28 18 12	5♌50 14	21D 5.3	17R 18.8	9 44.2	18R 34.2	26 39.8	4 32.3	23 7.7	24 37.6	3 21.8
3 Su	18 52 1	12 59 51	13♌20 46	20 48 48	21 5.9	16 3.0	10 59.7	18 23.4	26 52.1	4 33.5	23 9.3	24 39.4	3 23.9
4 M	18 55 58	14 0 59	28 13 26	5♍33 54	21 6.5	14 43.2	12 15.2	18 11.7	27 4.5	4 34.6	23 11.0	24 41.2	3 26.1
5 Tu	18 59 54	15 2 8	12♍49 37	20 0 7	21 7.1	13 22.0	13 30.7	17 59.2	27 17.0	4 35.5	23 12.7	24 43.0	3 28.2
6 W	19 3 51	16 3 16	27 5 6	4♎ 4 22	21 7.5	12 2.1	14 46.1	17 45.9	27 29.5	4 36.3	23 14.4	24 44.9	3 30.4
7 Th	19 7 48	17 4 25	10♎57 54	17 45 46	21R 7.6	10 46.0	16 1.6	17 31.8	27 42.1	4 37.1	23 16.2	24 46.8	3 32.5
8 F	19 11 44	18 5 34	24 28 6	1♏ 5 8	21 7.5	9 35.7	17 17.1	17 16.9	27 54.8	4 37.7	23 18.0	24 48.7	3 34.6
9 Sa	19 15 41	19 6 43	7♏37 8	14 4 25	21 7.3	8 32.9	18 32.6	17 1.4	28 7.6	4 38.2	23 19.9	24 50.6	3 36.8
10 Su	19 19 37	20 7 52	20 27 20	26 46 12	21 7.2	7 38.9	19 48.1	16 45.0	28 20.4	4 38.6	23 21.8	24 52.6	3 38.9
11 M	19 23 34	21 9 1	3♐ 1 22	9♐13 11	21D 7.1	6 54.4	21 3.6	16 28.0	28 33.3	4 38.9	23 23.8	24 54.5	3 41.0
12 Tu	19 27 30	22 10 11	15 21 58	21 28 3	21 7.2	6 19.7	22 19.1	16 10.2	28 46.3	4 39.1	23 25.8	24 56.5	3 43.1
13 W	19 31 27	23 11 19	27 31 42	3♑33 14	21 7.3	5 54.9	23 34.5	15 51.8	28 59.3	4R 39.2	23 27.8	24 58.5	3 45.2
14 Th	19 35 23	24 12 28	9♑32 54	15 30 58	21 7.5	5 39.6	24 50.0	15 32.8	29 12.4	4 39.1	23 29.9	25 0.5	3 47.2
15 F	19 39 20	25 13 36	21 27 41	27 23 18	21R 7.5	5D 33.4	26 5.5	15 13.2	29 25.6	4 39.0	23 32.1	25 2.5	3 49.3
16 Sa	19 43 17	26 14 44	3♒18 3	9♒12 13	21 7.2	5 35.9	27 20.9	14 52.9	29 38.8	4 38.7	23 34.2	25 4.6	3 51.4
17 Su	19 47 13	27 15 51	15 6 3	20 59 49	21 6.6	5 46.3	28 36.4	14 32.2	29 52.1	4 38.3	23 36.4	25 6.6	3 53.4
18 M	19 51 10	28 16 58	26 53 51	2♓48 27	21 5.7	6 4.1	29 51.8	14 10.9	0♓ 5.5	4 37.9	23 38.7	25 8.7	3 55.4
19 Tu	19 55 6	29 18 3	8♓43 58	14 40 46	21 4.5	6 28.7	1♒ 7.3	13 49.2	0 18.9	4 37.3	23 41.0	25 10.8	3 57.5
20 W	19 59 3	0♒19 8	20 39 16	26 39 53	21 3.3	6 59.3	2 22.7	13 27.0	0 32.3	4 36.6	23 43.3	25 12.9	3 59.5
21 Th	20 2 59	1 20 12	2♈43 4	8♈49 18	21 2.1	7 35.5	3 38.1	13 4.4	0 45.8	4 35.8	23 45.7	25 15.0	4 1.5
22 F	20 6 56	2 21 16	14 59 4	21 12 53	21 1.3	8 16.6	4 53.5	12 41.6	0 59.4	4 34.9	23 48.1	25 17.2	4 3.4
23 Sa	20 10 52	3 22 18	27 31 14	3♉54 38	21D 1.1	9 2.4	6 8.9	12 18.4	1 13.0	4 33.9	23 50.5	25 19.3	4 5.4
24 Su	20 14 49	4 23 19	10♉23 31	16 58 20	21 1.4	9 52.2	7 24.3	11 54.9	1 26.7	4 32.7	23 53.0	25 21.5	4 7.3
25 M	20 18 46	5 24 19	23 39 27	0♊27 9	21 2.3	10 45.7	8 39.7	11 31.3	1 40.4	4 31.5	23 55.5	25 23.6	4 9.3
26 Tu	20 22 42	6 25 19	7♊21 37	14 22 54	21 3.5	11 42.5	9 55.1	11 7.5	1 54.2	4 30.2	23 58.0	25 25.8	4 11.2
27 W	20 26 39	7 26 17	21 30 56	28 45 28	21 4.7	12 42.4	11 10.4	10 43.6	2 8.0	4 28.8	24 0.6	25 28.0	4 13.1
28 Th	20 30 35	8 27 14	6♋ 6 2	13♋32 3	21 5.4	13 45.1	12 25.8	10 19.6	2 21.8	4 27.2	24 3.2	25 30.2	4 15.0
29 F	20 34 32	9 28 10	21 2 41	28 36 58	21R 5.4	14 50.3	13 41.1	9 55.5	2 35.7	4 25.6	24 5.9	25 32.4	4 16.9
30 Sa	20 38 28	10 29 5	6♌13 47	13♌51 53	21 4.4	15 57.7	14 56.4	9 31.5	2 49.6	4 23.9	24 8.5	25 34.6	4 18.7
31 Su	20 42 25	11 29 59	21 30 1	29 6 50	21 2.4	17 7.3	16 11.7	9 7.6	3 3.6	4 22.0	24 11.2	25 36.8	4 20.5

LONGITUDE — FEBRUARY 2010

Day	Sid.Time	☉	0 hr ☽	Noon ☽	True ☊	☿	♀	♂	♃	♄	♅	♆	♇
1 M	20 46 22	12♒30 52	6♍41 6	14♍11 38	20♑59.6	18♑18.8	17♒27.0	8♌43.8	3♓17.6	4♎20.1	24♓14.0	25♒39.0	4♑22.4
2 Tu	20 50 18	13 31 44	21 37 26	28 57 37	20R 56.5	19 32.1	18 42.3	8R 20.1	3 31.6	4R 18.0	24 16.8	25 41.3	4 24.2
3 W	20 54 15	14 32 35	6♎11 32	13♎18 42	20 53.6	20 47.0	19 57.6	7 56.6	3 45.7	4 15.9	24 19.5	25 43.5	4 25.9
4 Th	20 58 11	15 33 25	20 18 52	27 11 55	20 51.3	22 3.5	21 12.9	7 33.4	3 59.8	4 13.7	24 22.4	25 45.8	4 27.7
5 F	21 2 8	16 34 15	3♏57 57	10♏37 10	20 50.1	23 21.5	22 28.1	7 10.4	4 13.9	4 11.3	24 25.2	25 48.0	4 29.4
6 Sa	21 6 4	17 35 4	17 9 53	23 36 31	20D 50.1	24 40.8	23 43.4	6 47.8	4 28.1	4 8.9	24 28.1	25 50.3	4 31.1
7 Su	21 10 1	18 35 52	29 57 34	6♐13 32	20 51.2	26 1.3	24 58.6	6 25.5	4 42.3	4 6.4	24 31.0	25 52.5	4 32.8
8 M	21 13 57	19 36 38	12♐24 59	18 32 28	20 52.9	27 23.1	26 13.8	6 3.6	4 56.5	4 3.8	24 34.0	25 54.8	4 34.5
9 Tu	21 17 54	20 37 24	24 36 31	0♑37 42	20 54.7	28 46.1	27 29.0	5 42.2	5 10.8	4 1.1	24 36.9	25 57.1	4 36.2
10 W	21 21 51	21 38 9	6♑36 31	12 33 27	20 56.0	0♒10.2	28 44.2	5 21.3	5 25.1	3 58.3	24 39.9	25 59.4	4 37.8
11 Th	21 25 47	22 38 53	18 28 57	24 23 26	20R 56.3	1 35.3	29 59.4	5 0.9	5 39.4	3 55.4	24 42.9	26 1.6	4 39.4
12 F	21 29 44	23 39 35	0♒17 17	6♒10 52	20 55.1	3 1.5	1♓14.6	4 41.0	5 53.7	3 52.5	24 46.0	26 3.9	4 41.0
13 Sa	21 33 40	24 40 16	12 4 28	17 58 23	20 52.1	4 28.7	2 29.8	4 21.7	6 8.0	3 49.4	24 49.0	26 6.2	4 42.6
14 Su	21 37 37	25 40 56	23 52 52	29 48 10	20 47.3	5 56.9	3 44.9	4 3.1	6 22.4	3 46.3	24 52.1	26 8.5	4 44.1
15 M	21 41 33	26 41 34	5♓44 29	11♓42 2	20 41.1	7 26.0	5 0.0	3 45.1	6 36.8	3 43.0	24 55.2	26 10.8	4 45.6
16 Tu	21 45 30	27 42 11	17 41 2	23 41 40	20 34.0	8 56.1	6 15.2	3 27.7	6 51.2	3 39.7	24 58.3	26 13.0	4 47.1
17 W	21 49 26	28 42 46	29 44 10	5♈48 47	20 26.8	10 27.1	7 30.2	3 11.0	7 5.6	3 36.4	25 1.5	26 15.3	4 48.6
18 Th	21 53 23	29 43 19	11♈55 43	18 5 17	20 20.0	11 59.1	8 45.3	2 55.1	7 20.0	3 32.9	25 4.7	26 17.6	4 50.0
19 F	21 57 19	0♓43 51	24 17 45	0♉33 27	20 14.6	13 32.0	10 0.4	2 39.8	7 34.5	3 29.4	25 7.8	26 19.9	4 51.4
20 Sa	22 1 16	1 44 21	6♉52 42	13 15 53	20 10.9	15 5.9	11 15.4	2 25.3	7 48.9	3 25.8	25 11.1	26 22.2	4 52.8
21 Su	22 5 13	2 44 49	19 43 22	26 15 32	20 9.1	16 40.7	12 30.4	2 11.6	8 3.4	3 22.1	25 14.3	26 24.4	4 54.2
22 M	22 9 9	3 45 15	2♊52 43	9♊35 16	20D 9.1	18 16.4	13 45.4	1 58.7	8 17.9	3 18.4	25 17.5	26 26.7	4 55.5
23 Tu	22 13 6	4 45 40	16 23 29	23 17 37	20 10.1	19 53.1	15 0.4	1 46.5	8 32.4	3 14.6	25 20.8	26 29.0	4 56.8
24 W	22 17 2	5 46 2	0♋17 46	7♋23 58	20 11.4	21 30.7	16 15.3	1 35.1	8 46.9	3 10.7	25 24.0	26 31.2	4 58.1
25 Th	22 20 59	6 46 23	14 36 8	21 53 59	20R 11.9	23 9.3	17 30.3	1 24.5	9 1.4	3 6.8	25 27.3	26 33.5	4 59.4
26 F	22 24 55	7 46 41	29 17 3	6♌44 43	20 10.8	24 48.9	18 45.2	1 14.6	9 15.8	3 2.8	25 30.6	26 35.7	5 0.6
27 Sa	22 28 52	8 46 58	14♌16 8	21 50 19	20 7.5	26 29.5	20 0.0	1 5.6	9 30.3	2 58.8	25 33.9	26 38.0	5 1.8
28 Su	22 32 48	9 47 12	29 26 8	7♍ 2 18	20 1.9	28 11.0	21 14.9	0 57.3	9 44.8	2 54.6	25 37.3	26 40.2	5 3.0

Astro Data (Dy Hr Mn)

	Dy Hr Mn
☽0S	5 11:10
♄ R	13 15:57
☿ D	15 16:53
☽0N	19 21:43
♄□♇	31 21:28
☽0S	1 20:40
♃⚻♄	5 8:15
♃✶♇	6 17:52
☽0N	16 3:59

Planet Ingress (Dy Hr Mn)

		Dy Hr Mn
♀	♒	18 14:36
♃	♓	18 2:11
☉	♒	20 4:29
☿	♒	10 9:07
♀	♓	11 12:11
☉	♓	18 18:37

Last Aspect / ☽ Ingress (January)

Last Aspect Dy Hr Mn			☽ Ingress	Dy Hr Mn
1 15:44	♅	△	♌	2 2:42
3 21:56	♃	☍	♍	4 2:54
5 17:26	♅	☍	♎	6 4:59
8 6:08	♃	△	♏	8 10:01
10 15:03	♃	□	♐	10 18:11
13 2:44	♃	✶	♑	13 4:55
15 9:04	♀	☌	♒	15 17:18
17 20:24	♆	☌	♓	18 6:18
20 6:07	♅	☌	♈	20 18:37
22 19:47	♆	✶	♉	23 4:41
25 3:04	♆	□	♊	25 11:12
27 6:33	♆	△	♋	27 14:02
29 4:50	♅	△	♌	29 14:11
31 6:28	♆	☍	♍	31 13:24

Last Aspect / ☽ Ingress (February)

Last Aspect Dy Hr Mn			☽ Ingress	Dy Hr Mn
2 4:18	♅	☍	♎	2 13:43
4 9:28	♆	△	♏	4 16:57
6 16:12	♆	□	♐	7 0:05
9 4:59	♀	✶	♑	9 10:45
11 12:40	♅	✶	♒	11 23:25
14 4:34	♆	☌	♓	14 12:24
16 14:33	♅	☌	♈	17 0:31
19 3:53	♆	✶	♉	19 10:56
21 12:16	♆	□	♊	21 18:48
23 17:30	♆	△	♋	23 23:30
25 17:49	♅	△	♌	26 1:09
27 20:16	☿	☍	♍	28 0:53

☽ Phases & Eclipses (Dy Hr Mn)

Dy Hr Mn		
7 10:41	☾	17♎01
15 7:12	●	25♑01
15 7:07:40	● A	11'07"
23 10:54	☽	3♉20
30 6:19	○	10♌15
5 23:50	☾	17♏04
14 2:52	●	25♒18
22 0:43	☽	3♊17
28 16:39	○	9♍59

Astro Data

1 JANUARY 2010
Julian Day # 40178
Galactic Ctr 26♐59.4
SVP 05♓06'56"
Obliquity 23°26'20"
⚷ Chiron 23♒08.6
☽ Mean ☊ 21♑36.5

1 FEBRUARY 2010
Julian Day # 40209
Galactic Ctr 26♐59.4
SVP 05♓06'50"
Obliquity 23°26'20"
⚷ Chiron 25♒08.4
☽ Mean ☊ 19♑58.0

*Giving the positions of planets daily at noon, in LONGITUDE Greenwich Mean Time (UT)
Each planet's retrograde period is shaded gray.

2010 Planetary Ephemeris (Noon GMT*)

MARCH 2010 — LONGITUDE

Day	Sid.Time	☉	0 hr ☽	Noon ☽	True ☊	☿	♀	♂	♃	♄	♅	♆	♇
1 M	22 36 45	10♓47 25	14♍37 32	22♍10 30	19♑54.6	29♒53.6	22♓29.7	0♌49.9	9♓59.3	2♎50.5	25♓40.6	26♒42.5	5♑ 4.1
2 Tu	22 40 42	11 47 36	29 39 58	7♎ 4 47	19R 46.2	1♓37.3	23 44.5	0R 43.2	10 13.8	2R 46.3	25 43.9	26 44.7	5 5.2
3 W	22 44 38	12 47 46	14♎23 59	21 36 47	19 38.0	3 22.0	24 59.3	0 37.3	10 28.3	2 42.0	25 47.3	26 46.9	5 6.3
4 Th	22 48 35	13 47 54	28 42 37	5♏41 7	19 31.0	5 7.7	26 14.1	0 32.2	10 42.8	2 37.7	25 50.7	26 49.1	5 7.4
5 F	22 52 31	14 48 0	12♏32 8	19 15 43	19 25.8	6 54.5	27 28.8	0 27.9	10 57.3	2 33.4	25 54.0	26 51.3	5 8.4
6 Sa	22 56 28	15 48 5	25 52 4	2♐21 32	19 22.7	8 42.5	28 43.5	0 24.3	11 11.8	2 29.0	25 57.4	26 53.5	5 9.4
7 Su	23 0 24	16 48 9	8♐44 35	15 1 46	19D 21.7	10 31.5	29 58.2	0 21.5	11 26.2	2 24.5	26 0.8	26 55.7	5 10.4
8 M	23 4 21	17 48 10	21 13 41	27 20 59	19 22.0	12 21.6	1♈12.9	0 19.5	11 40.7	2 20.1	26 4.2	26 57.8	5 11.4
9 Tu	23 8 17	18 48 11	3♑24 20	9♑24 25	19 22.9	14 12.8	2 27.5	0 18.2	11 55.2	2 15.6	26 7.6	26 60.0	5 12.3
10 W	23 12 14	19 48 9	15 21 52	21 17 20	19R 23.2	16 5.1	3 42.2	0D 17.7	12 9.6	2 11.0	26 11.1	27 2.1	5 13.2
11 Th	23 16 11	20 48 6	27 11 26	3♒ 4 45	19 22.1	17 58.4	4 56.8	0 17.9	12 24.0	2 6.5	26 14.5	27 4.3	5 14.0
12 F	23 20 7	21 48 1	8♒57 47	14 51 3	19 18.8	19 52.8	6 11.4	0 18.9	12 38.4	2 1.9	26 17.9	27 6.4	5 14.8
13 Sa	23 24 4	22 47 54	20 44 58	26 39 56	19 12.8	21 48.3	7 25.9	0 20.5	12 52.8	1 57.2	26 21.3	27 8.5	5 15.6
14 Su	23 28 0	23 47 45	2♓36 16	8♓34 15	19 4.1	23 44.7	8 40.4	0 22.9	13 7.2	1 52.6	26 24.7	27 10.6	5 16.4
15 M	23 31 57	24 47 35	14 34 7	20 36 4	18 53.1	25 42.0	9 54.9	0 26.0	13 21.6	1 47.9	26 28.2	27 12.7	5 17.1
16 Tu	23 35 53	25 47 22	26 40 15	2♈46 46	18 40.7	27 40.2	11 9.4	0 29.7	13 35.9	1 43.3	26 31.6	27 14.7	5 17.8
17 W	23 39 50	26 47 8	8♈55 43	15 7 10	18 27.9	29 39.1	12 23.9	0 34.2	13 50.3	1 38.6	26 35.0	27 16.8	5 18.5
18 Th	23 43 46	27 46 51	21 21 12	27 37 51	18 15.8	1♈38.6	13 38.3	0 39.3	14 4.6	1 33.8	26 38.5	27 18.8	5 19.1
19 F	23 47 43	28 46 33	3♉57 14	10♉19 24	18 5.5	3 38.6	14 52.7	0 45.1	14 18.9	1 29.1	26 41.9	27 20.8	5 19.7
20 Sa	23 51 40	29 46 12	16 44 29	23 12 37	17 57.8	5 38.8	16 7.0	0 51.6	14 33.1	1 24.4	26 45.3	27 22.9	5 20.3
21 Su	23 55 36	0♈45 49	29 43 59	6♊18 44	17 52.9	7 39.2	17 21.3	0 58.7	14 47.3	1 19.7	26 48.8	27 24.8	5 20.9
22 M	23 59 33	1 45 24	12♊57 7	19 39 21	17 50.6	9 39.4	18 35.6	1 6.4	15 1.6	1 15.0	26 52.2	27 26.8	5 21.4
23 Tu	0 3 29	2 44 56	26 25 39	3♋16 13	17D 50.1	11 39.2	19 49.9	1 14.7	15 15.7	1 10.2	26 55.6	27 28.8	5 21.8
24 W	0 7 26	3 44 26	10♋11 14	17 10 49	17R 50.3	13 38.3	21 4.1	1 23.6	15 29.9	1 5.5	26 59.0	27 30.7	5 22.3
25 Th	0 11 22	4 43 54	24 15 1	1♌23 45	17 49.7	15 36.3	22 18.3	1 33.1	15 44.0	1 0.8	27 2.4	27 32.6	5 22.7
26 F	0 15 19	5 43 19	8♌36 51	15 53 59	17 47.4	17 32.9	23 32.5	1 43.2	15 58.1	0 56.1	27 5.8	27 34.5	5 23.1
27 Sa	0 19 15	6 42 43	23 14 38	0♍38 11	17 42.4	19 27.7	24 46.6	1 53.9	16 12.1	0 51.4	27 9.2	27 36.4	5 23.4
28 Su	0 23 12	7 42 3	8♍ 3 49	15 30 36	17 34.6	21 20.2	26 0.7	2 5.1	16 26.1	0 46.7	27 12.6	27 38.3	5 23.8
29 M	0 27 9	8 41 22	22 57 29	0♎23 21	17 24.5	23 10.2	27 14.7	2 16.8	16 40.1	0 42.1	27 16.0	27 40.1	5 24.1
30 Tu	0 31 5	9 40 38	7♎47 6	15 7 37	17 13.0	24 57.1	28 28.8	2 29.1	16 54.0	0 37.4	27 19.4	27 41.9	5 24.3
31 W	0 35 2	10 39 53	22 23 53	29 35 3	17 1.4	26 40.6	29 42.7	2 41.8	17 7.9	0 32.8	27 22.7	27 43.7	5 24.5

APRIL 2010 — LONGITUDE

Day	Sid.Time	☉	0 hr ☽	Noon ☽	True ☊	☿	♀	♂	♃	♄	♅	♆	♇
1 Th	0 38 58	11♈39 5	6♏40 22	13♏39 17	16♑50.9	28♈20.2	0♉56.7	2♌55.1	17♓21.8	0♎28.2	27♓26.1	27♒45.5	5♑24.7
2 F	0 42 55	12 38 16	20 31 28	27 16 44	16R 42.6	29 55.7	2 10.6	3 8.9	17 35.6	0R 23.6	27 29.4	27 47.3	5 24.9
3 Sa	0 46 51	13 37 25	3♐55 7	10♐26 46	16 37.0	1♉26.6	3 24.5	3 23.1	17 49.4	0 19.1	27 32.8	27 49.0	5 25.0
4 Su	0 50 48	14 36 33	16 52 0	23 11 16	16 33.8	2 52.6	4 38.4	3 37.8	18 3.2	0 14.6	27 36.1	27 50.7	5 25.1
5 M	0 54 44	15 35 38	29 25 4	5♑34 0	16 32.7	4 13.4	5 52.2	3 53.0	18 16.9	0 10.1	27 39.4	27 52.4	5 25.2
6 Tu	0 58 41	16 34 42	11♑38 43	17 39 54	16 32.5	5 28.9	7 6.0	4 8.6	18 30.5	0 5.7	27 42.7	27 54.1	5 25.2
7 W	1 2 38	17 33 44	23 38 13	29 34 24	16 32.3	6 38.7	8 19.7	4 24.7	18 44.1	0 1.3	27 46.0	27 55.7	5R 25.2
8 Th	1 6 34	18 32 44	5♒29 7	11♒23 3	16 30.8	7 42.6	9 33.4	4 41.2	18 57.7	29♍56.9	27 49.3	27 57.3	5 25.2
9 F	1 10 31	19 31 42	17 16 49	23 11 1	16 27.2	8 40.5	10 47.1	4 58.2	19 11.2	29 52.6	27 52.5	27 58.9	5 25.1
10 Sa	1 14 27	20 30 38	29 6 14	5♓ 2 57	16 20.9	9 32.3	12 0.8	5 15.5	19 24.6	29 48.3	27 55.7	28 0.5	5 25.0
11 Su	1 18 24	21 29 33	11♓ 1 37	17 2 38	16 11.9	10 17.8	13 14.4	5 33.3	19 38.0	29 44.1	27 59.0	28 2.0	5 24.9
12 M	1 22 20	22 28 26	23 6 19	29 12 55	16 0.4	10 57.0	14 28.0	5 51.4	19 51.4	29 39.9	28 2.2	28 3.6	5 24.8
13 Tu	1 26 17	23 27 16	5♈22 38	11♈35 36	15 47.3	11 29.7	15 41.5	6 10.0	20 4.7	29 35.7	28 5.4	28 5.1	5 24.6
14 W	1 30 13	24 26 5	17 51 51	24 11 25	15 33.8	11 56.0	16 55.0	6 29.0	20 17.9	29 31.7	28 8.5	28 6.5	5 24.4
15 Th	1 34 10	25 24 52	0♉34 16	7♉ 0 18	15 21.0	12 15.9	18 8.5	6 48.3	20 31.1	29 27.7	28 11.7	28 8.0	5 24.1
16 F	1 38 6	26 23 37	13 29 26	20 1 34	15 10.0	12 29.3	19 21.9	7 8.0	20 44.2	29 23.7	28 14.8	28 9.4	5 23.8
17 Sa	1 42 3	27 22 20	26 36 33	3♊14 18	15 1.7	12 36.5	20 35.3	7 28.0	20 57.3	29 19.8	28 17.9	28 10.8	5 23.5
18 Su	1 46 0	28 21 1	9♊54 42	16 37 43	14 56.3	12R 37.6	21 48.7	7 48.4	21 10.3	29 16.0	28 21.0	28 12.1	5 23.2
19 M	1 49 56	29 19 40	23 23 17	0♋11 25	14 53.6	12 32.7	23 2.0	8 9.2	21 23.2	29 12.2	28 24.1	28 13.5	5 22.8
20 Tu	1 53 53	0♉18 16	7♋ 2 6	13 55 23	14D 52.9	12 22.1	24 15.3	8 30.3	21 36.1	29 8.5	28 27.1	28 14.8	5 22.4
21 W	1 57 49	1 16 51	20 51 17	27 49 51	14R 53.1	12 6.1	25 28.5	8 51.7	21 48.9	29 4.9	28 30.1	28 16.1	5 22.0
22 Th	2 1 46	2 15 23	4♌51 4	11♌54 52	14 52.8	11 45.2	26 41.7	9 13.5	22 1.6	29 1.3	28 33.1	28 17.3	5 21.5
23 F	2 5 42	3 13 53	19 1 11	26 9 47	14 50.9	11 19.7	27 54.8	9 35.5	22 14.3	28 57.8	28 36.1	28 18.5	5 21.0
24 Sa	2 9 39	4 12 20	3♍20 25	10♍32 42	14 46.8	10 50.3	29 7.9	9 57.9	22 26.9	28 54.4	28 39.1	28 19.7	5 20.5
25 Su	2 13 35	5 10 45	17 46 7	25 0 7	14 40.0	10 17.4	0♊21.0	10 20.5	22 39.4	28 51.0	28 42.0	28 20.9	5 20.0
26 M	2 17 32	6 9 9	2♎14 0	9♎27 3	14 31.0	9 41.9	1 34.0	10 43.5	22 51.9	28 47.8	28 44.9	28 22.0	5 19.4
27 Tu	2 21 29	7 7 30	16 38 28	23 47 27	14 20.7	9 4.2	2 47.0	11 6.7	23 4.3	28 44.6	28 47.7	28 23.1	5 18.8
28 W	2 25 25	8 5 50	0♏53 17	7♏55 13	14 10.2	8 25.2	3 59.9	11 30.2	23 16.6	28 41.5	28 50.6	28 24.2	5 18.2
29 Th	2 29 22	9 4 7	14 52 39	21 45 4	14 0.7	7 45.5	5 12.7	11 54.0	23 28.8	28 38.4	28 53.4	28 25.3	5 17.5
30 F	2 33 18	10 2 23	28 32 6	5♐13 29	13 53.1	7 6.0	6 25.6	12 18.1	23 40.9	28 35.5	28 56.2	28 26.3	5 16.8

Astro Data Dy Hr Mn	Planet Ingress Dy Hr Mn	Last Aspect Dy Hr Mn	☽ Ingress Dy Hr Mn	Last Aspect Dy Hr Mn	☽ Ingress Dy Hr Mn	☽ Phases & Eclipses Dy Hr Mn	Astro Data
☽0S 1 8:05	☿ ♓ 1 13:29	1 17:37 ♅ ☍	♎ 2 0:32	2 12:55 ♆ □	♐ 2 16:54	7 15:43 ☾ 16♐57	1 MARCH 2010
♀0N 9 18:57	♀ ♈ 7 12:34	3 20:45 ♆ △	♏ 4 2:12	4 20:59 ♆ ✶	♑ 5 1:08	15 21:02 ● 25♓10	Julian Day # 40237
♂ D 10 17:10	☿ ♈ 17 16:13	6 4:33 ♀ △	♐ 6 7:37	7 8:19 ♅ ✶	♒ 7 12:52	23 11:01 ☽ 2♋43	Galactic Ctr 26♐59.5
☽0N 15 10:20	☉ ♈ 20 17:33	8 11:14 ♆ ✶	♑ 8 17:14	9 21:45 ♆ ☌	♓ 10 1:49	30 2:27 ○ 9♎17	SVP 05♓06'47"
☿0N 18 19:58	♀ ♉ 31 17:36	10 22:00 ♅ ✶	♒ 11 5:43	12 12:52 ♄ ☍	♈ 12 13:32		Obliquity 23°26'20"
☽0S 28 18:43		13 12:58 ♆ ☌	♓ 13 18:45	14 19:24 ♆ ✶	♉ 14 22:56	6 9:38 ☾ 16♑29	⚷ Chiron 27♒06.2
	☿ ♉ 2 13:07	16 0:02 ☿ ☌	♈ 16 6:33	17 4:58 ♄ △	♊ 17 6:09	14 12:30 ● 24♈27	☽ Mean ☊ 18♑29.0
♇ R 7 2:35	♄ ♍ 7 18:52	18 11:24 ♆ ✶	♉ 18 16:30	19 10:22 ☉ ✶	♋ 19 11:40	21 18:21 ☽ 1♌32	
☽0N 11 17:02	☉ ♉ 20 4:31	20 19:42 ♆ □	♊ 21 0:29	21 14:08 ♄ ✶	♌ 21 15:43	28 12:20 ○ 8♏07	1 APRIL 2010
♅⚺♆ 13 7:44	♀ ♊ 25 5:06	23 1:50 ♆ △	♋ 23 6:17	23 15:36 ♆ ☍	♍ 23 18:25		Julian Day # 40268
☿ R 18 4:07		25 4:40 ♅ △	♌ 25 9:40	25 18:22 ♄ ☌	♎ 25 20:18		Galactic Ctr 26♐59.6
☽0S 25 2:42		27 7:05 ♆ ☍	♍ 27 10:58	27 19:46 ♆ △	♏ 27 22:30		SVP 05♓06'44"
♄☍♅ 26 23:24		29 6:56 ♅ ☍	♎ 29 11:22	30 0:41 ♅ △	♐ 30 2:37		Obliquity 23°26'20"
		31 12:14 ♀ ☍	♏ 31 12:42				⚷ Chiron 29♒04.2
							☽ Mean ☊ 16♑50.5

*Giving the positions of planets daily at noon, in LONGITUDE Greenwich Mean Time (UT)

Each planet's retrograde period is shaded gray.

2010 Planetary Ephemeris (Noon GMT*)

LONGITUDE — MAY 2010

Day	Sid.Time	☉	0 hr ☽	Noon ☽	True ☊	☿	♀	♂	♃	♄	♅	♆	♇
1 Sa	2 37 15	11♉ 0 38	11♐49 7	18♐19 1	13♑47.8	6♉27.2	7♊38.4	12♌42.4	23♓53.0	28♍32.6	28♓58.9	28♒27.3	5♑16.1
2 Su	2 41 11	11 58 51	24 43 21	1♑ 2 22	13R45.0	5R49.9	8 51.1	13 6.9	24 5.0	28R29.8	29 1.7	28 28.2	5R15.4
3 M	2 45 8	12 57 2	7♑16 27	13 26 3	13D44.1	5 14.7	10 3.8	13 31.7	24 16.9	28 27.1	29 4.4	28 29.2	5 14.6
4 Tu	2 49 4	13 55 12	19 31 39	25 33 53	13 44.6	4 42.1	11 16.5	13 56.8	24 28.7	28 24.5	29 7.1	28 30.1	5 13.8
5 W	2 53 1	14 53 20	1♒33 19	7♒30 37	13 45.4	4 12.6	12 29.1	14 22.1	24 40.5	28 22.0	29 9.7	28 30.9	5 13.0
6 Th	2 56 58	15 51 27	13 26 26	19 21 27	13R45.6	3 46.7	13 41.6	14 47.6	24 52.1	28 19.5	29 12.3	28 31.8	5 12.2
7 F	3 0 54	16 49 32	25 16 19	1♓11 41	13 44.3	3 24.7	14 54.2	15 13.4	25 3.7	28 17.2	29 14.9	28 32.6	5 11.3
8 Sa	3 4 51	17 47 36	7♓ 8 10	13 6 22	13 41.1	3 6.8	16 6.6	15 39.4	25 15.2	28 14.9	29 17.4	28 33.3	5 10.4
9 Su	3 8 47	18 45 39	19 6 51	25 10 5	13 35.7	2 53.3	17 19.1	16 5.6	25 26.6	28 12.8	29 19.9	28 34.1	5 9.5
10 M	3 12 44	19 43 40	1♈16 32	7♈26 34	13 28.3	2 44.4	18 31.4	16 32.1	25 37.9	28 10.7	29 22.4	28 34.8	5 8.6
11 Tu	3 16 40	20 41 40	13 40 30	19 58 33	13 19.6	2D40.0	19 43.8	16 58.7	25 49.1	28 8.7	29 24.9	28 35.4	5 7.6
12 W	3 20 37	21 39 38	26 20 51	2♉47 29	13 10.4	2 40.3	20 56.1	17 25.6	26 0.2	28 6.8	29 27.3	28 36.1	5 6.6
13 Th	3 24 33	22 37 35	9♉18 24	15 53 32	13 1.6	2 45.3	22 8.3	17 52.7	26 11.2	28 5.1	29 29.6	28 36.7	5 5.6
14 F	3 28 30	23 35 31	22 32 41	29 15 38	12 54.1	2 54.8	23 20.5	18 20.0	26 22.1	28 3.4	29 32.0	28 37.3	5 4.6
15 Sa	3 32 27	24 33 25	6♊ 2 6	12♊51 47	12 48.7	3 9.0	24 32.7	18 47.5	26 32.9	28 1.8	29 34.3	28 37.8	5 3.5
16 Su	3 36 23	25 31 17	19 44 19	26 39 23	12 45.4	3 27.6	25 44.8	19 15.2	26 43.6	28 0.3	29 36.6	28 38.3	5 2.4
17 M	3 40 20	26 29 8	3♋36 38	10♋35 46	12D44.3	3 50.5	26 56.8	19 43.1	26 54.2	27 58.9	29 38.8	28 38.8	5 1.3
18 Tu	3 44 16	27 26 57	17 36 28	24 38 28	12 44.7	4 17.7	28 8.8	20 11.2	27 4.7	27 57.6	29 41.0	28 39.3	5 0.2
19 W	3 48 13	28 24 45	1♌41 33	8♌45 28	12 45.9	4 49.1	29 20.8	20 39.5	27 15.0	27 56.4	29 43.1	28 39.7	4 59.1
20 Th	3 52 9	29 22 31	15 50 2	22 55 3	12 46.9	5 24.5	0♋32.6	21 7.9	27 25.3	27 55.3	29 45.3	28 40.1	4 57.9
21 F	3 56 6	0♊20 15	0♍ 0 19	7♍ 5 39	12R46.8	6 3.8	1 44.5	21 36.6	27 35.5	27 54.3	29 47.3	28 40.4	4 56.7
22 Sa	4 0 2	1 17 57	14 10 49	21 15 33	12 45.2	6 46.8	2 56.2	22 5.4	27 45.5	27 53.4	29 49.4	28 40.7	4 55.5
23 Su	4 3 59	2 15 38	28 19 34	5♎22 33	12 41.8	7 33.6	4 7.9	22 34.4	27 55.5	27 52.6	29 51.4	28 41.0	4 54.3
24 M	4 7 56	3 13 17	12♎24 10	19 24 0	12 36.9	8 23.9	5 19.6	23 3.5	28 5.3	27 51.9	29 53.3	28 41.3	4 53.1
25 Tu	4 11 52	4 10 55	26 21 41	3♏16 48	12 31.1	9 17.6	6 31.2	23 32.8	28 15.0	27 51.4	29 55.2	28 41.5	4 51.8
26 W	4 15 49	5 8 31	10♏ 8 57	16 57 46	12 25.1	10 14.6	7 42.7	24 2.3	28 24.6	27 50.9	29 57.1	28 41.7	4 50.5
27 Th	4 19 45	6 6 6	23 42 55	0♐24 7	12 19.7	11 15.0	8 54.1	24 31.9	28 34.1	27 50.5	29 59.0	28 41.8	4 49.3
28 F	4 23 42	7 3 40	7♐ 1 8	13 33 48	12 15.4	12 18.4	10 5.5	25 1.7	28 43.4	27 50.2	0♈ 0.8	28 42.0	4 48.0
29 Sa	4 27 38	8 1 13	20 2 4	26 25 55	12 12.7	13 25.0	11 16.9	25 31.6	28 52.6	27 50.0	0 2.5	28 42.1	4 46.6
30 Su	4 31 35	8 58 45	2♑45 26	9♑ 0 47	12D11.6	14 34.6	12 28.1	26 1.7	29 1.7	27D50.0	0 4.2	28 42.1	4 45.3
31 M	4 35 32	9 56 16	15 12 12	21 19 59	12 11.9	15 47.2	13 39.3	26 31.9	29 10.7	27 50.0	0 5.9	28R42.1	4 44.0

LONGITUDE — JUNE 2010

Day	Sid.Time	☉	0 hr ☽	Noon ☽	True ☊	☿	♀	♂	♃	♄	♅	♆	♇
1 Tu	4 39 28	10♊53 46	27♑24 31	3♒26 13	12♑13.2	17♉ 2.6	14♋50.5	27♌ 2.3	29♓19.6	27♍50.1	0♈ 7.5	28♒42.1	4♑42.6
2 W	4 43 25	11 51 15	9♒25 34	15 23 5	12 14.9	18 20.9	16 1.6	27 32.8	29 28.3	27 50.3	0 9.1	28R42.1	4R41.2
3 Th	4 47 21	12 48 43	21 19 19	27 14 50	12 16.5	19 42.1	17 12.6	28 3.5	29 36.9	27 50.7	0 10.7	28 42.0	4 39.8
4 F	4 51 18	13 46 11	3♓10 16	9♓ 6 11	12R17.4	21 6.0	18 23.5	28 34.3	29 45.4	27 51.1	0 12.2	28 41.9	4 38.4
5 Sa	4 55 14	14 43 38	15 3 14	21 2 0	12 17.3	22 32.6	19 34.4	29 5.2	29 53.7	27 51.6	0 13.6	28 41.8	4 37.0
6 Su	4 59 11	15 41 4	27 3 5	3♈ 7 4	12 16.1	24 2.0	20 45.2	29 36.3	0♈ 1.9	27 52.3	0 15.0	28 41.6	4 35.6
7 M	5 3 7	16 38 29	9♈14 27	15 25 45	12 13.7	25 34.1	21 56.0	0♍ 7.5	0 9.9	27 53.0	0 16.4	28 41.4	4 34.2
8 Tu	5 7 4	17 35 54	21 41 25	28 1 47	12 10.6	27 8.9	23 6.6	0 38.9	0 17.8	27 53.8	0 17.7	28 41.2	4 32.7
9 W	5 11 1	18 33 18	4♉27 10	10♉57 45	12 7.1	28 46.4	24 17.2	1 10.4	0 25.6	27 54.8	0 19.0	28 40.9	4 31.3
10 Th	5 14 57	19 30 42	17 33 41	24 14 56	12 3.7	0♊26.5	25 27.8	1 42.0	0 33.2	27 55.8	0 20.2	28 40.6	4 29.8
11 F	5 18 54	20 28 5	1♊ 1 25	7♊52 55	12 0.8	2 9.3	26 38.3	2 13.8	0 40.7	27 57.0	0 21.4	28 40.3	4 28.3
12 Sa	5 22 50	21 25 28	14 49 9	21 49 42	11 58.9	3 54.7	27 48.7	2 45.6	0 48.1	27 58.2	0 22.5	28 39.9	4 26.8
13 Su	5 26 47	22 22 49	28 54 4	6♋ 1 43	11D58.0	5 42.7	28 59.0	3 17.7	0 55.3	27 59.6	0 23.6	28 39.5	4 25.4
14 M	5 30 43	23 20 10	13♋12 2	20 24 24	11 58.1	7 33.2	0♌ 9.2	3 49.8	1 2.3	28 1.0	0 24.6	28 39.1	4 23.9
15 Tu	5 34 40	24 17 30	27 38 9	4♌52 40	11 58.9	9 26.3	1 19.4	4 22.0	1 9.2	28 2.6	0 25.6	28 38.7	4 22.4
16 W	5 38 36	25 14 50	12♌ 7 19	19 21 32	12 0.0	11 21.7	2 29.5	4 54.4	1 15.9	28 4.2	0 26.6	28 38.2	4 20.8
17 Th	5 42 33	26 12 8	26 34 47	3♍46 37	12 1.1	13 19.5	3 39.4	5 26.9	1 22.5	28 5.9	0 27.5	28 37.7	4 19.3
18 F	5 46 30	27 9 25	10♍56 36	18 4 23	12 1.8	15 19.6	4 49.4	5 59.5	1 28.9	28 7.8	0 28.3	28 37.1	4 17.8
19 Sa	5 50 26	28 6 42	25 9 41	2♎12 15	12R 1.9	17 21.7	5 59.2	6 32.2	1 35.2	28 9.7	0 29.1	28 36.5	4 16.3
20 Su	5 54 23	29 3 58	9♎11 52	16 8 24	12 1.4	19 25.8	7 8.9	7 5.1	1 41.3	28 11.8	0 29.9	28 35.9	4 14.8
21 M	5 58 19	0♋ 1 13	23 1 42	29 51 41	12 0.4	21 31.6	8 18.5	7 38.0	1 47.2	28 13.9	0 30.6	28 35.3	4 13.2
22 Tu	6 2 16	0 58 27	6♏38 17	13♏21 25	11 59.1	23 39.0	9 28.0	8 11.1	1 53.0	28 16.1	0 31.3	28 34.6	4 11.7
23 W	6 6 12	1 55 41	20 1 5	26 37 13	11 57.8	25 47.7	10 37.5	8 44.2	1 58.6	28 18.4	0 31.9	28 33.9	4 10.2
24 Th	6 10 9	2 52 54	3♐ 9 50	9♐38 56	11 56.6	27 57.4	11 46.8	9 17.5	2 4.1	28 20.9	0 32.5	28 33.2	4 8.6
25 F	6 14 5	3 50 7	16 4 32	22 26 42	11 55.8	0♋ 7.9	12 56.0	9 50.9	2 9.4	28 23.4	0 33.0	28 32.5	4 7.1
26 Sa	6 18 2	4 47 20	28 45 30	5♑ 1 1	11 55.4	2 18.9	14 5.2	10 24.3	2 14.5	28 26.0	0 33.4	28 31.7	4 5.6
27 Su	6 21 59	5 44 32	11♑13 23	17 22 45	11D55.4	4 30.2	15 14.2	10 57.9	2 19.4	28 28.7	0 33.9	28 30.9	4 4.0
28 M	6 25 55	6 41 44	23 29 18	29 33 18	11 55.7	6 41.3	16 23.1	11 31.6	2 24.2	28 31.5	0 34.2	28 30.1	4 2.5
29 Tu	6 29 52	7 38 56	5♒34 58	11♒34 38	11 56.1	8 52.2	17 31.9	12 5.3	2 28.8	28 34.4	0 34.6	28 29.2	4 0.9
30 W	6 33 48	8 36 7	17 32 37	23 29 19	11 56.5	11 2.4	18 40.6	12 39.2	2 33.3	28 37.3	0 34.8	28 28.3	3 59.4

Astro Data	Planet Ingress	Last Aspect	☽ Ingress	Last Aspect	☽ Ingress	☽ Phases & Eclipses	Astro Data
Dy Hr Mn	Dy Hr Mn	Dy Hr Mn	Dy Hr Mn	Dy Hr Mn	Dy Hr Mn	Dy Hr Mn	1 MAY 2010
♄⊼♆ 2 22:23	♀ ♋ 20 1:06	2 8:09 ♅ □	♑ 2 10:01	1 3:42 ♃ ✶	♒ 1 5:09	6 4:16 ☾ 15♒33	Julian Day # 40298
☽0N 9 0:09	☉ ♊ 21 3:35	4 19:08 ♅ ✶	♒ 4 20:53	3 14:57 ♆ ☌	♓ 3 17:35	14 1:05 ● 23♉09	Galactic Ctr 26♐59.6
☿ D 11 22:28	♅ ♈ 28 1:45	7 6:37 ♆ ☌	♓ 7 9:35	6 5:50 ♃ ☌	♈ 6 5:51	20 23:44 ☽ 29♌51	SVP 05♓06'40"
☽0S 22 8:10		9 20:13 ♅ ☌	♈ 9 21:30	8 13:14 ♆ ✶	♉ 8 15:42	27 23:08 ○ 6♐33	Obliquity 23°26'19"
♃☍♄ 23 5:38	♃ ♈ 6 6:29	12 4:12 ♆ ✶	♉ 12 6:49	10 19:51 ♆ □	♊ 10 22:12		⚷ Chiron 0♓25.4
♃⊻♆ 28 8:15	♂ ♍ 7 6:12	14 12:29 ♅ ✶	♊ 14 13:19	12 23:36 ♆ △	♋ 13 1:51	4 22:14 ☾ 14♓11	☽ Mean ☊ 15♑15.2
♄ D 30 18:10	☿ ♊ 10 5:42	16 17:07 ♅ □	♋ 16 17:47	15 0:39 ♄ ✶	♌ 15 3:55	12 11:16 ● 21♊24	
♆ R 31 18:49	♀ ♌ 14 8:51	18 20:36 ♅ △	♌ 18 21:07	17 3:25 ♆ ☍	♍ 17 5:42	19 4:31 ☽ 27♍49	1 JUNE 2010
	☉ ♋ 21 11:30	20 23:44 ☉ □	♍ 20 23:59	19 5:05 ♄ ☌	♎ 19 8:14	26 11:31 ○ 4♑46	Julian Day # 40329
☽0N 5 7:35	☿ ♋ 25 10:33	23 2:35 ♅ ☍	♎ 23 2:51	21 9:46 ♆ △	♏ 21 12:15	26 11:40 ☍P 0.537	Galactic Ctr 26♐59.7
♃☌♅ 8 11:28		25 4:02 ♆ △	♏ 25 6:18	23 15:33 ♆ □	♐ 23 18:11		SVP 05♓06'35"
☽0S 18 13:07		27 11:15 ♅ △	♐ 27 11:17	25 23:34 ♆ ✶	♑ 26 2:22		Obliquity 23°26'18"
♄⊼♆ 28 2:47		29 16:41 ♃ □	♑ 29 18:45	28 9:57 ♄ △	♒ 28 12:53		⚷ Chiron 0♓59.2
							☽ Mean ☊ 13♑36.7

*Giving the positions of planets daily at noon, in LONGITUDE Greenwich Mean Time (UT)

2010 Planetary Ephemeris (Noon GMT*)

JULY 2010

LONGITUDE

Day	Sid.Time	☉	0 hr ☽	Noon ☽	True ☊	☿	♀	♂	♃	♄	♅	♆	♇
1 Th	6 37 45	9♋33 19	29♒25 7	5♓20 30	11♑56.8	13♋11.9	19♌49.2	13♍13.2	2♈37.5	28♍40.4	0♈35.1	28♒27.4	3♑57.9
2 F	6 41 41	10 30 31	11♓15 54	17 11 51	11 57.0	15 20.3	20 57.7	13 47.3	2 41.6	28 43.5	0 35.2	28R26.5	3R56.4
3 Sa	6 45 38	11 27 43	23 8 51	29 7 29	11 57.1	17 27.5	22 6.1	14 21.4	2 45.5	28 46.8	0 35.4	28 25.5	3 54.8
4 Su	6 49 34	12 24 55	5♈ 8 16	11♈11 47	11 57.1	19 33.3	23 14.3	14 55.7	2 49.2	28 50.1	0 35.5	28 24.5	3 53.3
5 M	6 53 31	13 22 7	17 18 35	23 29 13	11 57.1	21 37.7	24 22.4	15 30.1	2 52.8	28 53.5	0R35.5	28 23.5	3 51.8
6 Tu	6 57 28	14 19 20	29 44 13	6♉ 4 4	11 57.2	23 40.4	25 30.5	16 4.5	2 56.1	28 57.0	0 35.5	28 22.5	3 50.3
7 W	7 1 24	15 16 33	12♉29 11	18 59 58	11 57.5	25 41.4	26 38.4	16 39.1	2 59.3	29 0.6	0 35.4	28 21.4	3 48.8
8 Th	7 5 21	16 13 46	25 36 43	2♊19 36	11 57.9	27 40.7	27 46.1	17 13.7	3 2.3	29 4.3	0 35.3	28 20.3	3 47.3
9 F	7 9 17	17 11 0	9♊ 8 44	16 4 3	11 58.3	29 38.2	28 53.8	17 48.5	3 5.1	29 8.0	0 35.2	28 19.2	3 45.8
10 Sa	7 13 14	18 8 14	23 5 24	0♋12 27	11 58.6	1♌33.8	0♍ 1.3	18 23.3	3 7.7	29 11.9	0 34.9	28 18.1	3 44.3
11 Su	7 17 10	19 5 29	7♋24 44	14 41 39	11R58.8	3 27.5	1 8.7	18 58.3	3 10.1	29 15.8	0 34.7	28 16.9	3 42.9
12 M	7 21 7	20 2 43	22 2 27	29 26 18	11 58.5	5 19.3	2 15.9	19 33.3	3 12.3	29 19.8	0 34.4	28 15.7	3 41.4
13 Tu	7 25 3	20 59 58	6♌52 16	14♌19 22	11 57.8	7 9.2	3 23.0	20 8.4	3 14.4	29 23.9	0 34.0	28 14.5	3 39.9
14 W	7 29 0	21 57 13	21 46 36	29 12 59	11 56.8	8 57.3	4 30.0	20 43.7	3 16.2	29 28.0	0 33.6	28 13.3	3 38.5
15 Th	7 32 57	22 54 28	6♍37 36	13♍59 35	11 55.6	10 43.3	5 36.8	21 19.0	3 17.9	29 32.3	0 33.2	28 12.1	3 37.1
16 F	7 36 53	23 51 42	21 18 13	28 32 53	11 54.5	12 27.5	6 43.4	21 54.4	3 19.3	29 36.6	0 32.7	28 10.8	3 35.6
17 Sa	7 40 50	24 48 57	5♎43 5	12♎48 28	11 53.7	14 9.8	7 49.9	22 29.8	3 20.6	29 41.0	0 32.2	28 9.5	3 34.2
18 Su	7 44 46	25 46 13	19 48 50	26 44 3	11D53.5	15 50.2	8 56.3	23 5.4	3 21.7	29 45.5	0 31.6	28 8.2	3 32.8
19 M	7 48 43	26 43 28	3♏34 8	10♏19 10	11 53.8	17 28.6	10 2.4	23 41.0	3 22.6	29 50.0	0 30.9	28 6.9	3 31.4
20 Tu	7 52 39	27 40 43	16 59 17	23 34 42	11 54.7	19 5.2	11 8.4	24 16.8	3 23.2	29 54.7	0 30.3	28 5.5	3 30.1
21 W	7 56 36	28 37 59	0♐ 5 40	6♐32 27	11 56.0	20 39.8	12 14.2	24 52.6	3 23.7	29 59.4	0 29.5	28 4.2	3 28.7
22 Th	8 0 32	29 35 15	12 55 20	19 14 35	11 57.3	22 12.5	13 19.8	25 28.5	3 24.0	0♎ 4.1	0 28.8	28 2.8	3 27.4
23 F	8 4 29	0♌32 31	25 30 31	1♑43 23	11 58.2	23 43.3	14 25.3	26 4.5	3R24.1	0 9.0	0 27.9	28 1.4	3 26.0
24 Sa	8 8 26	1 29 48	7♑53 27	14 0 59	11R58.5	25 12.2	15 30.5	26 40.5	3 24.0	0 13.9	0 27.1	28 0.0	3 24.7
25 Su	8 12 22	2 27 6	20 6 14	26 9 24	11 57.9	26 39.1	16 35.6	27 16.7	3 23.7	0 18.9	0 26.2	27 58.6	3 23.4
26 M	8 16 19	3 24 24	2♒10 45	8♒10 29	11 56.2	28 4.0	17 40.4	27 52.9	3 23.2	0 23.9	0 25.2	27 57.2	3 22.1
27 Tu	8 20 15	4 21 42	14 8 51	20 6 5	11 53.4	29 27.0	18 45.1	28 29.2	3 22.5	0 29.1	0 24.2	27 55.7	3 20.9
28 W	8 24 12	5 19 2	26 2 25	1♓58 7	11 49.9	0♍47.8	19 49.5	29 5.6	3 21.7	0 34.2	0 23.2	27 54.2	3 19.6
29 Th	8 28 8	6 16 22	7♓53 29	13 48 49	11 45.9	2 6.6	20 53.7	29 42.1	3 20.6	0 39.5	0 22.1	27 52.7	3 18.4
30 F	8 32 5	7 13 43	19 44 26	25 40 43	11 41.9	3 23.3	21 57.7	0♎18.6	3 19.3	0 44.8	0 21.0	27 51.2	3 17.2
31 Sa	8 36 2	8 11 5	1♈38 4	7♈36 53	11 38.3	4 37.8	23 1.5	0 55.2	3 17.8	0 50.2	0 19.8	27 49.7	3 16.0

AUGUST 2010

LONGITUDE

Day	Sid.Time	☉	0 hr ☽	Noon ☽	True ☊	☿	♀	♂	♃	♄	♅	♆	♇
1 Su	8 39 58	9♌ 8 28	13♈37 38	19♈40 47	11♑35.7	5♍50.1	24♍ 5.0	1♎31.9	3♈16.2	0♎55.6	0♈18.6	27♒48.2	3♑14.8
2 M	8 43 55	10 5 52	25 46 51	1♉56 20	11R34.2	7 0.0	25 8.3	2 8.7	3R14.3	1 1.1	0R17.4	27R46.7	3R13.6
3 Tu	8 47 51	11 3 18	8♉ 9 47	14 27 42	11D33.9	8 7.6	26 11.4	2 45.6	3 12.2	1 6.7	0 16.1	27 45.1	3 12.5
4 W	8 51 48	12 0 44	20 50 37	27 19 0	11 34.7	9 12.7	27 14.2	3 22.5	3 10.0	1 12.3	0 14.8	27 43.6	3 11.4
5 Th	8 55 44	12 58 12	3♊53 19	10♊33 55	11 36.1	10 15.2	28 16.8	3 59.5	3 7.6	1 18.0	0 13.4	27 42.0	3 10.3
6 F	8 59 41	13 55 42	17 21 6	24 15 4	11 37.6	11 15.1	29 19.1	4 36.7	3 4.9	1 23.8	0 12.0	27 40.4	3 9.2
7 Sa	9 3 37	14 53 12	1♋15 50	8♋23 20	11R38.4	12 12.1	0♎21.1	5 13.8	3 2.1	1 29.6	0 10.6	27 38.9	3 8.2
8 Su	9 7 34	15 50 44	15 37 15	22 57 9	11 38.0	13 6.2	1 22.9	5 51.1	2 59.1	1 35.5	0 9.1	27 37.3	3 7.1
9 M	9 11 31	16 48 17	0♌22 21	7♌52 0	11 36.0	13 57.3	2 24.4	6 28.5	2 55.9	1 41.4	0 7.6	27 35.7	3 6.1
10 Tu	9 15 27	17 45 50	15 25 6	23 0 28	11 32.4	14 45.1	3 25.6	7 5.9	2 52.5	1 47.4	0 6.0	27 34.1	3 5.1
11 W	9 19 24	18 43 25	0♍36 52	8♍13 0	11 27.6	15 29.5	4 26.5	7 43.4	2 48.9	1 53.4	0 4.4	27 32.5	3 4.2
12 Th	9 23 20	19 41 1	15 47 35	23 19 23	11 22.1	16 10.4	5 27.0	8 21.0	2 45.1	1 59.5	0 2.8	27 30.8	3 3.2
13 F	9 27 17	20 38 38	0♎47 17	8♎10 22	11 16.8	16 47.4	6 27.3	8 58.6	2 41.2	2 5.6	0 1.1	27 29.2	3 2.3
14 Sa	9 31 13	21 36 16	15 27 51	22 39 10	11 12.5	17 20.5	7 27.2	9 36.4	2 37.1	2 11.8	29♓59.4	27 27.6	3 1.4
15 Su	9 35 10	22 33 55	29 43 57	6♏42 2	11 9.7	17 49.4	8 26.8	10 14.2	2 32.8	2 18.0	29 57.7	27 26.0	3 0.6
16 M	9 39 6	23 31 35	13♏33 25	20 18 13	11D 8.5	18 13.9	9 25.9	10 52.0	2 28.3	2 24.3	29 55.9	27 24.3	2 59.7
17 Tu	9 43 3	24 29 16	26 56 42	3♐29 14	11 8.8	18 33.8	10 24.8	11 30.0	2 23.7	2 30.6	29 54.1	27 22.7	2 58.9
18 W	9 47 0	25 26 58	9♐56 13	16 18 9	11 10.0	18 48.8	11 23.2	12 8.0	2 18.9	2 37.0	29 52.3	27 21.1	2 58.1
19 Th	9 50 56	26 24 41	22 35 31	28 48 48	11 11.3	18 58.7	12 21.2	12 46.1	2 13.9	2 43.4	29 50.4	27 19.4	2 57.4
20 F	9 54 53	27 22 25	4♑58 31	11♑ 5 8	11R12.0	19R 3.2	13 18.9	13 24.3	2 8.8	2 49.9	29 48.5	27 17.8	2 56.6
21 Sa	9 58 49	28 20 10	17 9 8	23 10 55	11 11.1	19 2.3	14 16.1	14 2.6	2 3.5	2 56.4	29 46.6	27 16.1	2 55.9
22 Su	10 2 46	29 17 56	29 10 53	5♒ 9 23	11 8.3	18 55.7	15 12.8	14 40.9	1 58.0	3 3.0	29 44.6	27 14.5	2 55.2
23 M	10 6 42	0♍15 44	11♒ 6 46	17 3 18	11 3.3	18 43.2	16 9.1	15 19.3	1 52.4	3 9.6	29 42.7	27 12.9	2 54.6
24 Tu	10 10 39	1 13 33	22 59 16	28 54 54	10 56.2	18 24.9	17 4.9	15 57.7	1 46.7	3 16.2	29 40.7	27 11.2	2 53.9
25 W	10 14 35	2 11 24	4♓50 24	10♓46 1	10 47.3	18 0.8	18 0.2	16 36.3	1 40.8	3 22.9	29 38.6	27 9.6	2 53.3
26 Th	10 18 32	3 9 16	16 41 55	22 38 19	10 37.4	17 30.8	18 55.0	17 14.9	1 34.8	3 29.6	29 36.6	27 8.0	2 52.8
27 F	10 22 28	4 7 9	28 35 26	4♈33 29	10 27.4	16 55.3	19 49.3	17 53.5	1 28.6	3 36.3	29 34.5	27 6.3	2 52.2
28 Sa	10 26 25	5 5 4	10♈32 43	16 33 26	10 18.2	16 14.5	20 43.1	18 32.3	1 22.3	3 43.1	29 32.4	27 4.7	2 51.7
29 Su	10 30 22	6 3 1	22 35 54	28 40 30	10 10.6	15 29.0	21 36.3	19 11.1	1 15.8	3 49.9	29 30.2	27 3.1	2 51.2
30 M	10 34 18	7 1 0	4♉47 34	10♉57 31	10 5.1	14 39.3	22 28.9	19 50.0	1 9.3	3 56.8	29 28.1	27 1.5	2 50.7
31 Tu	10 38 15	7 59 1	17 10 48	23 27 51	10 1.9	13 46.1	23 20.9	20 29.0	1 2.6	4 3.7	29 25.9	26 59.9	2 50.3

Astro Data Dy Hr Mn	Planet Ingress Dy Hr Mn	Last Aspect Dy Hr Mn	☽ Ingress Dy Hr Mn	Last Aspect Dy Hr Mn	☽ Ingress Dy Hr Mn	☽ Phases & Eclipses Dy Hr Mn	Astro Data
☽0N 2 15:01	☿ ♌ 9 16:30	30 22:04 ♆ ☌	♓ 1 1:11	2 3:55 ♆ ⚹	♉ 2 8:14	4 14:36 ☾ 12♈31	1 JULY 2010
♅ R 5 16:50	♀ ♍ 10 11:33	3 11:18 ♄ ☍	♈ 3 13:45	4 12:45 ♆ □	♊ 4 16:55	11 19:42 ● 19♋24	Julian Day # 40359
♃0N 8 17:52	♄ ♎ 21 15:11	5 21:25 ♆ ⚹	♉ 6 0:30	6 21:23 ♀ □	♋ 6 21:51	11 19:34:39 ● T 5'20"	Galactic Ctr 26♐59.8
☽0S 15 19:44	☉ ♌ 22 22:22	8 6:11 ♄ △	♊ 8 7:52	7 18:47 ☿ ⚹	♌ 8 23:24	18 10:12 ☽ 25♎42	SVP 05♓06'30"
♃ R 23 12:04	☿ ♍ 27 21:44	10 10:18 ♄ □	♋ 10 11:39	10 19:11 ♆ ☍	♍ 10 23:02	26 1:38 ○ 2♒60	Obliquity 23°26'18"
♃□♇ 25 4:21	♂ ♎ 29 23:47	12 11:49 ♄ ⚹	♌ 12 12:55	12 0:05 ☿ ☌	♎ 12 22:44		⚷ Chiron 0♓37.8R
♄☍♅ 26 17:08		14 10:24 ♆ ☍	♍ 14 13:16	14 20:07 ♆ △	♏ 15 0:27		☽ Mean ☊ 12♑01.4
☽0N 29 22:06	♀ ♎ 7 3:49	16 13:47 ♄ ☌	♎ 16 14:25	17 5:25 ♅ △	♐ 17 5:35	3 5:00 ☾ 10♉47	
♂0S 31 17:46	♅ ♓ 14 3:38	18 14:27 ♆ △	♏ 18 17:43	19 13:59 ♅ □	♑ 19 14:18	10 3:09 ● 17♌25	1 AUGUST 2010
♃0S 31 2:24	☉ ♍ 23 5:28	20 23:44 ♄ ⚹	♐ 20 23:50	22 1:09 ♅ ⚹	♒ 22 1:38	16 18:15 ☽ 23♏47	Julian Day # 40390
♃□♇ 3 5:33		23 4:52 ♆ ⚹	♑ 23 8:40	24 8:31 ♆ ☌	♓ 24 14:12	24 17:06 ○ 1♓26	Galactic Ctr 26♐59.8
♀0S 6 10:16	☿ R 20 20:00	25 14:21 ♂ △	♒ 25 19:39	27 2:01 ♅ ☌	♈ 27 2:50		SVP 05♓06'25"
☽0S 12 4:54	♄□♇ 21 10:17	28 3:47 ♆ ☌	♓ 28 8:01	29 8:49 ♆ ⚹	♉ 29 14:36		Obliquity 23°26'18"
♃☍♄ 16 20:46	☽0N 26 4:38	30 3:45 ♀ ☍	♈ 30 20:43				⚷ Chiron 29♒28.6R
							☽ Mean ☊ 10♑22.9

*Giving the positions of planets daily at noon, in LONGITUDE Greenwich Mean Time (UT)

2010 Planetary Ephemeris (Noon GMT*)

LONGITUDE — SEPTEMBER 2010

Day	Sid.Time	☉	0 hr ☽	Noon ☽	True ☊	☿	♀	♂	♃	♄	♅	♆	♇
1 W	10 42 11	8♍57 4	29♉49 11	6♊15 16	10♑ 0.7	12♍50.5	24♎12.3	21♎ 8.0	0♈55.8	4♎10.6	29♓23.7	26♒58.3	2♑49.9
2 Th	10 46 8	9 55 8	12♊46 35	19 23 36	10D 1.0	11R 53.5	25 3.1	21 47.1	0R 48.9	4 17.5	29R 21.5	26R 56.7	2R 49.5
3 F	10 50 4	10 53 15	26 6 42	2♋56 14	10 1.6	10 56.1	25 53.2	22 26.3	0 41.9	4 24.5	29 19.3	26 55.1	2 49.2
4 Sa	10 54 1	11 51 24	9♋52 27	16 55 28	10R 1.6	9 59.7	26 42.6	23 5.6	0 34.7	4 31.5	29 17.0	26 53.5	2 48.9
5 Su	10 57 57	12 49 34	24 5 14	1♌21 31	9 59.9	9 5.6	27 31.3	23 44.9	0 27.5	4 38.6	29 14.8	26 52.0	2 48.6
6 M	11 1 54	13 47 46	8♌43 54	16 11 45	9 55.8	8 14.9	28 19.2	24 24.3	0 20.2	4 45.7	29 12.5	26 50.4	2 48.3
7 Tu	11 5 51	14 46 1	23 44 10	1♍20 7	9 49.2	7 28.8	29 6.4	25 3.8	0 12.8	4 52.8	29 10.2	26 48.9	2 48.1
8 W	11 9 47	15 44 17	8♍58 20	16 37 29	9 40.5	6 48.6	29 52.8	25 43.4	0 5.3	4 59.9	29 7.9	26 47.3	2 47.9
9 Th	11 13 44	16 42 34	24 16 6	1♎52 47	9 30.7	6 15.2	0♏38.4	26 23.0	29♓57.7	5 7.0	29 5.5	26 45.8	2 47.7
10 F	11 17 40	17 40 54	9♎26 10	16 55 2	9 21.0	5 49.3	1 23.0	27 2.7	29 50.1	5 14.2	29 3.2	26 44.3	2 47.6
11 Sa	11 21 37	18 39 15	24 18 20	1♏35 14	9 12.5	5 31.7	2 6.8	27 42.5	29 42.4	5 21.4	29 0.8	26 42.8	2 47.5
12 Su	11 25 33	19 37 38	8♏45 9	15 47 43	9 6.1	5D 23.0	2 49.7	28 22.3	29 34.6	5 28.6	28 58.5	26 41.3	2 47.4
13 M	11 29 30	20 36 2	22 42 47	29 30 24	9 2.1	5 23.3	3 31.5	29 2.3	29 26.8	5 35.8	28 56.1	26 39.8	2 47.4
14 Tu	11 33 26	21 34 28	6♐10 48	12♐44 20	9 0.4	5 32.9	4 12.4	29 42.2	29 19.0	5 43.1	28 53.7	26 38.4	2D 47.4
15 W	11 37 23	22 32 56	19 11 27	25 32 43	9D 0.1	5 51.8	4 52.1	0♏22.3	29 11.1	5 50.3	28 51.3	26 37.0	2 47.4
16 Th	11 41 20	23 31 25	1♑48 44	8♑ 0 6	9R 0.3	6 19.8	5 30.8	1 2.4	29 3.2	5 57.6	28 49.0	26 35.5	2 47.5
17 F	11 45 16	24 29 56	14 7 27	20 11 24	8 59.9	6 56.7	6 8.3	1 42.6	28 55.2	6 4.9	28 46.6	26 34.1	2 47.6
18 Sa	11 49 13	25 28 28	26 12 35	2♒11 33	8 57.7	7 42.2	6 44.5	2 22.9	28 47.2	6 12.2	28 44.2	26 32.7	2 47.7
19 Su	11 53 9	26 27 2	8♒ 8 51	14 4 58	8 53.1	8 35.7	7 19.6	3 3.2	28 39.2	6 19.6	28 41.8	26 31.4	2 47.8
20 M	11 57 6	27 25 38	20 0 22	25 55 26	8 45.6	9 36.8	7 53.3	3 43.6	28 31.2	6 26.9	28 39.4	26 30.0	2 48.0
21 Tu	12 1 2	28 24 15	1♓50 31	7♓45 57	8 35.4	10 44.9	8 25.6	4 24.1	28 23.2	6 34.2	28 36.9	26 28.7	2 48.2
22 W	12 4 59	29 22 55	13 41 59	19 38 50	8 22.9	11 59.4	8 56.6	5 4.6	28 15.2	6 41.6	28 34.5	26 27.4	2 48.5
23 Th	12 8 55	0♎21 36	25 36 42	1♈35 45	8 9.1	13 19.5	9 26.1	5 45.2	28 7.2	6 49.0	28 32.1	26 26.1	2 48.7
24 F	12 12 52	1 20 19	7♈36 7	13 37 57	7 55.0	14 44.7	9 54.0	6 25.9	27 59.2	6 56.3	28 29.7	26 24.8	2 49.0
25 Sa	12 16 49	2 19 4	19 41 22	25 46 30	7 41.9	16 14.4	10 20.4	7 6.6	27 51.2	7 3.7	28 27.3	26 23.5	2 49.4
26 Su	12 20 45	3 17 52	1♉53 32	8♉ 2 38	7 30.8	17 47.9	10 45.2	7 47.4	27 43.2	7 11.1	28 24.9	26 22.3	2 49.7
27 M	12 24 42	4 16 41	14 13 59	20 27 50	7 22.3	19 24.7	11 8.3	8 28.3	27 35.3	7 18.5	28 22.5	26 21.1	2 50.1
28 Tu	12 28 38	5 15 33	26 44 27	3♊ 4 9	7 16.8	21 4.1	11 29.6	9 9.2	27 27.4	7 25.9	28 20.1	26 19.9	2 50.6
29 W	12 32 35	6 14 27	9♊27 17	15 54 12	7 13.9	22 45.8	11 49.1	9 50.2	27 19.6	7 33.3	28 17.8	26 18.7	2 51.0
30 Th	12 36 31	7 13 24	22 25 17	29 0 57	7 13.1	24 29.2	12 6.8	10 31.3	27 11.8	7 40.7	28 15.4	26 17.6	2 51.5

LONGITUDE — OCTOBER 2010

Day	Sid.Time	☉	0 hr ☽	Noon ☽	True ☊	☿	♀	♂	♃	♄	♅	♆	♇
1 F	12 40 28	8♎12 22	5♋41 33	12♋27 27	7♑13.0	26♍14.0	12♏22.5	11♏12.5	27♓ 4.1	7♎48.1	28♓13.0	26♒16.4	2♑52.1
2 Sa	12 44 24	9 11 23	19 18 56	26 16 14	7R 12.5	27 59.8	12 36.2	11 53.7	26R 56.4	7 55.5	28R 10.7	26R 15.3	2 52.6
3 Su	12 48 21	10 10 27	3♌19 27	10♌28 32	7 10.2	29 46.3	12 47.9	12 35.0	26 48.8	8 2.9	28 8.3	26 14.3	2 53.2
4 M	12 52 18	11 9 32	17 43 18	25 3 22	7 5.5	1♎33.2	12 57.5	13 16.4	26 41.2	8 10.3	28 6.0	26 13.2	2 53.8
5 Tu	12 56 14	12 8 40	2♍28 8	9♍56 50	6 58.1	3 20.4	13 5.0	13 57.8	26 33.8	8 17.7	28 3.7	26 12.2	2 54.5
6 W	13 0 11	13 7 50	17 28 29	25 1 57	6 48.2	5 7.6	13 10.2	14 39.3	26 26.4	8 25.1	28 1.4	26 11.2	2 55.1
7 Th	13 4 7	14 7 2	2♎35 58	10♎ 9 14	6 37.0	6 54.7	13 13.2	15 20.9	26 19.1	8 32.5	27 59.1	26 10.2	2 55.8
8 F	13 8 4	15 6 16	17 40 24	25 8 14	6 25.7	8 41.5	13R 13.9	16 2.5	26 11.9	8 39.9	27 56.8	26 9.3	2 56.6
9 Sa	13 12 0	16 5 33	2♏31 34	9♏49 25	6 15.6	10 28.0	13 12.3	16 44.2	26 4.8	8 47.3	27 54.5	26 8.3	2 57.4
10 Su	13 15 57	17 4 51	17 1 2	24 5 49	6 7.7	12 14.0	13 8.2	17 26.0	25 57.8	8 54.6	27 52.3	26 7.5	2 58.2
11 M	13 19 53	18 4 11	1♐ 3 25	7♐53 43	6 2.4	13 59.5	13 1.8	18 7.9	25 51.0	9 2.0	27 50.1	26 6.6	2 59.0
12 Tu	13 23 50	19 3 33	14 36 46	21 12 46	5 59.8	15 44.5	12 53.0	18 49.8	25 44.2	9 9.3	27 47.9	26 5.8	2 59.9
13 W	13 27 46	20 2 56	27 42 5	4♑ 5 10	5D 59.0	17 28.9	12 41.7	19 31.8	25 37.6	9 16.7	27 45.7	26 5.0	3 0.8
14 Th	13 31 43	21 2 22	10♑22 36	16 34 58	5R 59.2	19 12.6	12 28.0	20 13.8	25 31.1	9 24.0	27 43.6	26 4.2	3 1.7
15 F	13 35 40	22 1 49	22 42 55	28 47 8	5 59.0	20 55.7	12 11.9	20 56.0	25 24.7	9 31.3	27 41.4	26 3.4	3 2.6
16 Sa	13 39 36	23 1 18	4♒48 16	10♒47 0	5 57.5	22 38.1	11 53.5	21 38.1	25 18.5	9 38.6	27 39.3	26 2.7	3 3.6
17 Su	13 43 33	24 0 48	16 43 56	22 39 42	5 53.9	24 19.9	11 32.8	22 20.4	25 12.4	9 45.8	27 37.2	26 2.0	3 4.6
18 M	13 47 29	25 0 21	28 34 51	4♓29 54	5 47.6	26 1.1	11 9.9	23 2.7	25 6.4	9 53.1	27 35.2	26 1.4	3 5.6
19 Tu	13 51 26	25 59 55	10♓25 21	16 21 37	5 38.7	27 41.5	10 44.9	23 45.1	25 0.6	10 0.3	27 33.1	26 0.7	3 6.7
20 W	13 55 22	26 59 31	22 19 3	28 17 58	5 27.6	29 21.4	10 17.9	24 27.5	24 54.9	10 7.5	27 31.1	26 0.1	3 7.8
21 Th	13 59 19	27 59 9	4♈18 39	10♈21 17	5 15.2	1♏ 0.6	9 49.1	25 10.0	24 49.4	10 14.7	27 29.1	25 59.6	3 8.9
22 F	14 3 15	28 58 48	16 26 3	22 33 4	5 2.5	2 39.1	9 18.5	25 52.5	24 44.1	10 21.8	27 27.2	25 59.0	3 10.1
23 Sa	14 7 12	29 58 30	28 42 26	4♉54 11	4 50.6	4 17.1	8 46.4	26 35.2	24 38.9	10 29.0	27 25.3	25 58.5	3 11.2
24 Su	14 11 9	0♏58 14	11♉ 8 24	17 25 5	4 40.6	5 54.5	8 13.0	27 17.9	24 33.9	10 36.1	27 23.4	25 58.0	3 12.5
25 M	14 15 5	1 58 0	23 44 19	0♊ 6 7	4 33.1	7 31.3	7 38.5	28 0.6	24 29.0	10 43.2	27 21.5	25 57.6	3 13.7
26 Tu	14 19 2	2 57 48	6♊30 33	12 57 44	4 28.3	9 7.6	7 3.1	28 43.4	24 24.4	10 50.2	27 19.7	25 57.2	3 14.9
27 W	14 22 58	3 57 38	19 27 46	26 0 48	4 26.2	10 43.4	6 27.0	29 26.3	24 19.9	10 57.3	27 17.9	25 56.8	3 16.2
28 Th	14 26 55	4 57 30	2♋37 0	9♋16 33	4D 25.9	12 18.6	5 50.6	0♐ 9.3	24 15.6	11 4.3	27 16.1	25 56.5	3 17.5
29 F	14 30 51	5 57 25	15 59 39	22 46 30	4 26.7	13 53.3	5 13.9	0 52.3	24 11.4	11 11.2	27 14.4	25 56.2	3 18.9
30 Sa	14 34 48	6 57 21	29 37 16	6♌32 6	4R 27.2	15 27.5	4 37.4	1 35.4	24 7.5	11 18.2	27 12.7	25 55.9	3 20.2
31 Su	14 38 44	7 57 20	13♌31 5	20 34 12	4 26.4	17 1.3	4 1.2	2 18.6	24 3.7	11 25.1	27 11.1	25 55.6	3 21.6

Astro Data Dy Hr Mn	Planet Ingress Dy Hr Mn	Last Aspect Dy Hr Mn	☽ Ingress Dy Hr Mn	Last Aspect Dy Hr Mn	☽ Ingress Dy Hr Mn	☽ Phases & Eclipses Dy Hr Mn
☽0S 8 15:45	♀ ♏ 8 15:46	31 23:14 ♅ ✶	♊ 1 0:20	2 15:23 ☿ ✶	♌ 2 18:22	1 17:23 ☾ 9♊10
♄0S 8 13:58	♃ ♓ 9 4:51	3 5:41 ♅ □	♋ 3 6:52	4 13:53 ♆ ☍	♍ 4 20:01	8 10:31 ● 15♍41
☿ D 12 23:10	♂ ♏ 14 22:39	5 8:32 ♅ △	♌ 5 9:46	6 16:44 ♅ ☍	♎ 6 19:53	15 5:51 ☽ 22♐18
♇ D 14 4:37	☉ ♎ 23 3:10	7 8:18 ♀ ✶	♍ 7 9:54	8 13:39 ♆ △	♏ 8 19:53	23 9:18 ○ 0♈15
♃☌♅ 19 1:04		9 9:00 ♃ ☍	♎ 9 9:02	10 18:28 ♅ △	♐ 10 22:10	
☽0N 22 10:45	☿ ♎ 3 15:05	11 5:17 ♂ ☌	♏ 11 9:22	13 0:09 ♅ □	♑ 13 4:18	1 3:53 ☾ 7♋52
	☿ ♏ 20 21:20	13 11:54 ♃ △	♐ 13 12:53	15 9:50 ♅ ✶	♒ 15 14:25	7 18:46 ● 14♎24
☿0S 5 22:28	☉ ♏ 23 12:36	15 18:53 ♃ □	♑ 15 20:31	17 18:50 ♆ ☌	♓ 18 2:53	14 21:29 ☽ 21♑26
☽0S 6 2:17	♂ ♐ 28 6:49	18 5:14 ♃ ✶	♒ 18 7:36	20 10:26 ♅ ☌	♈ 20 15:24	23 1:38 ○ 29♈33
♃⚺♆ 8 22:15		20 13:10 ♆ ☌	♓ 20 20:16	23 1:38 ☉ ☍	♉ 23 2:31	30 12:47 ☾ 6♌59
♀ R 8 7:06		23 5:53 ♅ ☌	♈ 23 8:48	25 7:50 ♂ ☍	♊ 25 11:49	
☽0N 19 16:54		25 13:13 ♆ ✶	♉ 25 20:18	27 14:20 ♅ □	♋ 27 19:15	
♄⚼♆ 27 10:31		28 3:04 ♅ ✶	♊ 28 6:12	29 19:49 ♅ △	♌ 30 0:40	
		30 10:38 ♅ □	♋ 30 13:47			

Astro Data

1 SEPTEMBER 2010
Julian Day # 40421
Galactic Ctr 26♐59.9
SVP 05♓06'21"
Obliquity 23°26'18"
⚷ Chiron 27♒57.3R
☽ Mean ☊ 8♑44.4

1 OCTOBER 2010
Julian Day # 40451
Galactic Ctr 27♐00.0
SVP 05♓06'18"
Obliquity 23°26'18"
⚷ Chiron 26♒41.0R
☽ Mean ☊ 7♑09.1

*Giving the positions of planets daily at noon, in LONGITUDE Greenwich Mean Time (UT)

2010 Planetary Ephemeris (Noon GMT*)

NOVEMBER 2010 — LONGITUDE

Day	Sid.Time	☉	0 hr ☽	Noon ☽	True ☊	☿	♀	♂	♃	♄	♅	♆	♇
1 M	14 42 41	8♏57 21	27♌41 22	4♍52 21	4♑23.7	18♏34.6	3♏25.5	3♐ 1.8	24♓ 0.1	11♎32.0	27♓ 9.4	25♒55.4	3♑23.0
2 Tu	14 46 38	9 57 24	12♍ 6 49	19 24 16	4R 18.7	20 7.5	2R 50.7	3 45.0	23R 56.7	11 38.8	27R 7.8	25R 55.2	3 24.5
3 W	14 50 34	10 57 30	26 44 5	4♎ 5 30	4 11.6	21 39.9	2 17.0	4 28.4	23 53.5	11 45.6	27 6.3	25 55.1	3 25.9
4 Th	14 54 31	11 57 37	11♎27 39	18 49 34	4 3.4	23 11.9	1 44.5	5 11.8	23 50.5	11 52.4	27 4.8	25 55.0	3 27.4
5 F	14 58 27	12 57 46	26 10 17	3♏28 47	3 54.9	24 43.6	1 13.4	5 55.3	23 47.7	11 59.1	27 3.3	25 54.9	3 28.9
6 Sa	15 2 24	13 57 58	10♏44 7	17 55 26	3 47.2	26 14.8	0 44.0	6 38.8	23 45.1	12 5.8	27 1.9	25 54.8	3 30.5
7 Su	15 6 20	14 58 11	25 1 57	2♐ 3 4	3 41.3	27 45.5	0 16.4	7 22.4	23 42.7	12 12.4	27 0.5	25D 54.8	3 32.0
8 M	15 10 17	15 58 25	8♐58 19	15 47 25	3 37.6	29 15.9	29♎50.7	8 6.1	23 40.5	12 19.0	26 59.2	25 54.9	3 33.6
9 Tu	15 14 13	16 58 42	22 30 13	29 6 44	3D 36.0	0♐45.9	29 27.1	8 49.8	23 38.5	12 25.6	26 57.9	25 54.9	3 35.2
10 W	15 18 10	17 59 0	5♑37 8	12♑ 1 41	3 36.2	2 15.5	29 5.7	9 33.6	23 36.7	12 32.1	26 56.6	25 55.0	3 36.8
11 Th	15 22 7	18 59 19	18 20 47	24 34 53	3 37.5	3 44.6	28 46.5	10 17.5	23 35.1	12 38.6	26 55.4	25 55.2	3 38.5
12 F	15 26 3	19 59 40	0♒44 30	6♒50 15	3 38.9	5 13.4	28 29.6	11 1.4	23 33.7	12 45.0	26 54.2	25 55.3	3 40.2
13 Sa	15 30 0	21 0 2	12 52 43	18 52 34	3R 39.8	6 41.6	28 15.1	11 45.3	23 32.5	12 51.4	26 53.1	25 55.5	3 41.8
14 Su	15 33 56	22 0 26	24 50 24	0♓46 54	3 39.3	8 9.4	28 3.1	12 29.4	23 31.5	12 57.7	26 52.0	25 55.7	3 43.6
15 M	15 37 53	23 0 50	6♓42 40	12 38 19	3 37.1	9 36.6	27 53.5	13 13.4	23 30.7	13 4.0	26 51.0	25 56.0	3 45.3
16 Tu	15 41 49	24 1 17	18 34 25	24 31 31	3 33.1	11 3.3	27 46.4	13 57.6	23 30.2	13 10.2	26 50.0	25 56.3	3 47.0
17 W	15 45 46	25 1 44	0♈30 7	6♈30 39	3 27.5	12 29.4	27 41.8	14 41.8	23 29.8	13 16.3	26 49.1	25 56.6	3 48.8
18 Th	15 49 42	26 2 13	12 33 33	18 39 7	3 21.0	13 54.9	27D 39.6	15 26.0	23D 29.7	13 22.4	26 48.2	25 57.0	3 50.6
19 F	15 53 39	27 2 44	24 47 40	0♉59 24	3 14.1	15 19.6	27 39.9	16 10.3	23 29.7	13 28.5	26 47.3	25 57.4	3 52.4
20 Sa	15 57 36	28 3 15	7♉14 29	13 33 2	3 7.6	16 43.5	27 42.6	16 54.7	23 30.0	13 34.5	26 46.5	25 57.8	3 54.2
21 Su	16 1 32	29 3 49	19 55 4	26 20 36	3 2.3	18 6.5	27 47.6	17 39.1	23 30.5	13 40.4	26 45.7	25 58.3	3 56.0
22 M	16 5 29	0♐ 4 23	2♊49 35	9♊21 56	2 58.4	19 28.6	27 55.0	18 23.6	23 31.2	13 46.3	26 45.0	25 58.8	3 57.9
23 Tu	16 9 25	1 5 0	15 57 32	22 36 15	2 56.4	20 49.4	28 4.7	19 8.2	23 32.1	13 52.1	26 44.4	25 59.3	3 59.8
24 W	16 13 22	2 5 38	29 17 56	6♋ 2 28	2D 56.0	22 9.0	28 16.6	19 52.8	23 33.2	13 57.9	26 43.8	25 59.9	4 1.7
25 Th	16 17 18	3 6 17	12♋49 42	19 39 30	2 56.8	23 27.1	28 30.7	20 37.4	23 34.5	14 3.6	26 43.2	26 0.5	4 3.6
26 F	16 21 15	4 6 58	26 31 44	3♌26 17	2 58.4	24 43.6	28 46.9	21 22.1	23 36.0	14 9.3	26 42.7	26 1.2	4 5.5
27 Sa	16 25 11	5 7 40	10♌23 3	17 21 55	2 59.9	25 58.1	29 5.2	22 6.9	23 37.7	14 14.8	26 42.2	26 1.8	4 7.4
28 Su	16 29 8	6 8 24	24 22 44	1♍25 24	3R 0.8	27 10.4	29 25.5	22 51.7	23 39.6	14 20.3	26 41.8	26 2.5	4 9.4
29 M	16 33 5	7 9 10	8♍29 43	15 35 29	3 0.6	28 20.3	29 47.6	23 36.6	23 41.7	14 25.8	26 41.5	26 3.3	4 11.3
30 Tu	16 37 1	8 9 57	22 42 26	29 50 17	2 59.2	29 27.2	0♏11.7	24 21.5	23 44.0	14 31.2	26 41.1	26 4.1	4 13.3

DECEMBER 2010 — LONGITUDE

Day	Sid.Time	☉	0 hr ☽	Noon ☽	True ☊	☿	♀	♂	♃	♄	♅	♆	♇
1 W	16 40 58	9♐10 46	6♎58 39	14♎ 7 8	2♑56.8	0♑30.9	0♏37.5	25♐ 6.5	23♓46.5	14♎36.5	26♓40.9	26♒ 4.9	4♑15.3
2 Th	16 44 54	10 11 36	21 15 15	28 22 29	2R 53.6	1 30.8	1 5.1	25 51.6	23 49.2	14 41.7	26R 40.7	26 5.7	4 17.3
3 F	16 48 51	11 12 28	5♏28 20	12♏32 13	2 50.3	2 26.4	1 34.3	26 36.7	23 52.2	14 46.9	26 40.5	26 6.6	4 19.3
4 Sa	16 52 47	12 13 21	19 33 37	26 31 58	2 47.3	3 17.1	2 5.1	27 21.8	23 55.3	14 52.0	26 40.4	26 7.5	4 21.4
5 Su	16 56 44	13 14 15	3♐26 49	10♐17 44	2 45.1	4 2.1	2 37.5	28 7.1	23 58.6	14 57.0	26 40.3	26 8.4	4 23.4
6 M	17 0 40	14 15 10	17 4 21	23 46 24	2 43.9	4 40.9	3 11.3	28 52.3	24 2.1	15 1.9	26D 40.3	26 9.4	4 25.5
7 Tu	17 4 37	15 16 6	0♑23 42	6♑56 9	2D 43.8	5 12.5	3 46.6	29 37.6	24 5.8	15 6.8	26 40.4	26 10.4	4 27.5
8 W	17 8 34	16 17 3	13 23 47	19 46 39	2 44.4	5 36.2	4 23.2	0♑23.0	24 9.7	15 11.6	26 40.5	26 11.4	4 29.6
9 Th	17 12 30	17 18 1	26 4 58	2♒18 59	2 45.7	5 51.0	5 1.1	1 8.4	24 13.8	15 16.3	26 40.6	26 12.5	4 31.7
10 F	17 16 27	18 19 0	8♒29 3	14 35 32	2 47.1	5R 56.1	5 40.3	1 53.9	24 18.1	15 20.9	26 40.8	26 13.6	4 33.8
11 Sa	17 20 23	19 19 59	20 38 55	26 39 41	2 48.3	5 50.8	6 20.8	2 39.4	24 22.6	15 25.5	26 41.1	26 14.7	4 35.9
12 Su	17 24 20	20 20 59	2♓38 23	8♓35 35	2 49.2	5 34.5	7 2.3	3 25.0	24 27.2	15 30.0	26 41.4	26 15.9	4 38.0
13 M	17 28 16	21 21 59	14 31 51	20 27 49	2R 49.6	5 6.6	7 45.0	4 10.6	24 32.1	15 34.3	26 41.7	26 17.0	4 40.1
14 Tu	17 32 13	22 23 0	26 24 4	2♈21 11	2 49.3	4 27.3	8 28.8	4 56.2	24 37.1	15 38.6	26 42.1	26 18.3	4 42.2
15 W	17 36 10	23 24 1	8♈19 47	14 20 26	2 48.6	3 36.7	9 13.7	5 41.9	24 42.3	15 42.9	26 42.6	26 19.5	4 44.3
16 Th	17 40 6	24 25 3	20 23 39	26 29 57	2 47.7	2 35.9	9 59.5	6 27.7	24 47.7	15 47.0	26 43.1	26 20.8	4 46.5
17 F	17 44 3	25 26 5	2♉39 47	8♉53 33	2 46.6	1 26.2	10 46.3	7 13.5	24 53.3	15 51.1	26 43.7	26 22.1	4 48.6
18 Sa	17 47 59	26 27 8	15 11 36	21 34 12	2 45.6	0 9.6	11 34.0	7 59.3	24 59.0	15 55.0	26 44.3	26 23.4	4 50.7
19 Su	17 51 56	27 28 12	28 1 32	4♊33 42	2 44.9	28♐48.5	12 22.7	8 45.2	25 5.0	15 58.9	26 45.0	26 24.8	4 52.9
20 M	17 55 52	28 29 15	11♊10 44	17 52 34	2 44.5	27 25.6	13 12.1	9 31.1	25 11.1	16 2.7	26 45.7	26 26.2	4 55.0
21 Tu	17 59 49	29 30 20	24 39 1	1♋29 51	2D 44.4	26 3.8	14 2.5	10 17.1	25 17.3	16 6.4	26 46.4	26 27.6	4 57.2
22 W	18 3 45	0♑31 25	8♋24 45	15 23 17	2 44.5	24 45.6	14 53.6	11 3.1	25 23.8	16 10.0	26 47.3	26 29.0	4 59.3
23 Th	18 7 42	1 32 30	22 25 2	29 29 28	2 44.6	23 33.5	15 45.5	11 49.1	25 30.4	16 13.5	26 48.1	26 30.5	5 1.5
24 F	18 11 39	2 33 36	6♌36 5	13♌44 19	2R 44.7	22 29.4	16 38.1	12 35.2	25 37.2	16 17.0	26 49.1	26 32.0	5 3.7
25 Sa	18 15 35	3 34 42	20 53 38	28 3 31	2 44.7	21 34.7	17 31.5	13 21.4	25 44.1	16 20.3	26 50.0	26 33.5	5 5.8
26 Su	18 19 32	4 35 49	5♍13 28	12♍23 1	2 44.5	20 50.3	18 25.5	14 7.5	25 51.2	16 23.5	26 51.0	26 35.1	5 8.0
27 M	18 23 28	5 36 57	19 31 45	26 39 19	2 44.4	20 16.5	19 20.2	14 53.8	25 58.5	16 26.7	26 52.1	26 36.7	5 10.1
28 Tu	18 27 25	6 38 5	3♎45 22	10♎49 39	2D 44.4	19 53.3	20 15.5	15 40.0	26 5.9	16 29.7	26 53.2	26 38.3	5 12.3
29 W	18 31 21	7 39 14	17 51 56	24 51 59	2 44.6	19 40.6	21 11.5	16 26.3	26 13.5	16 32.7	26 54.4	26 39.9	5 14.5
30 Th	18 35 18	8 40 23	1♏49 40	8♏44 49	2 45.0	19D 37.7	22 8.0	17 12.7	26 21.2	16 35.5	26 55.6	26 41.5	5 16.6
31 F	18 39 14	9 41 33	15 37 18	22 27 0	2 45.6	19 43.9	23 5.1	17 59.1	26 29.1	16 38.3	26 56.9	26 43.2	5 18.8

Astro Data	Planet Ingress	Last Aspect	☽ Ingress	Last Aspect	☽ Ingress	☽ Phases & Eclipses	Astro Data
Dy Hr Mn	Dy Hr Mn	Dy Hr Mn	Dy Hr Mn	Dy Hr Mn	Dy Hr Mn	Dy Hr Mn	1 NOVEMBER 2010
☽0S 2 10:38	☿ ♐ 8 23:44	31 21:02 ♆ ☍	♍ 1 3:52	2 8:09 ♆ △	♏ 2 14:45	6 4:53 ● 13♏40	Julian Day # 40482
☿ D 7 6:05	♀ ♎ 8 3:07	3 0:37 ♅ ☍	♎ 3 5:20	4 12:15 ♅ △	♐ 4 18:00	13 16:40 ☽ 21♒12	Galactic Ctr 27♐00.1
☽0N 15 23:37	☉ ♐ 22 10:16	4 23:35 ♆ △	♏ 5 6:17	6 21:47 ♂ ☌	♑ 6 23:17	21 17:28 ○ 29♉18	SVP 05♓06'15"
♀ D 18 21:19	♀ ♏ 30 0:34	7 3:45 ☿ ☌	♐ 7 8:29	9 1:08 ♅ ✶	♒ 9 7:32	28 20:38 ☾ 6♍30	Obliquity 23°26'18"
♃ D 18 16:54		9 12:36 ♀ ✶	♑ 9 13:38	11 11:10 ♅ ☌	♓ 11 18:42		⚷ Chiron 26♒04.7R
☽0S 29 16:25	☿ ♑ 1 0:12	11 19:58 ♀ □	♒ 11 22:33	14 0:36 ♅ ☌	♈ 14 7:16	5 17:37 ● 13♐28	☽ Mean ☊ 5♑30.6
	♂ ♑ 7 23:50	14 6:34 ♀ △	♓ 14 10:25	16 11:42 ♆ ✶	♉ 16 18:50	13 14:00 ☽ 21♓27	
♅ D 6 1:51	☿ ♐ 18 14:54	16 16:38 ♅ ☌	♈ 16 23:00	18 21:38 ♅ ✶	♊ 19 3:38	21 8:15 ○ 29♊21	1 DECEMBER 2010
☿ R 10 12:05	☉ ♑ 21 23:40	19 5:34 ♀ ☍	♉ 19 10:05	21 8:15 ☉ ☍	♋ 21 9:23	21 8:18 ☍T 1.256	Julian Day # 40512
☽0N 13 7:14		21 17:28 ☉ ☍	♊ 21 18:47	23 7:27 ♅ △	♌ 23 12:52	28 4:20 ☾ 6♎19	Galactic Ctr 27♐00.1
☽0S 26 21:34		23 21:58 ♀ △	♋ 24 1:15	25 9:29 ♆ ☍	♍ 25 15:15		SVP 05♓06'10"
☿ D 30 7:22		26 3:45 ♀ □	♌ 26 6:02	27 12:22 ♅ ☍	♎ 27 17:39		Obliquity 23°26'17"
		28 8:31 ♀ ✶	♍ 28 9:35	29 15:06 ♆ △	♏ 29 20:51		⚷ Chiron 26♒24.6
		30 11:18 ☿ □	♎ 30 12:16				☽ Mean ☊ 3♑55.3

*Giving the positions of planets daily at noon, in LONGITUDE Greenwich Mean Time (UT)

January
1
2
3
4
5
6
7
8
9
10
11
12
13
14
15
16
17
18
19
20
21
22
23
24
31
25
26
27
28
29
30

Sunday
Monday
Tuesday
Wednesday
Thursday
Friday
Saturday
1
2
3
4
5
6
7
8
9
10
11
12
13
14
15
16
17
18
19
20
21
22
23
24
25
26
27
28
February

March

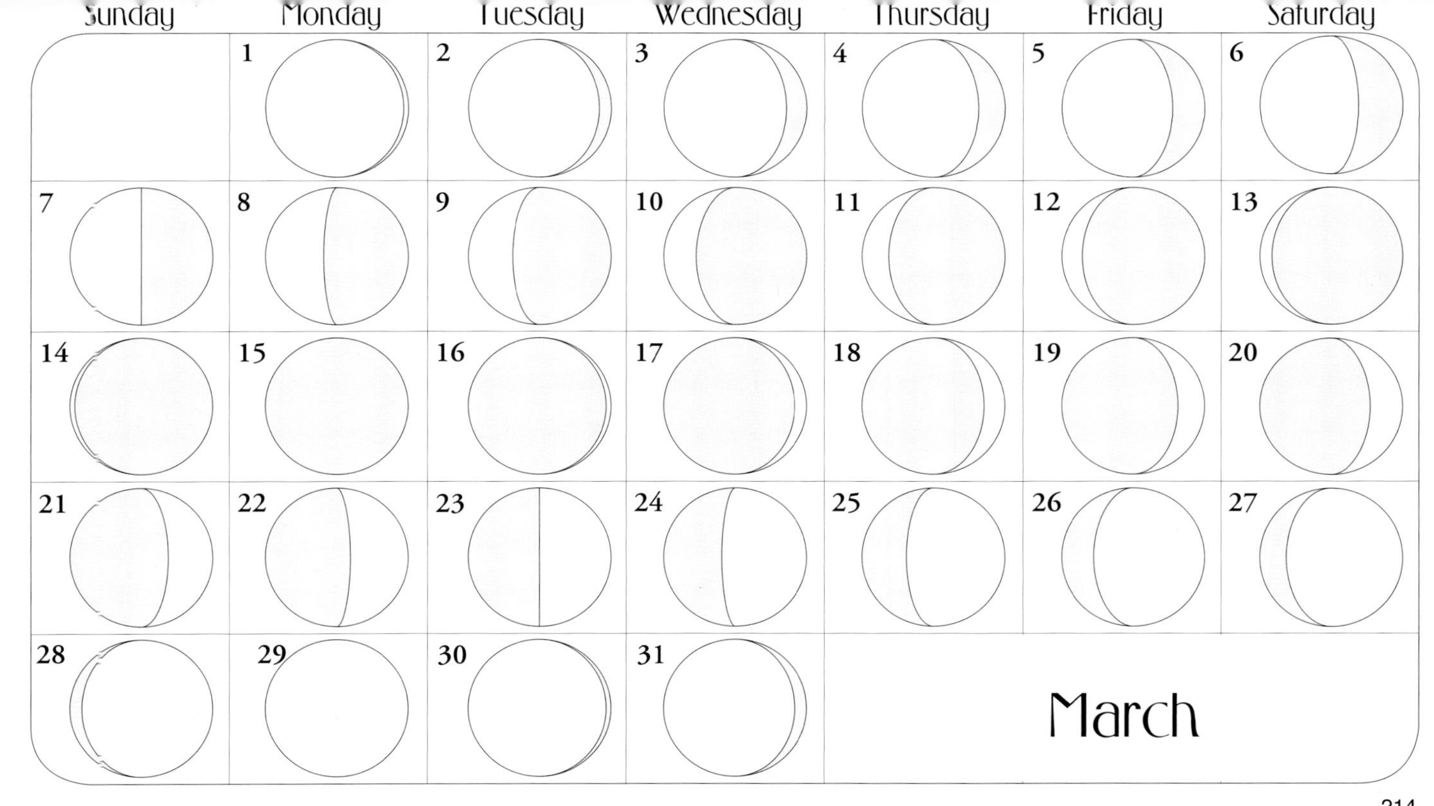

Sunday	Monday	Tuesday	Wednesday	Thursday	Friday	Saturday
	1	2	3	4	5	6
7	8	9	10	11	12	13
14	15	16	17	18	19	20
21	22	23	24	25	26	27
28	29	30	31			

Sunday
Monday
Tuesday
Wednesday
Thursday
Friday
Saturday
April
1
2
3
4
5
6
7
8
9
10
11
12
13
14
15
16
17
18
19
20
21
22
23
24
25
26
27
28
29
30

Sunday
Monday
Tuesday
Wednesday
Thursday
Friday
Saturday
May
1
2
3
4
5
6
7
8
9
10
11
12
13
14
15
16
17
18
19
20
21
22
23
24
25
26
27
28
29
30
31

June

Sunday	Monday	Tuesday	Wednesday	Thursday	Friday	Saturday
		1	2	3	4	5
6	7	8	9	10	11	12
13	14	15	16	17	18	19
20	21	22	23	24	25	26
27	28	29	30			

July

Sunday	Monday	Tuesday	Wednesday	Thursday	Friday	Saturday
				1	2	3
4	5	6	7	8	9	10
11	12	13	14	15	16	17
18	19	20	21	22	23	24
25	26	27	28	29	30	31

Sunday
Monday
Tuesday
Wednesday
Thursday
Friday
Saturday
1
2
3
4
5
6
7
8
9
10
11
12
13
14
15
16
17
18
19
20
21
22
23
24
25
26
27
28
29
30
31
August

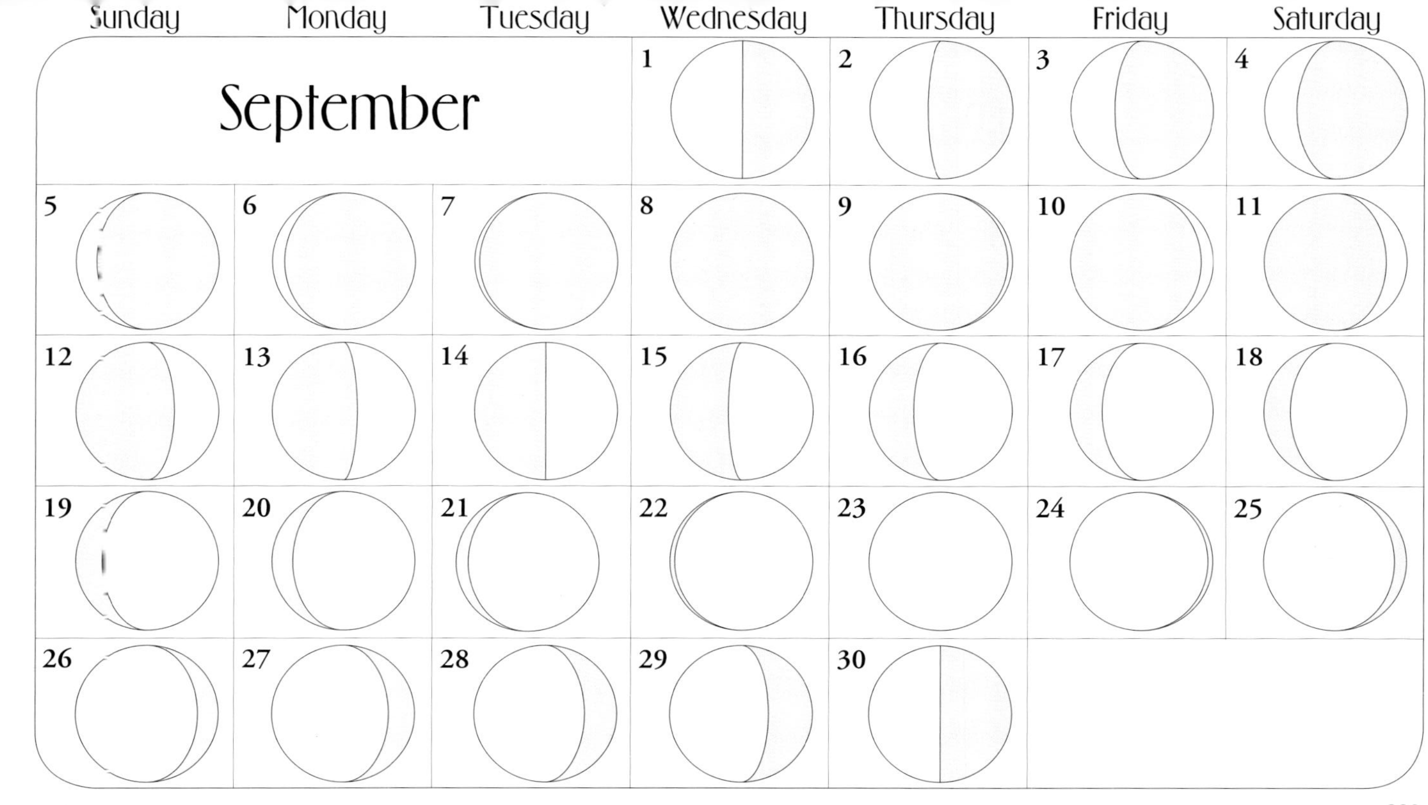

September

Sunday	Monday	Tuesday	Wednesday	Thursday	Friday	Saturday
			1	2	3	4
5	6	7	8	9	10	11
12	13	14	15	16	17	18
19	20	21	22	23	24	25
26	27	28	29	30		

Sunday
Monday
Tuesday
Wednesday
Thursday
Friday
Saturday
1
2
3
4
5
6
7
8
9
10
11
12
13
14
15
16
17
18
19
20
21
22
23
24
25
26
27
28
29
30
31
October

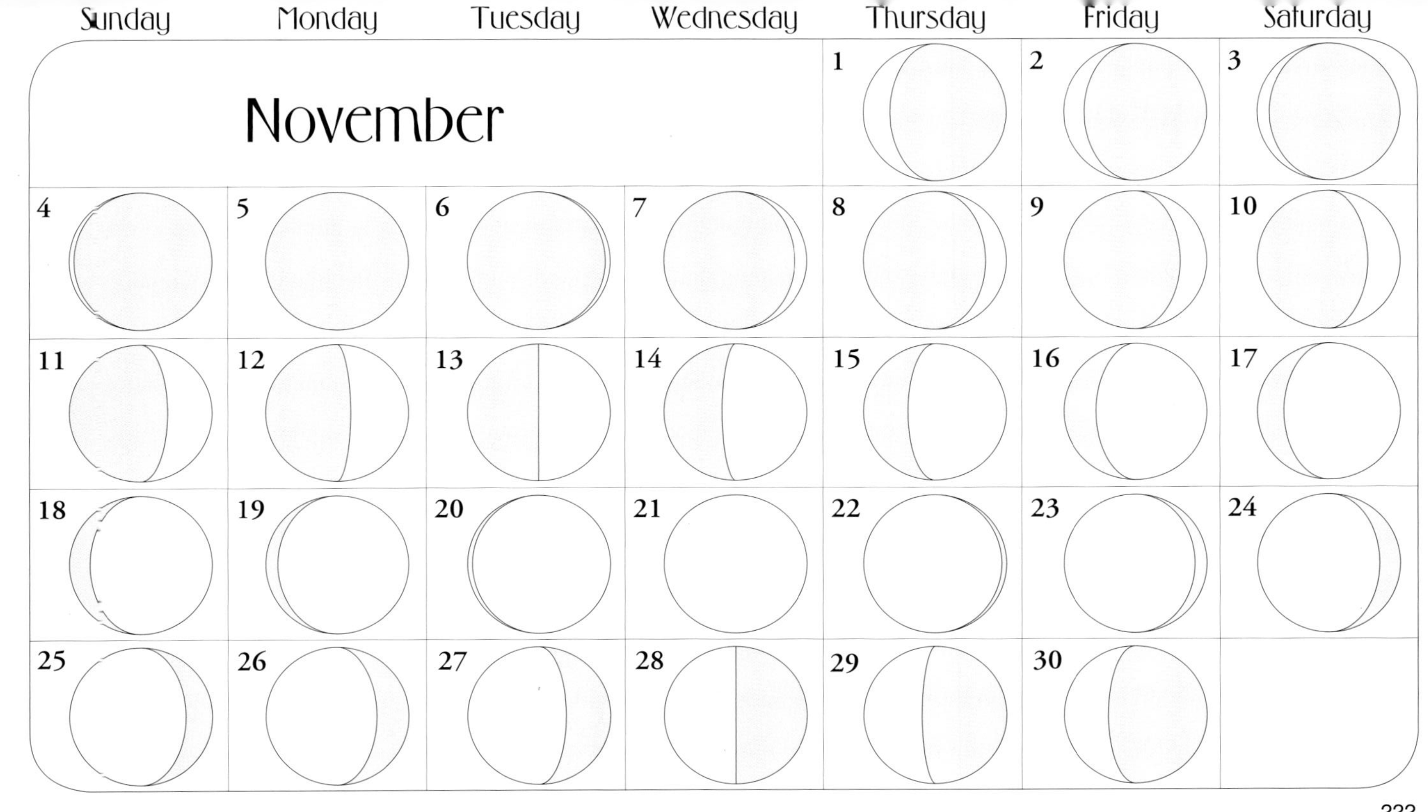
Sunday
Monday
Tuesday
Wednesday
Thursday
Friday
Saturday
November
1
2
3
4
5
6
7
8
9
10
11
12
13
14
15
16
17
18
19
20
21
22
23
24
25
26
27
28
29
30

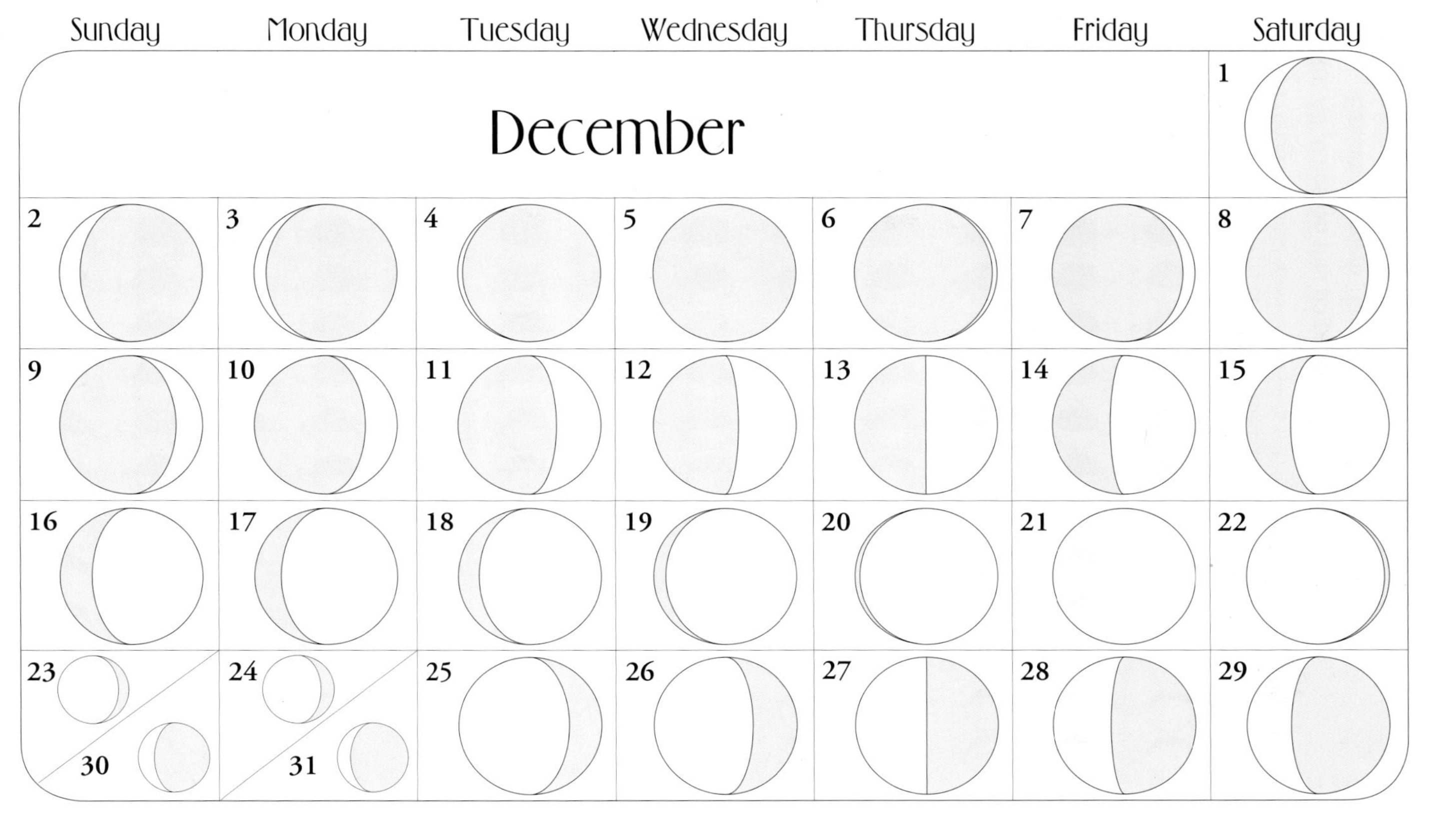
December
Sunday
Monday
Tuesday
Wednesday
Thursday
Friday
Saturday
1
2
3
4
5
6
7
8
9
10
11
12
13
14
15
16
17
18
19
20
21
22
23
30
24
31
25
26
27
28
29

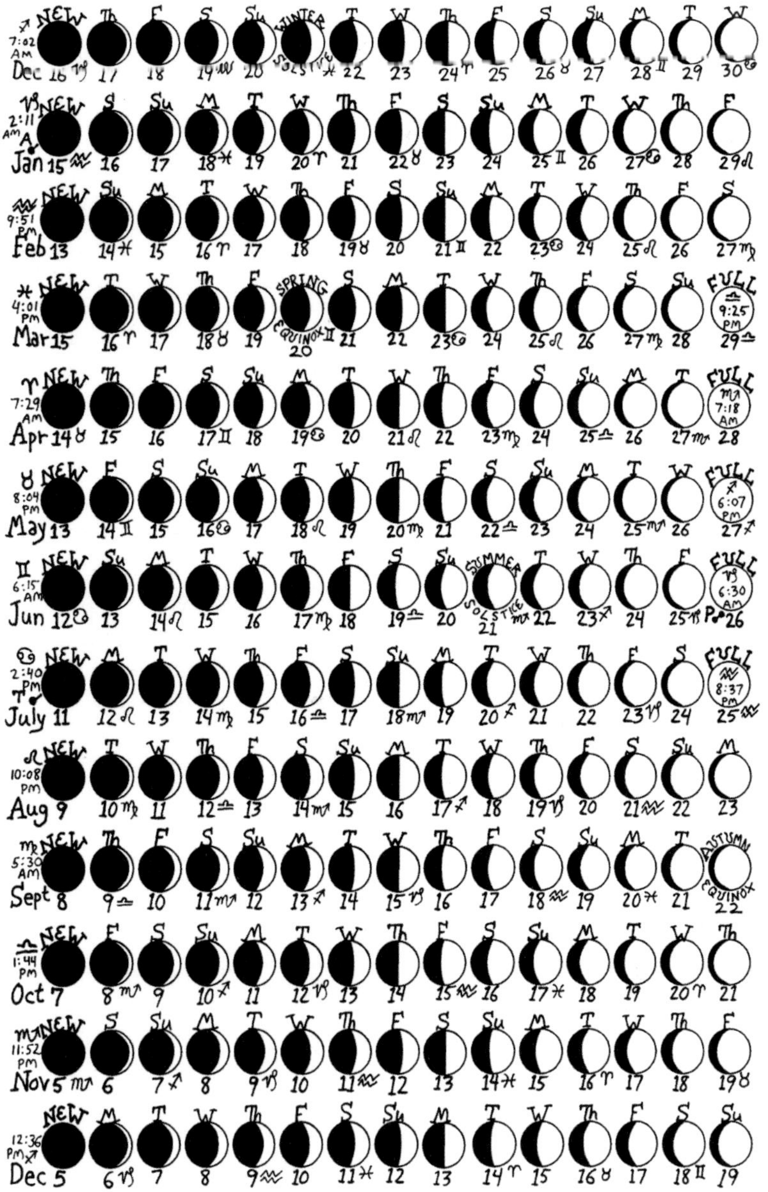

♐ NEW 7:02 AM Dec 16 ♑ | Th 17 | F 18 | S 19 ♒ | Su 20 | WINTER SOLSTICE ♓ | T 22 | W 23 | Th 24 ♈ | F 25 | S 26 ♉ | Su 27 | M 28 ♊ | T 29 | W 30 ♋

♑ NEW 2:11 AM A Jan 15 ♒ | S 16 | Su 17 | M 18 ♓ | T 19 | W 20 ♈ | Th 21 | F 22 ♉ | S 23 | Su 24 | M 25 ♊ | T 26 | W 27 ♋ | Th 28 | F 29 ♌

♒ NEW 9:51 PM Feb 13 | Su 14 ♓ | M 15 | T 16 ♈ | W 17 | Th 18 | F 19 ♉ | S 20 | Su 21 ♊ | M 22 | T 23 ♋ | W 24 | Th 25 ♌ | F 26 | S 27 ♍

♓ NEW 4:01 PM Mar 15 | T 16 ♈ | W 17 | Th 18 ♉ | F 19 | SPRING EQUINOX ♊ 20 | S 21 | M 22 | T 23 ♋ | W 24 | Th 25 ♌ | F 26 | S 27 ♍ | Su 28 | FULL ♎ 9:25 PM 29 ♎

♈ NEW 7:29 AM Apr 14 ♉ | Th 15 | F 16 | S 17 ♊ | Su 18 | M 19 ♋ | T 20 | W 21 ♌ | Th 22 | F 23 ♍ | S 24 | Su 25 ♎ | M 26 | T 27 ♏ | FULL ♏ 7:18 AM 28

♉ NEW 8:04 PM May 13 | F 14 ♊ | S 15 | Su 16 ♋ | M 17 | T 18 ♌ | W 19 | Th 20 ♍ | F 21 | S 22 ♎ | Su 23 | M 24 | T 25 ♏ | W 26 | FULL ♐ 6:07 PM 27 ♐

♊ NEW 6:15 AM Jun 12 ♋ | Su 13 | M 14 ♌ | T 15 | W 16 | Th 17 ♍ | F 18 | S 19 ♎ | Su 20 | SUMMER SOLSTICE 21 ♏ | T 22 | W 23 ♐ | Th 24 | F 25 ♑ | FULL ♑ 6:30 AM P 26

♋ NEW 2:40 PM T July 11 | M 12 ♌ | T 13 | W 14 ♍ | Th 15 | F 16 ♎ | S 17 | Su 18 ♏ | M 19 | T 20 ♐ | W 21 | Th 22 | F 23 ♑ | S 24 | FULL ♒ 8:37 PM 25 ♒

♌ NEW 10:08 PM Aug 9 | T 10 ♍ | W 11 | Th 12 ♎ | F 13 | S 14 ♏ | Su 15 | M 16 | T 17 ♐ | W 18 | Th 19 ♑ | F 20 | S 21 ♒ | Su 22 | M 23

♍ NEW 5:30 AM Sept 8 | Th 9 ♎ | F 10 | S 11 ♏ | Su 12 | M 13 ♐ | T 14 | W 15 ♑ | Th 16 | F 17 | S 18 ♒ | Su 19 | M 20 ♓ | T 21 | AUTUMN EQUINOX 22

♎ NEW 1:44 PM Oct 7 | F 8 ♏ | S 9 | Su 10 ♐ | M 11 | T 12 ♑ | W 13 | Th 14 | F 15 ♒ | S 16 | Su 17 ♓ | M 18 | T 19 | W 20 ♈ | Th 21

♏ NEW 11:52 PM Nov 5 ♏ | S 6 | Su 7 ♐ | M 8 | T 9 ♑ | W 10 | Th 11 ♒ | F 12 | S 13 | Su 14 ♓ | M 15 | T 16 ♈ | W 17 | Th 18 | F 19 ♉

NEW 12:36 PM ♐ Dec 5 | M 6 ♑ | T 7 | W 8 | Th 9 ♒ | F 10 | S 11 ♓ | Su 12 | M 13 | T 14 ♈ | W 15 | Th 16 ♉ | F 17 | S 18 ♊ | Su 19

Eclipse Key: ✓ =Solar ♪ =Lunar A=Annular T=Total P = Penumbral or Partial
Lunar Eclipses are visible wherever it is night and cloud free around time of full moon.

Attn: All times on this page in EST

Eastern Standard Time (-5 from GMT)

Add one hour during Daylight Savings.

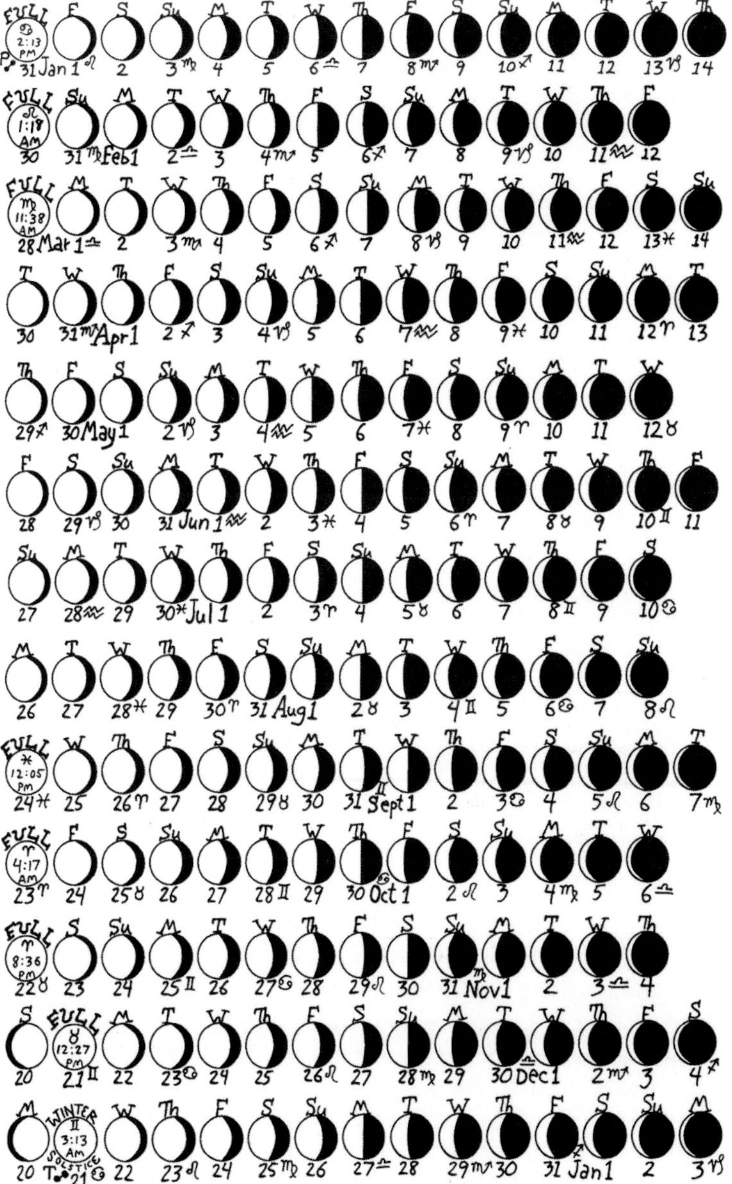

2010 Lunar Phases

This format available on cards from: **http://snakeandsnake.com**

Snake and Snake Productions 3037 Dixon Rd Durham, NC 27707

World Time Zones

ID LW	NT BT	CA HT	YST	PST	MST	CST	EST	AST	BST	AT	WAT	GMT	CET	EET	BT	USSR Z3	USSR Z4	USSR Z5	SST	CCT	JST	GST	USSR Z10	ID LE
-12	-11	-10	-9	-8	-7	-6	-5	-4	-3	-2	-1	**0**	+1	+2	+3	+4	+5	+6	+7	+8	+9	+10	+11	+12
-4	-3	-2	-1	**0**	+1	+2	+3	+4	+5	+6	+7	+8	+9	+10	+11	+12	+13	+14	+15	+16	+17	+18	+19	+20

Standard Time Zones from West to East Calculated from PST as Zero Point:

IDLW:	International Date Line West	-4
NT/BT:	Nome Time/Bering Time	-3
CA/HT:	Central Alaska & Hawaiian Time	-2
YST:	Yukon Standard Time	-1
PST:	Pacific Standard Time	0
MST:	Mountain Standard Time	+1
CST:	Central Standard Time	+2
EST:	Eastern Standard Time	+3
AST:	Atlantic Standard Time	+4
NFT:	Newfoundland Time	+4 1/2
BST:	Brazil Standard Time	+5
AT:	Azores Time	+6
WAT:	West African Time	+7
GMT:	Greenwich Mean Time	+8
WET:	Western European Time (England)	+8
CET:	Central European Time	+9
EET:	Eastern European Time	+10
BT:	Bagdhad Time	+11
IT:	Iran Time	+11 1/2
USSR	Zone 3	+12
USSR	Zone 4	+13
IST:	Indian Standard Time	+13 1/2
USSR	Zone 5	+14
NST:	North Sumatra Time	+14 1/2
SST:	South Sumatra Time & USSR Zone 6	+15
JT:	Java Time	+15 1/2
CCT:	China Coast Time	+16
MT:	Moluccas Time	+16 1/2
JST:	Japanese Standard Time	+17
SAST:	South Australian Standard Time	+17 1/2
GST:	Guam Standard Time	+18
USSR	Zone 10	+19
IDLE:	International Date Line East	+20

How to Calculate Time Zone Corrections in Your Area:

ADD if you are **east** of PST (Pacific Standard Time); **SUBTRACT** if you are **west** of PST on this map (see right-hand column of chart above).

All times in this calendar are calculated from the West Coast of North America where it is made. Pacific Standard Time (PST Zone 8) is zero point for this calendar, except during Daylight Savings Time (March 14–November 7, 2010, during which times are given for PDT Zone 7). If your time zone does not use Daylight Savings Time, add one hour to the standard correction during this time. At the bottom of each page, EST/EDT (Eastern Standard or Daylight Time) and GMT (Greenwich Mean Time) times are also given. For all other time zones, calculate your time zone correction(s) from this map and write it on the inside cover for easy reference.

Planets

<u>Personal Planets</u> are closest to Earth.

☉ **Sun**: self radiating outward, character, ego

☽ **Moon**: inward sense of self, emotions, psyche

☿ **Mercury**: communication, travel, thought

♀ **Venus**: relationship, love, sense of beauty, empathy

♂ **Mars**: will to act, initiative, ambition

<u>Asteroids</u> are between Mars and Jupiter and reflect the awakening of feminine-defined energy centers in human consciousness. See "Emerging Planets" (p.205).

<u>Social Planets</u> are between personal and outer planets.

♃ **Jupiter**: expansion, opportunities, leadership

Note: The days of the week are named in various languages after the above 7 dieties/heavenly bodies.

♄ **Saturn**: limits, structure, discipline

⚷ **Chiron**: is a small planetary body between Saturn and Uranus representing the wounded healer.

<u>Transpersonal Planets</u> are the outer planets.

♅ **Uranus**: cosmic consciousness, revolutionary change

♆ **Neptune**: spiritual awakening, cosmic love, all one

♇ **Pluto**: death and rebirth, deep, total change

Zodiac Signs

♈ **Aries**

♉ **Taurus**

♊ **Gemini**

♋ **Cancer**

♌ **Leo**

♍ **Virgo**

♎ **Libra**

♏ **Scorpio**

♐ **Sagittarius**

♑ **Capricorn**

♒ **Aquarius**

♓ **Pisces**

Aspects

Aspects show the angle between planets; this informs how the planets influence each other and us. **We'Moon** lists only significant aspects:

☌ CONJUNCTION (planets are 0–5° apart)
linked together, energy of aspected planets is mutually enhancing

☍ OPPOSITION (planets are 180° apart)
polarizing or complementing, energies are diametrically opposite

△ TRINE (planets are 120° apart)
harmonizing, energies of this aspect are in the same element

□ SQUARE (planets are 90° apart)
challenging, energies of this aspect are different from each other

⚹ SEXTILE (planets are 60° apart)
cooperative, energies of this aspect blend well

⚻ QUINCUNX (planets are 150° apart)
variable, energies of this aspect combine contrary elements

Other Symbols

☽ **v/c**–Moon is void of course from last lunar aspect till it enters new sign.

ApG–Apogee: Point in the orbit of a planet that's farthest from Earth.

PrG–Perigee: Point in the orbit of a planet that's nearest to Earth.

D or R–Direct or Retrograde: Describes when a planet moves forward (D) through the zodiac or appears to move backward (R).

2011

JANUARY

S	M	T	W	T	F	S
						1
2	3	4	5	6	7	8
9	10	11	12	13	14	15
16	17	18	19	20	21	22
23	24	25	26	27	28	29
30	31					

FEBRUARY

S	M	T	W	T	F	S
		1	2	3	4	5
6	7	8	9	10	11	12
13	14	15	16	17	18	19
20	21	22	23	24	25	26
27	28					

MARCH

S	M	T	W	T	F	S
		1	2	3	4	5
6	7	8	9	10	11	12
13	14	15	16	17	18	19
20	21	22	23	24	25	26
27	28	29	30	31		

APRIL

S	M	T	W	T	F	S
					1	2
3	4	5	6	7	8	9
10	11	12	13	14	15	16
17	18	19	20	21	22	23
24	25	26	27	28	29	30

MAY

S	M	T	W	T	F	S
1	2	3	4	5	6	7
8	9	10	11	12	13	14
15	16	17	18	19	20	21
22	23	24	25	26	27	28
29	30	31				

JUNE

S	M	T	W	T	F	S
			1	2	3	4
5	6	7	8	9	10	11
12	13	14	15	16	17	18
19	20	21	22	23	24	25
26	27	28	29	30		

JULY

S	M	T	W	T	F	S
					1	2
3	4	5	6	7	8	9
10	11	12	13	14	15	16
17	18	19	20	21	22	23
24	25	26	27	28	29	30
31						

AUGUST

S	M	T	W	T	F	S
	1	2	3	4	5	6
7	8	9	10	11	12	13
14	15	16	17	18	19	20
21	22	23	24	25	26	27
28	29	30	31			

SEPTEMBER

S	M	T	W	T	F	S
				1	2	3
4	5	6	7	8	9	10
11	12	13	14	15	16	17
18	19	20	21	22	23	24
25	26	27	28	29	30	

OCTOBER

S	M	T	W	T	F	S
						1
2	3	4	5	6	7	8
9	10	11	12	13	14	15
16	17	18	19	20	21	22
23	24	25	26	27	28	29
30	31					

NOVEMBER

S	M	T	W	T	F	S
		1	2	3	4	5
6	7	8	9	10	11	12
13	14	15	16	17	18	19
20	21	22	23	24	25	26
27	28	29	30			

DECEMBER

S	M	T	W	T	F	S
				1	2	3
4	5	6	7	8	9	10
11	12	13	14	15	16	17
18	19	20	21	22	23	24
25	26	27	28	29	30	31

= NEW MOON, PST/PDT

= FULL MOON, PST/PDT

Green Sea Turtles

Announcing New Mother Tongue Ink Products!

New!

The Last Wild Witch

by Starhawk – illustrations by Lindy Kehoe

An Eco-Fable for Kids and Other Free Spirits

In the very heart of the last magic forest lived the last wild Witch... This is the story of how the children of the perfect town let a little wildness get inside of them, found their joy and courage, and saved the last wild Witch and the last magic forest from disappearing. The first children's book by visionary author and earth activist **Starhawk**, magically illustrated by painter **Lindy Kehoe**, *The Last Wild Witch* is a fable for our time. Hardcover, 34 pages 8x10 $18.95

***The Last Wild Witch* Poster** is an 11x17 glossy image from this soon-be-be classic children's book. To order book or poster, see page 231.

30 Years of We'Moon: An Anthology

To be released in the Fall of 2010, along with the 30th edtion (**We'Moon 2011**). Visit www.wemoon.ws to find out how to order in advance. All contributors to **We'Moon** over the years: please send in your current contact information: anthology@wemoon.ws

How to Order Mother Tongue Ink Products:

We'Moon 2010: Reinvent the Wheel

• **Datebook:** Choice of 3 bindings: **Spiral, Layflat & Unbound.** An empowering handbook in natural rhythms, with inspirational art and writing by women on the growing edge of global women's culture. $17.95

• **Cover Poster:**
Full-color front cover poster with a stunning painting by Teresa Wild: *"Firedancer"* 11x17 $10

We'Moon 2010 Cards:

• **Greeting Cards**

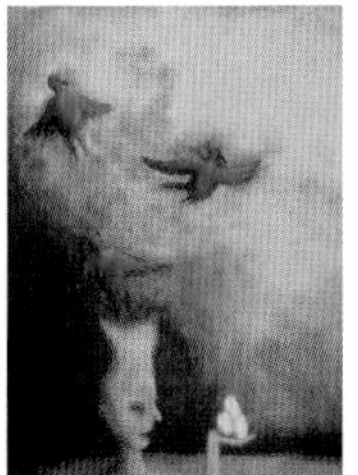

Full color cards featuring gorgeous, inspirational art from *We'Moon 2010: Reinvent the Wheel.* Bright and beautiful, each card pack has four different images. Choose from our Greeting or Solstice packs. All are 5x7, bio-cellophane wrapped, and blank inside. $10 per pack or $6.95 with other products: see Card Special* (next page).

• **Solstice Cards**

• **We'Moon on the Wall 2010:** Full-color, 12x12, lunar wall calendar featuring gorgeous art and inspiring writing from **We'Moon 2010 Datebook**, complete with daily moon phases, signs and key astrological information. $13.95

• **We'Moon Datebooks—Back Issues:** Collector's editions of select past **We'Moon** datebooks. $10

• **We'Moon Greeting Cards '08, '07, '06:** 4 colorful images for every occasion, 5x7, blank inside. $6.95

• **Nostalgia Mystery Card Pack:** 10 assorted cards from past **We'Moons**, bio-wrapped, 5x7. $10

• **Lunar Power Packs:** Big pack of thirteen luscious greeting cards, 5x7 blank inside. $13

Mother Tongue Ink Specials:

• Buy over $50, get 5% off!
• Buy over $85, get 10% off!!
• Buy over $105, get 15% off!!!

***Card Special:** Get each 4 Pack for $6.95 with purchase of any **We'Moon 2010** datebook, wall calendar or poster.

Shipping Special: FREE shipping on a **2010** card pack with purchase of any Mother Tongue Ink product!

ORDER NOW—WHILE THEY LAST!
Visit **www.wemoon.ws** ***for specials, product info and to order online! Or email*** **weorder@wemoon.ws**
US toll free **877-693-6666 (877-O-WeMoon)**
Local & International **541-956-6052** ***Wholesale*** **503-288-3588**

SHIPPING AND HANDLING

•Prices vary depending on what you order and where you live.
See www.wemoon.ws for specifics, or call 1-877-693-6666 or 541-956-6052

All products printed in full color on recycled paper with soy-based ink.

Accepting contributions June through August 2010 for

We'Moon 2012: The 31st Edition!

Tentative Themes: Radical Trust/Transcendence

Call for Contributions: Sent out by June 1, 2010

Due Date for all art and writing: September 1, 2010

Note: It is too late to contribute to ***We'Moon 2011: Uprising!***

Become a We'Moon Contributor!

We'Moon *is an exploration of a world created in Her image. We welcome work by, for and about womyn. Our focus on womyn is an affirmation of the range and richness of a world where womyn are whole unto themselves. Many earth-based cultures traditionally have womyn-only spaces and times, which, through deepening the female experience, are seen to enhance womyn's contributions to the whole of society.* ***We'Moon*** *invites all womyn who love and honor womyn to join us in this spirit, and we offer what we create from such a space for the benefit of all beings.*

We invite you to send in your art and writing for the 31st edition of We'Moon! Here's how:

Step 1: Send your request for a Call for Contributions, along with a self-addressed business-size envelope (#10 USA) and adequate postage (US stamps or an international postal coupon) to **We'Moon Submissions, 181 Brimstone Rd., Wolf Creek, OR 97497**. The Call contains current information about the theme (it may change) and how to submit your art and writing (with exact specifications), and terms of compensation.

Step 2: Fill in the accompanying Contributor's License, giving all the requested information and return it with your art/writing as specified by the due date. *No work will be accepted without a signed license!*

Step 3: Think ahead! To assure your work is considered for **We'Moon 2012**, get your submissions in by Sept. 1, 2010.

***Visit *www.wemoon.ws* to download the Contributor's License and get all the latest *We'Moon on the Web* info!**

Give **We'Moon Solstice Cards 2010** for the holidays!
...and for special occasions all year around!

The above images are from **We'Moon Solstice Cards 2010** and are credited as follows: *Nature Diva: January ¤ Diane Melanie 2002 (p. 53); Raven Reflection © Cathy McClelland 2008 (p. 185); Goddess of Laussel ¤ Lisa A. Tayerle 2000 (p. 41); She Changes Everything She Touches © Jakki Moore 2008 (p. 105)*

Note images are from **We'Moon Greeting Cards 2010** and are credited as follows: *La Fortuna© Luz-Marie López 2007 (p. 233); Night of One Thousand Birds © Rebecca Guberman-Bloom 2005 (p. 115); Burdock Spirit © Asha Croggon 2005 (p. 237); Keepers of the Water © Leah Marie Dorion 2008 (p. 239)*

Notes

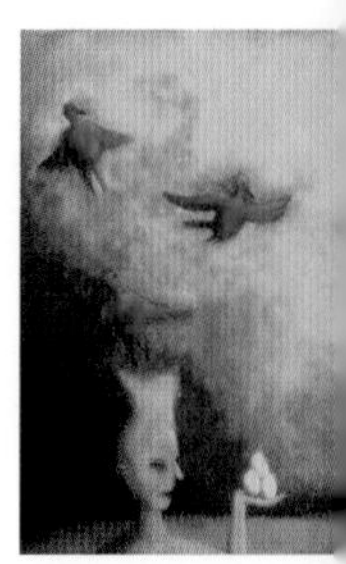

Notes

Notes